Market Towns

Market towns are frequently identified as being among the most desirable places to live. Yet, paradoxically, they are also the focus of government efforts to bring economic regeneration to the countryside as a means of achieving a more sustainable pattern of development. But, with the loss of livestock and produce markets in most towns, there is no longer a clear picture of what defines a market town. This absence of definition has served to inhibit our ability to undertake analysis, develop policy and understand what works where and why.

Through a detailed analysis of the characteristics of over two hundred towns and in-depth studies of eleven towns in different parts of England, this book identifies and explores a number of key roles for market towns: as retirement or commuter towns; as employment centres; as service centres or as tourist towns. It sets the results in the context of past and current policy and considers in more detail some critical issues, including increased personal mobility, aging populations, housing growth and affordability, employment, and retail competitiveness. Drawing on this detailed case study material, a final section explores the future role of market towns as sustainable communities and how they might best assure their futures.

Market Towns draws on original research to address issues which have not yet been covered in contemporary planning literature. This comprehensive volume provides a wide-ranging discussion that is likely to appeal to those involved at all levels of practice related to market towns as well as to academics and students working in both rural and urban geography and planning.

Neil Powe is a lecturer in planning at the University of Newcastle. His main research interests include non-market environmental valuation and rural planning. Market towns research has provided the focus of his rural planning research and he has co-authored a number of journal articles on the subject. He has published a book on environmental valuation.

Trevor Hart is visiting research fellow in the School of Architecture, Planning and Landscape, University of Newcastle. He has a number of years' experience of practice in planning and economic development in rural areas and has recently been engaged in a number of evaluation studies involving the impact of enterprise policy in deprived communities, graduate recruitment in small businesses and the impact of social enterprise.

Tim Shaw is head of the School of Architecture, Planning and Landscape, University of Newcastle. His research has covered various aspects of regional planning and he has many years' experience dealing with issues of rural planning. He has co-authored journal articles on market towns and is currently editing a special issue on green belts for the *Journal of Environmental Planning and Management*.

Market Towns

Roles, challenges and prospects

Edited by Neil Powe, Trevor Hart
and Tim Shaw

LONDON AND NEW YORK

Cover photographs: *left* – a view from the castle of the marketplace in Richmond; *right* – the new marketplace in Downham Market.

First published 2007
by Routledge
2 Park Square, Milton Park, Abingdon, Oxon OX14 4RN

Simultaneously published in the USA and Canada
by Routledge
270 Madison Ave, New York, NY 10016

Routledge is an imprint of the Taylor & Francis Group, an informa business

© 2007 Neil Powe, Trevor Hart and Tim Shaw for selection and editorial matter; individual chapters, the contributors

Typeset in Frutiger Light by
Florence Production Ltd, Stoodleigh, Devon
Printed and bound in Great Britain by
TJ International Ltd, Padstow, Cornwall

British Library Cataloguing in Publication Data
A catalogue record for this book is available from the British Library

Library of Congress Cataloging in Publication Data
A catalog record for this book has been requested

ISBN13: 978–0–415–38962–4 (hbk)
ISBN13: 978–0–203–08944–6 (ebk)

ISBN10: 0–415–38962–3 (hbk)
ISBN10: 0–203–08944–8 (ebk)

Contents

List of illustrations		vii
Notes on contributors		ix
Foreword		xi
Acknowledgements		xii
List of abbreviations		xiii

1 The challenges of understanding market towns
Neil Powe, Trevor Hart and Tim Shaw — 1

Part 1
Characteristics, roles and policy — 9

2 Market town characteristics
Neil Powe and Trevor Hart — 11

3 Exploring contemporary functional roles
Neil Powe, Trevor Hart and Tim Shaw — 27

4 Policies for market towns
Trevor Hart — 43

Part 2
Issues and challenges — 57

5 Transport and mobility in the English market town
Geoff Vigar — 59

6 Ready or not: the ageing of the market towns' population
Rose Gilroy, Liz Brooks and Tim Shaw — 69

7 Market towns, housing and social inclusion
Stuart Cameron and Mark Shucksmith — 81

Contents

8 Capacity vs. need: exploring regional differences in housing provision
in market towns   93
Susannah Gunn and Neil Powe

9 Market towns and rural employment   105
Trevor Hart and Neil Powe

10 Visiting the shops: rural service centre or visitor attraction?   118
Neil Powe and Trevor Hart

Part 3
What prospects for market towns?   135

11 Drivers for change in the case study towns   137
Trevor Hart and Neil Powe

12 Market towns: roles, challenges and prospects   148
Trevor Hart and Neil Powe

Appendix 1: A short history of market towns   157
Neil Powe and Trevor Hart

Appendix 2: A short guide to the English development planning system   160
Trevor Hart

Bibliography   163
Index   177

Illustrations

Figures

5.1	Passenger travel by car and other modes, 1980–2004: Great Britain	60
5.2	Changes in the costs of travel and disposable income, 1980–2004: Great Britain	61
5.3	Difficulties of accessing services in households with no access to a car: England	63
5.4	Households within 13 minutes of an hourly bus service by area type: Great Britain	64

Tables

1.1	Data collected	6
2.1	Population change 1991–2001	13
2.2	Regression models explaining market town characteristics	16
2.3	Economic and service roles of the towns	17
2.4	Cluster analysis results	21
2.5	Illustration for towns in the North East region	22
2.6	Illustration for towns in the East of England region	23
3.1	Characteristics of case study towns	39
5.1	Two towns' travel patterns compared	66
6.1	Mosaic UK group and type descriptions	70
7.1	Affordability of rural housing by area and settlement type	83
7.2	Tenure of rural housing by area and settlement type, 2001	84
8.1	Description of the case study 'market towns'	98
8.2	In-migrators' engagement with activities within the town	101
8.3	Respondents' perception of town's changes	102
8.4	Respondents' perception of housing issues	103
9.1	Engagement of working residents	113
10.1	Description of retail in surveyed towns	126
10.2	What do residents like about shopping in the towns?	127
10.3	How to encourage customers to visit the town centres more often	128
10.4	Residents visiting the town centre in the month prior to interview	128
10.5	How to encourage residents to visit towns more in the evening	129
10.6	Choice of most typical and popular market towns	130
10.7	Facilities visited in country towns	131

Boxes

2.1 Cluster analysis   19
3.1 Rural service use in Alnwick   31
3.2 Keswick: a major visitor attraction   32
3.3 Minehead: a coastal tourist town   33
3.4 Richmond: the effect of being located near a large defence establishment   34
3.5 Wymondham: a commuter town planned for further expansion   36
3.6 Hunstanton: a remote coastal town in Norfolk   38
3.7 Oswestry: a traditional market town   40
3.8 Todmorden: a town looking for a new role   41
4.1 Yorkshire Forward's approach to market town regeneration   53
4.2 Key actors in market towns partnerships   55
9.1 Alnwick: rural employment centre   111
9.2 Downham Market: housing rural employees   112
10.1 Supermarkets in Alnwick   121
11.1 Keswick's Business Improvement District   139
11.2 Todmorden Market   141

Plates

Plates fall between pages 98 and 99

1   Market cross in Alnwick
2   Market cross in Wymondham
3   Obelisk, which replaced the market cross within Richmond's (North Yorkshire) large market place in Georgian times
4   Keswick's mountainous backdrop
5   Keswick's pedestrianised town centre
6   Wymondham town plaque and the town's oldest inn – the 'Green Dragon'
7   Housing estate on the outskirts of Wymondham
8   New housing in Downham Market
9   Sculptures in the pedestrianised main shopping street of Aurich, North Germany
10 One of three sculptured seats in Alnwick's medieval market square
11 Independent department store in Morpeth
12 Independent furniture store in Downham Market
13 Traditional shop frontage in Richmond
14 Marketplace in Downham Market and Victorian clock tower
15 The Playhouse in Alnwick
16 The Theatre by the Lake in Keswick
17 Inside Todmorden market
18 Redeveloped marketplace in Morpeth
19 Crediton redeveloped town square
20 Canal in the centre of Todmorden

Contributors

All contributors are based in the School of Architecture, Planning and Landscape, Newcastle University. Reflecting the 'intermediary' position of market towns, not truly rural and not truly urban, the background of the contributors is mixed between urban and rural specialists.

Liz Brooks is a mature student studying for a PhD on rural ageing issues. Prior to this she worked as a researcher for a national older people's charity and specialised in the areas of older people's services, participatory research and service evaluation.

Stuart Cameron is a senior lecturer in the School of Architecture, Planning and Landscape. His research and publication are in the areas of urban regeneration and governance, social exclusion and housing. His current research and writing focuses mainly on housing market renewal.

Rose Gilroy is a senior lecturer in planning and an experienced qualitative researcher. Her work has covered urban regeneration, the housing of offenders, women's issues in housing and planning, and in recent years has focused on the impact of the ageing population.

Susannah Gunn is a lecturer in planning. She has specialised in housing research considering issues of housing capacity and the role of regions within housing's delivery. She is currently working on an Economic and Social Research Council-funded research project 'Intra-regional co-ordination: through the lens of housing strategies'.

Trevor Hart is visiting research fellow in the School of Architecture, Planning and Landscape. He has a number of years' experience of practice in planning and economic development in rural areas, coupled with research activity in areas such as tourism, skills and training, and small business. He has recently been engaged in a number of evaluation studies; of the impact of enterprise policy in deprived communities, of graduate recruitment in small business and on the impact of social enterprise.

Neil Powe is a lecturer teaching in planning. He has two key research interests: non-market environmental valuation and rural planning. Market towns research has provided the recent focus of his rural planning research and he has co-authored a number of journal articles on market towns. He has published a book on the subject of environmental valuation.

Tim Shaw is head of the School of Architecture, Planning and Landscape. His research interests include minerals and regional planning, and he has many years' experience dealing with issues of rural planning. He has co-authored journal articles on market towns and is currently editing a special issue on green belts for the *Journal of Environmental Planning and Management*.

Mark Shucksmith is a professor of planning, vice-president of the International Rural Sociological Association and a board member of the Commission for Rural Communities (formerly the Countryside Agency). During 2005–06 he was also a member of DEFRA/ DCLG's Affordable Rural Housing Commission and secretary to the Joseph Rowntree Foundation's Rural Housing Policy Forum. He has written a number of books on rural issues.

Geoff Vigar is director of the Global Urban Research Unit and senior lecturer in planning. His research focuses on governance issues with an emphasis on the construction and salience of environmental and social issues, and policy process concerns in the fields of transport and spatial planning. He has also written two books on transport issues.

Foreword

There comes a time in the emergence of any discipline, when it is important to take stock of what has been learnt so far. This can provide a platform on which future work can build and give the chance to take the collective understanding to the next level.

As this book recounts, it is now over a decade since market town regeneration became a theme in government policy. Indeed, Action for Market Towns itself this year celebrates its tenth anniversary of supporting locally based action to revitalise small, rural towns across the country. The current period is also one of transition from the national Market Towns Initiative to even higher levels of investment through targeted and regionally distinct regeneration programmes.

In its stated aim to bring some clarity about what a market town is and what role it performs in today's countryside, this book is therefore very timely. In doing this, it is performing a great service to all of us who are either paid or work voluntarily to improve the quality of life of the millions of people who live in and around our nation's market towns.

In many ways the book paints a necessarily complex picture. Just the range of issues that it covers – from dealing with an ageing population to the opportunities for improved economic development – underlines the significant challenges that market towns face in the future. By bringing this information together in one resource, the book is able to demonstrate the inter-linkages between different issues to a depth that I do not think has been achieved before.

Out of the apparent complexity of the issues, the book offers clarity to the practitioner. Thus, by describing the five functional roles for market towns identified from analysis – service centres; visitor attractions; employment centres; housing commuters and housing the retired – the book provides a vocabulary that practitioners and towns-folk can begin to use to discuss the similarities and differences that exist between towns. By spotting gaps in the current level of knowledge and supplementing this with new research, the book is providing additional insights. By pulling together many complex strands it can help the policy maker, the regeneration specialist or the community activist to each better understand and focus on the impacts of their work.

It is my hope and belief that this book will be well read, well received and well referred to. It very ably captures and adds to the learning gained from many people's work in the discipline over the last 10 years or more. I look forward to it informing ever more effective policies and interventions over the next decade.

Chris Wade, Chief Executive, Action for Market Towns

Acknowledgements

A number of people have been very helpful in the process of producing this book and we wish to thank them for their efforts. Invaluable advice has been given to us by Paul Courtney, Judith Fozzard, Colin Grant, Eveline van Leeuwen, Graham May, Dave Pope, James Shorten, Roger Turner and two anonymous referees, with special thanks to Chris Wade for his continued encouragement, advice and help choosing the case study towns. Although they will remain nameless, because we told them they would, a very warm thank you to all those in our 11 case study towns who gave up their time to talk to us. Thanks also go to Stephen Murray for his help editing and creating figures for the book. Special thanks also to Pat McGrellis, Lena Sünnenberg and Gilla Sünnenberg.

Abbreviations

ARHC   Affordable Rural Housing Commission
AONB   Area of Outstanding Natural Beauty
BID   Business Improvement District
CRC   Commission for Rural Communities
CP   Community Plan
DFT   Department for Transport
DPDs   Development Plan Documents
EEDA   East of England Development Agency
EERA   East of England Regional Assembly
FRESA   Frameworks for Regional Employment and Skills Actions
HMRP   Housing Market Renewal Pathfinder
HOPe   Housing for Older People
ICT   Information and Communication Technology
LAAs   Local Area Agreements
LDFs   Local Development Frameworks
LDS   Local Development Scheme
LSPs   Local Strategic Partnerships
MCTI   Market and Coastal Towns Initiative
MTI   Market Towns Initiative
NRF   Neighbourhood Renewal Fund
NEF   New Economics Foundation
ODPM   Office of the Deputy Prime Minister
PPS   Planning Policy Statement
RDA   Regional Development Agency
RES   Regional Economic Strategy
RSSs   Regional Spatial Strategies
RSLs   Registered Social Landlords
RMT   Renaissance Market Towns
SRB   Single Regeneration Budget
SME   Small and Medium-sized Enterprise
SERRL   South East Regional Research Laboratory
SCI   Statement of Community Involvement
SRPs   Sub-Regional Partnerships
SPDs   Supplementary Planning Documents

Chapter 1

The challenges of understanding market towns

Neil Powe, Trevor Hart and Tim Shaw

Introduction

Say the phrase 'market town' and it conjures up a place that teenagers would probably find boring, but their parents or grandparents would probably find comfortable or welcoming. These forty-year-olds and over are the people who help to put such towns on the lists of most desirable places to live in lifestyle surveys. But, if they are so desirable, why, as has been the case for much of the past decade, should these same market towns have become the focus of government policy initiatives to regenerate rural areas? Places in need of regeneration are rarely seen as desirable places to live and come at the opposite end of the spectrum in the same lifestyle surveys. These apparent contradictions provide an impetus for this book, which seeks to understand the similarities and differences between the many places that have come to be encompassed by the term 'market town', and to identify the trends and forces that are shaping them. This can then contribute to the development of policy for market towns, a better understanding of the impacts of policy, and help build a picture of what the future may hold for the towns.

In spite of a long-established policy to protect the countryside from development, rural areas have experienced growing populations, a trend often attributed to the catch-all term 'counter-urbanisation'. So, 'although professional and political opinion favours accommodating housing growth in cities, where the release of land is least controversial, the strongest demand for housing is in the very opposite types of locations, where the pressure not to build is at its most intense' (Buller *et al.* 2003: 5). Market towns have participated in this trend and Champion and Fielding (1992: 2) have observed that these flows of population 'have added small estates of owner occupied detached houses to small- and medium sized free-standing towns', a description that encompasses those places identified as 'market towns'. While functional motivations – such as taking up new employment – are part of the migration decisions that are driving this trend, moving to the countryside is often a 'lifestyle' choice.

Opportunities for exercising such a lifestyle choice have been enhanced through a combination of factors, perhaps the most fundamental of which relates to transport. With rising levels of car ownership, and the costs of motoring falling as a proportion of disposable income (DfT 2005), urban residents are able to widen their search for a residential location that offers the physical and social qualities they seem to prefer (Halfacree 1994). This greater mobility has facilitated the enjoyment of both a rural residence and the services available in larger urban areas, and contributed to the development of a less contained lifestyle, with many rural residents travelling significant distances for shopping and employment (SERRL 2004).

This increasing mobility, which has helped bring growth to market towns, also presents them with a challenge, in that they now have to compete for custom for the services that they have traditionally provided for local and hinterland residents. The strength of this challenge has been amplified by trends in retailing, which has increasingly sought to develop larger-scale facilities in centralised locations away from places like market towns, contributing to difficulties experienced in maintaining their role as rural service centres (English Market Towns Forum 2002). The leakage of expenditure from the towns that can result may start to undermine the economic rationale for their existence and pose a threat to their viability. A decline in physical fabric and environment may follow, resulting in boarded-up shop frontages and run-down buildings, detracting from the appeal of the town centres for retailers and customers and initiating a cycle of decline that may be difficult to arrest.

Increasing mobility also challenges current policy, which seeks to promote sustainable patterns of development and living. The agenda for promoting sustainable development in rural areas sees potential for settlements such as market towns in terms of co-locating homes, work and services (MAFF and DETR 2000; DEFRA 2004a). However, realising this potential relies on market towns offering the quantity and quality of facilities that residents are seeking. Housing growth in market towns also runs the risk of exacerbating another problem that is seen as endemic in rural areas – the shortage of affordable housing. Fuelled by external demand, rural house prices have increased markedly (CRC 2005a). The general shortage of affordable rented housing in rural areas, along with the wider choice of employment in urban areas (Green 1999), contributes to a continuing out-migration of young people. This in turn compromises the ability of the towns to fill the – often lower-paid – posts in service employment on which their success depends.

With declining levels of village services, market towns have become increasingly important for the less mobile in rural areas, and perhaps have a particular role in addressing rural social exclusion. Given the inadequacy of public transport, which may be largely irrelevant for the elderly (Moseley 1996), for some there may be little alternative other than to move to market towns, where the provision of services is increasingly focused. This additional challenge for market towns of playing a part in tackling social exclusion can be made more difficult by their 'intermediate' position, somewhere between the truly rural and the truly urban, making it less easy to access the government support required. As such, these towns may face 'urban' problems of disadvantaged households, communities and economic decline, without access to the funding for regeneration and social policy that is available only to larger towns and cities.

Clearly, circumstances will vary from place to place, and it is reasonable to expect market towns in booming regions to face different challenges from those in declining regions, or towns in the shadow of large conurbations to perform different roles from those that are more remotely located. It is also possible for challenges of growth in one dimension to coincide with decline in another. So, the challenges facing market towns are likely to be both complex and particular, and systematic study is necessary to develop a robust basis for both analysis and policy.

Policy and market towns

Although settlements such as market towns have long had a central role in policy guiding development in rural areas, they have recently become central to national and regional efforts to drive rural regeneration. Building on some work by the Civic Trust and the Rural Development Commission in England in the early 1990s, market towns initially emerged as a theme in the first Rural White Paper in 1995. The Labour government that took office in 1997 continued and developed this interest in its own Rural White Paper published in 2000 (MAFF and DETR), which presaged the introduction of a programme known as the Market Towns Initiative (MTI). Based on joint working between the Countryside Agency and the recently established Regional Development Agencies (RDAs), towns in each region were selected for support based on a perception of need. What was originally a national programme has gradually been absorbed into the work of the RDAs, which have developed regionally differentiated approaches, with RDAs continuing to give prominence to market towns in their activities in rural areas.

Throughout this period of increasing policy activity, the term 'market town' has been used consistently. Essentially, 'market town' is an historical term being applied to current circumstances that differ significantly from history (see Appendix 1 for a brief history of market towns). What is usually being referred to is one of the many towns in rural areas that act as some kind of service centre – a function that was, in the past, commonly associated with the presence of a cattle or produce market – for the surrounding area of hamlets and villages. Although most such towns no longer have cattle markets (Swain 1997), some form of local market continues to take place in many market towns. Marketplaces have remained important attractions and locations for such markets as well as festivals. Although the original 'market crosses' have often been replaced, they still provide a focus for many marketplaces and are part of the 'heritage' which helps define the attraction of many market towns (Plate 1, Plate 2, Plate 3).[1]

For policy purposes, 'market towns' have been identified mainly on the basis of size, but the chosen size band of between 2,000 and 30,000 residents can include many different types of places with differing characteristics. Our use of the term 'market town' in this book refers to this wide group of market towns but our purpose is to seek to develop a better understanding of the differences that exist within this diverse group of places.

Purpose of this book

In the future, the fortune of market towns is likely to depend on both sustaining traditional functions as service centres for their rural hinterland, and developing newer roles, for example, as locations for new housing or as visitor destinations. The aim of this book is to try to bring some clarity to the understanding of just what a market town is and what role it performs in today's countryside. In doing this, it is hoped to provide a better basis for considering the impact of trends and policy initiatives on the towns. It does this by:

- exploring market towns' contemporary roles and the policy framework that has sought to guide and manage their development;
- exploring relevant issues and challenges; and
- forming a judgement about the likely future prospects for market towns.

These three elements are addressed sequentially in the three sections of the book.

Content

Part 1: Characteristics, roles and policy

Part 1 provides the framework for the remainder of the book. Chapter 2 considers the meaning of the term 'market towns' in terms of both policy and public perceptions. The chapter then goes on to provide a descriptive analysis of over 200 market towns in England (details of the sample given at the end of this chapter), and, using regression and cluster analysis, explores this data further to identify the nature and extent of the similarities and differences between the towns. The chapter concludes by providing a list of contemporary functional roles, establishing the framework for Chapter 3. Chapter 3 reviews relevant literature on market towns, and illustrates the characteristics and roles of market towns, as well as giving more detailed profiles of the 11 towns we have studied in greater depth. Having established a good understanding of market towns, Chapter 4 then provides an overview of relevant policy, specifically considering rural settlement policy and initiatives to regenerate the towns.

Part 2: Issues and challenges

Part 2 provides greater detail on a number of topics emerging from the analysis in Part 1, all of which contribute to our understanding of the likely issues and challenges faced by market towns. The section begins with a review of trends in transport (Chapter 5), which has been identified in this chapter as a key factor shaping the future of market towns. Another important rural trend is the ageing of population that has accompanied the migration process. Chapter 6 considers the evidence of ageing in Britain's rural places and the implications this has for market towns. As part of the analysis it considers the extent to which there is a robust framework in place to meet the specific needs and aspirations of older people resident in market towns and their rural hinterlands.

Chapter 7 provides an overview of housing and regeneration in market towns. This chapter considers trends in house prices, the delivery of affordable housing and the role of regeneration funding in meeting the need for housing renewal. Given the importance of the housing role of market towns and the significant differences in levels of pressure of population growth between regions in England, Chapter 8 goes on to consider specifically the implications of regional housing allocations for market towns. This is achieved through detailed case studies of four towns in two regions, with the East of England providing an example of a region needing to accommodate high levels of population and household growth, and the North East of England an example of a region that, in aggregate terms at least, has a relatively low level of need for new housing. How these different regional characteristics are translated into policies at the local level and the implications these policies might have for the future character of the towns are examined, and consequent challenges and issues are highlighted.

Chapter 9 explores the scope for market towns to act as centres for employment, and considers the contribution of employment development to the fortunes and futures of the towns in a number of related dimensions. It begins by considering the context in which they operate, by reviewing employment trends in rural areas, before reviewing evidence on employment in market towns, from literature and from the work undertaken in the 11 case study towns.

The last chapter in this part (Chapter 10) explores the retail futures of market towns by considering their roles as rural service centres and visitor attractions; to do this it makes use of the results of surveys of both market town residents and potential visitors from urban areas. The chapter explores the synergies and inconsistencies between pursuing both these roles.

Part 3: What prospects for market towns?

This final part effectively provides the discussion and conclusion for the book, but is separated into two chapters. Drawing from 11 case study towns, Chapter 11 considers the context and challenges facing the towns; strategies adopted to improve the towns; developments occurring within the towns; and their experiences with the Market Towns Initiative. The overriding objective of this chapter is to identify some of the key drivers for change affecting the towns.

Chapter 12 reflects on the characteristics of the large and diverse group of rural settlements that are referred to by the term 'market town', and considers the challenges they face. In the light of these findings a vision is proposed and some of the factors affecting its implementation are identified. The chapter and book ends with some speculation about the likely future for market towns.

The information base of the book

In studying a hard-to-define subject such as market towns, inevitably some choices have to be made about where to focus work and which data to collect and analyse. Secondary data is clearly easier to access and has the virtue of often being comparable between places. But it is unlikely that data will be available for the areas and covering the range of topics considered by this study, rendering some primary research necessary. So, we have proceeded on the basis of using a combination of secondary and primary data for a selection of towns.

A choice of towns

If we start by using size as a tool for selecting towns to study we find that there are about 1,200 small towns in England with populations between 2,000 and 30,000. There was thus a need to work with a sample from these towns. Given their evident policy relevance, those towns taking part in the Market Towns Initiative provided an obvious group on which to focus. More specifically, 227 towns were listed in response to a parliamentary question as taking part in the Market Towns Initiative (Hansard 1 Mar 2004: Column 639W). Of those listed, owing to errors (typing and repetition) and towns too small to be included in the Population Census 2001 urban areas data sets (those below 1,500 in population), the number of towns to be studied was reduced to 202.

Secondary data collected

The following sources provided data for each of the 202 towns in the study:

* Population Census 2001, giving a range of key statistics for town areas;
* Land Registry, giving property price data for the postcode sectors appropriate to the town;
* Yellow Pages, identifying the presence of services within the towns; and
* Free-to-use maps provided by BTex Limited (www.streetmap.co.uk).

Table 1.1 provides a summary list of the key data collected, where the data has been presented by general characteristics: location and accessibility; characteristics of town residents; structure of the economy; affluence and deprivation; visitor attractions; and services. Although not exhaustive, this list is felt to cover the key issues facing market towns and was established through consultation with Action for Market Towns, the principal membership organisation for these towns. Data on town population does not fit easily into any of these categories, but because of its potential importance it has been included within 'characteristics of town residents'. This data provides the basis for the statistical analysis discussed in Chapter 2, which involved the use of two main techniques: regression analysis, to identify some key relationships between variables; and cluster analysis, to identify groups of town characteristics and a basis for constructing a classification of towns.

Data from market town surveys

Previous research has suggested that town and hinterland residents are the most important visitor groups for market towns. Maintaining existing trade and 'clawing back' trade from

Table 1.1 Data collected

Location and accessibility	
Time to drive to a large urban area	Distance to a large urban area
Number of urban areas within 10 km radius	% driving to work
Average distance travelled to work	Located in the South East region

Characteristics of town residents	
Population of the town	% retired
% aged below 18	Mean age
Change in the % retired	% British and white
% migrating from inside the UK	

Structure of the economy	
% employed in manufacturing	% wholesale and retail
% hotel and catering (including within tourism)	% public administration
% in financial intermediation	% health and social work
% real estate, renting and business activities	% construction
% education	

Affluence and deprivation	
% of households with no car	% change in unemployment (1991–2001)
% of unemployed	% change in house price (2000–4)
% of lone parent households	Average house price in 2004

Visitor attractions	
Number of campsites	Distance to the sea
% employed in hotels and catering	Distance to a National Park
Number of tourist attractions	

Services	
Number of banks	Number of doctors' surgeries
Number of solicitors	Number of supermarkets
Number of building societies	Number of services/town population
Number of ladies' clothes shops	

other areas can then become crucial to town regeneration. In order to consider retail usage and attitudes towards town services, questionnaire surveys were undertaken in 2005 and 2006 of town residents in the towns of Morpeth, Alnwick, Downham Market and Wymond-ham (Chapters 8, 9, 10 and 11 provide further discussion on these towns). The questionnaire surveys were undertaken house-to-house within the towns themselves. Using the house-to-house approach allowed both customers and potential customers to provide feedback, and this approach also enabled the respondents to complete the questionnaires in their own time and give more detailed responses to open-ended questions.

Urban residents' survey

Given the importance of visitors – and not just those who might be characterised as 'tourists' – to market towns, it was considered important to have a better understanding of attitudes and perceptions of urban residents to market towns. Attempts were made to remedy the lack of previous research in this area through a range of approaches to understand the range of behaviour and opinions regarding leisure trips to market towns.

First, two focus groups (defined by Krueger (1994) as 'carefully planned discussions designed to obtain perceptions on a defined area of interest' (6)) were held in Gosforth, a suburb not far from the centre of Newcastle upon Tyne. A location for the meeting was chosen around which there was a variety of housing (reflecting different socio-economic groups), and participants recruited door-to-door with a £20 incentive to encourage people with a range of experience to attend. Second, a questionnaire survey was undertaken in a range of areas of Newcastle exploring three issues: what people did on 'days out'; perceptions of market towns; and attitudes and preferences towards market towns. All this material was combined with information giving a profile of the respondents, to help identify similarities and differences between different groups in the community.

Case study visits

Finally, visits were made to eleven towns identified as representing a range of types identified by the statistical analysis. These were undertaken for: Crediton and Minehead in the South West; Haslemere in the South East; Downham Market and Wymondham in the East of England; Oswestry in the West Midlands; Keswick in the North West; Richmond and Todmorden in Yorkshire and Humber; and Alnwick and Morpeth in the North East. For each visit, detailed local profiles were developed through study of documentary sources, and this information was extended by interviews with a number of key local actors to gain a full understanding of the issues and initiatives shaping the development of the town. The researchers adopted something of a 'mystery shopper' approach to the visit, to help assess the nature of some of the issues that had emerged from other forms of study. The fruits of this work are used throughout the text to illustrate issues and findings, as well as providing a key input to Chapter 11 on the possible futures for market towns.

Notes

1   Matching the diversity of the country towns themselves, marketplaces come in many forms, whether in terms of a 'market cross' or covered market. Chamberlin (1983) suggests historically many markets were undertaken at the 'market cross' whose name comes from the original location of markets often under the cross in churchyards. The location of many markets changed in the thirteenth century following a proclamation of Edward I that they should no longer be located within church grounds.

Part 1
Characteristics, roles and policy

With the loss of livestock and produce markets in most towns, there is no clear picture of what defines a place as a 'market town'. This absence of a clear definition inhibits our ability to undertake analysis, develop policy and understand what works where and why. Through a detailed consideration of over 200 market towns, Chapter 2 provides a framework for analysis developed through consideration of their functional roles. This framework is developed using statistical analysis (descriptive, regression and cluster) and detailed data on: location and accessibility; characteristics of town residents; structure of the economy; affluence and deprivation, visitor attractions; and services. Through the use of literature review and case material, Chapter 3 then develops this examination of roles further and, in this context, describes the 11 case study towns. Having established a good understanding of market towns, Chapter 4 then provides an overview of the relevant government policy, specifically considering rural settlement policy and initiatives to regenerate towns. As such this first part provides the framework for the remainder of the book.

Chapter 2
Market town characteristics

Neil Powe and Trevor Hart

Introduction

Despite the recent interest in market towns and the importance they have assumed within policy, little is known in a systematic manner about their characteristics and the challenges they face. Although recognising that there is 'no such thing as a stereotypical town' (Countryside Agency 2004a: 216), current approaches to policy and implementation place great stress on the monitoring and evaluation of effectiveness, and on attempts to identify 'best practice' and transferable lessons. None of these tasks are easy – or may be possible – without some understanding of similarities and differences between towns.

Policy in this area contrasts sharply with urban areas, where within government the work of the Social Exclusion Unit and the Cabinet Office Strategy Unit, supported by academic study,[1] has provided a basis for analysis, explanation, policy development and evaluation. To date, the inclusion of market towns in the national or regional policy initiatives does not have a transparent and fully articulated basis, or certainly not one that differentiates between different types of settlements or problems faced. The absence of a framework for analysis and evaluation seems a serious shortcoming and is surprising given the current emphasis on performance measurement in most areas of public policy.

Through consideration of the characteristics of market towns this chapter helps to address some of these shortcomings. In order to provide a basis for analysis, explanation, policy development and evaluation, it is also necessary to provide a classification of towns. This will be achieved through the use of regression analysis (a statistical method for specifying and formally testing a functional relationship between variables) and cluster analysis (a statistical method for data reduction and classification). In the context of this book, classification is very useful in providing a framework for shaping and interpreting the findings of the more detailed case study research.

Defining market towns

Market towns are generally perceived to have in common a capacity to act as a focal point for trade and services for their hinterland. Within England, market towns have generally been defined as having a population somewhere between 2,000 and 30,000 (Swain 1997; Countryside Agency 2000; MAFF and DETR 2000). While larger towns may still perform the role of a 'market town', it is unlikely to be a defining function. In other countries where towns and larger villages may be more remotely located, market towns may be smaller in population (Bunce 1982), but the typical characteristic of a market town remains that, because of their rural linkages, they have more services and facilities than would be expected for their size. Located in the space between urban and rural, these towns play a key role within the settlement hierarchy. For example, Davies *et al*. (1998) illustrate the hierarchical service role of market towns in Western Victoria, Australia, where a cumulatively increasing range of commercial services are provided at each level.

There were estimated to be 1,274 small towns in England with populations between 2,000 and 30,000 (Countryside Agency 2004a)[2] of which 499 were categorised as 'service hubs'. These are defined by having a bank or building society or solicitor; more than ten retail outlets; an above average number of shops (2.4 per 1,000 residents); a doctors' surgery; and a small or large supermarket. This suggests that these 499 towns are providing a 'market town' function, but the number of shops may also reflect tourist trade. In addition, it was noted by the Countryside Agency (2004a) that not all 'non-hub' towns were located on the fringes of urban areas. Indeed, a number (not stated) were in freestanding rural locations (Countryside Agency 2004a). This data illustrates that the degree to which market towns perform a rural service centre role may vary markedly.

Perceptions of 'market towns'

It has been suggested that the term 'market town' has a deeper historical and cultural meaning than the dictionary definition of 'a town where a market is held' (Thompson 1995). It is this wider cultural and historical meaning of the term that is being used within publicity material for British towns. The results of the Newcastle residents' survey demonstrate the wider meaning of the term 'market town' (see Chapter 1 for details of the survey and Chapter 10 for further details of the findings).

Participants were asked to consider a list of fourteen small towns in the North East of England and to select the three towns that were closest to what they conceptualise as 'market towns'. Participants found this to be easy. Indeed, following this exercise, when asked about the meaning of the term 'market towns' they were able to articulate quite detailed definitions. Of the 148 responses to the questionnaire survey, only eleven respondents failed to give a meaning and a further six did not add to the dictionary definition.

The key distinction made concerning market towns was their 'difference from the city'. The most common responses related to the historic and traditional aspects of the towns (32 per cent), their size (31 per cent) and their rural location (29 per cent). Market towns were also seen by a number of participants (20 per cent) to provide a focus for their rural area, and other respondents noted their linkages with agriculture (7 per cent) and availability of local produce (9 per cent). The 'different from the city' nature of the shops was also noted by a number (15 per cent) of the respondents, suggesting shops tend not to belong to a chain and fall instead into that group often described as 'specialist shops'.

Discussion within the focus groups also enabled consideration of which towns were not considered to be 'market towns'. Such towns were seen not to have sufficient history, or their history was indicative of a different role such as seaside (Amble) and/or border town (Berwick-upon-Tweed) or based more on industry and coal mining (Bishop Auckland). Location was also important: one town – Prudhoe – was considered to be an urban suburb, while another – Wooler – too small to be classified as a market town. As such, the term 'market town' evidently has colloquial meaning. In the context of the development and marketing of the towns, this finding also provides justification to the wider use of the term within policy.

Understanding market town characteristics

The most detailed analysis of small towns available for England is provided by the Countryside Agency (2004a) in their State of the Countryside report.[3] Of the 1,274 small towns in England (between 2,000 and 30,000 in population), the majority (56 per cent) are very small (between 2,000 and 5,000) and only 255 (20 per cent) have populations over 10,000. Although referred to as 'market towns' by the Countryside Agency, some of these towns share many of the characteristics of suburbs and as such are unlikely to be commonly recognised as market towns. As noted above, only 499 of these towns were designated as providing a service hub function, but reflecting the distribution of town sizes, the majority of towns with a population over 5,000 do provide this characteristic service hub function. For towns under 5,000, however, very few are service hubs (16 per cent).

In terms of employment structure, small towns are not very different from the national average, with the exception being 'banking, finance and business services' where small towns perform much more weakly. The employment structure was also found to follow regional differences, for example, there is a strong showing for 'distribution, hotels and catering' in the South West reflecting a dependence on tourism in this region. Despite the detailed nature of the analysis by the Countryside Agency (2004a), many important questions remain unanswered: for example, questions such as how many towns perform a tourist function and the extent to which they have characteristics in common.

In order to explore the characteristics of market towns further, it was necessary to create our own data set. As described in Chapter 1, data were collected for 202 English towns taking part in the MTI (see Chapter 4 for a more detailed discussion of the MTI). The remainder of this chapter analyses the characteristics of these 202 towns through a descriptive discussion of the data, followed by the use of regression analysis to explore the degree of commonality occurring between diversely characterised towns and finally through the use of cluster analysis.

Descriptive analysis

Population

The average population of the sample of towns is approximately 10,000 but the majority of the towns are a little smaller than this. The diversity of the towns was illustrated by their population range of between 1,500 and 34,000, with towns at the lower end of the population range expected to differ markedly in terms of their functions. The data suggests that, on average, the towns had increased in population by approximately 11 per cent between the 1991 and 2001 Population Censuses.[4] Of those living in the town at the time of the 2001 Population Census, an average of 6.6 per cent had moved into the area from within the UK in the year prior to completion of the questionnaire (0.11 per cent for England and Wales).

The average age of residents within the towns (41 years) is slightly older than the national average (39). There is a higher proportion of retired population in towns (19 per cent) than the national average (16 per cent), and a similar trend was observed using 1991 data. Comparing 1991 and 2001 Population Census data, Table 2.1 shows an ageing population

Table 2.1 Population change 1991–2001

| | Population Census | | % change |
	1991	2001	
0–15	22.32	19.38	−13.17
16–24	12.61	9.21	−26.96
25–44	26.30	26.70	1.52
45–74	31.98	34.90	9.13
75+	6.80	9.80	44.12

with a big out-migration of people in the 16–24 age group and an even larger increase in the population over 75.[5]

In terms of ethnic groups, 97 per cent of those living in towns sampled are British, which is much higher than the 88 per cent national average.

Most of the towns (57 per cent) were located within less than 30 minutes' drive from a large urban area and the vast majority (87 per cent) within one hour. As such, there is potential for people within most towns to both work and shop in their nearest large urban area.

Economy

Generally, the structure of the economy within the towns considered was similar to that of the nation as a whole, but with slightly more 'manufacturing' (17.4 per cent within small towns and 15 per cent for the nation as a whole), and slightly less 'real estate renting and business activities' (2.8 per cent compared to 4.7 per cent) and 'financial intermediation' (10.1 per cent compared to 13 per cent). A small number of towns have a high proportion of employment in public administration; this can often be accounted for by the location of Ministry of Defence operations close by, or by local government offices being based in the town. Unemployment levels in the towns tend to be lower than the national average (2.8 per cent for market towns compared to 3.4 per cent England average at the 2001 Population Census) and they participated in the national downward trend in unemployment.

The 202 towns varied in the extent to which they were identified as visitor attractions. Most of the towns have a tourist information centre (45 per cent open all year and 11 per cent seasonally open) and 71 per cent have at least one identifiable visitor attraction, but few had a larger number of visitor attractions that would be likely to make them 'honey pots' attracting large numbers of visitors. 12 per cent of towns were seaside towns and a further 18 per cent within 5 km of a National Park. Seaside towns were readily identifiable as visitor attractions with 68 per cent having a campsite(s) and 92 per cent having at least one identifiable tourist attraction.

Although house prices lag behind the national average, there seems to have been a recent catching up. In 2000, the first year comprehensive records of house prices became available, the average house price in the market towns surveyed was £97,733 compared to £107,946 for England and Wales. Over the period 2000–4 national house prices rose by 65 per cent, but during the same period, the average house price rise for our sample of towns was 90 per cent, such that the average for market towns was comparable with the national averages (£177,663 compared to £178,227). This more rapid rate of increase no doubt reflects the pressure in the local housing market from in-migration.

Services

The level of services in the towns was assessed by considering the number of banks and building societies, solicitors, ladies' clothing shops, doctors' surgeries and supermarkets located in the towns. About 1.5 per cent of the towns had none of these services and 32 per cent lacked representation in one of the categories (7.4 per cent no bank, 9.9 per cent no solicitor, 18.8 per cent no ladies' clothing shops, 4.5 per cent no doctors' surgeries and 18.8 per cent no supermarket). It would be difficult to describe such towns as service hubs; indeed, this indicates that the sample – and the towns included in the MTI – represent a range of country towns rather than them all fully fulfilling the rural service centre role.

Common features between towns

The degree of commonality occurring between diversely characterised towns was explored using regression analysis. Regression analysis is a statistical method for specifying and formally testing a functional relationship between variables, where its use here is not necessarily to demonstrate causality but more the co-existence of town characteristics. By explaining the variation in a variable, for example the proportion of the local employment in hotels and catering, through a series of other variables, for example proximity to a National Park, regression enables the co-existence of factors to be explored. The proportion of variation explained can be summarised in the R^2 goodness of fit statistic, where for example 0.30 suggests the model explains 30 per cent of variation.

Tables 2.2 and 2.3 provide the results of the regression analysis. Based on their importance to the understanding of small rural towns, 11 dependent variables were chosen. The first three in Table 2.2 – percentage unemployed in the towns; percentage in-migrating from inside the UK and percentage retirement age – were chosen to indicate the state of towns in terms of their local economy and changing characteristics of the population. The remaining variables in Table 2.2 consider containment within the towns in terms of distance travelled to work and percentage in self-employment. The results of six models presented in Table 2.3 reflect the following functional roles of the towns: specialised employment (percentage employed in public administration and percentage employed in manufacturing); visitor attractions (percentage employed in hotels and catering, and number of tourist attractions in the towns); and services (number of services per head of population and the number of services).

There are a number of difficulties associated with the selection of independent variables. For example, the number of supermarkets can be misleading as it is unclear whether they are large or small. Similarly, the provision of one large doctors' surgery could provide the same level of service as a series of small surgeries. In order to consider which variables to include, bivariate correlation was undertaken. If two variables were highly correlated then the variable with the strongest contribution was included and the other dropped. The final selection of variables was based on prior expectations, statistical significance and contribution to the goodness of fit of the model. The variables included within Tables 2.2 and 2.3 are all significant at the 5 per cent level and all the models achieve at least a respectable R^2 goodness of fit of 0.30. The models were found to be robust and insensitive to the omission of variables and observations.

A number of significant observations emerge from the models detailed in Table 2.2. Unemployment was found to be lowest in towns with an older than average population (mean age of the town residents) and higher rates of in-migration (percentage in-migrating from inside the UK). Related to this, lower unemployment is most likely to occur where the pressure in the housing market is greatest (percentage change in house prices (2000–4)). Those towns more remote from urban areas (time to drive to a large urban area) and located on the coast (seaside town), were more likely to have a high unemployment.

Consistent with the 'unemployment' model, greater in-migration was observed in towns with lower unemployment. The opposite was also true for the percentage change in house prices, reflecting the affluence of the towns. Smaller towns, located further away from large urban areas and close to the sea or a National Park, were more likely to have a higher level of in-migration, indicating an in-migrant preference for smaller rural towns with nearby amenities. Interestingly, in-migrants are more likely to be self-employed, suggesting a positive effect of in-migration.

Those towns with a higher percentage of people of retirement age were more likely to be remote from large urban areas. Towns with a higher percentage of people of retirement age were also more likely to be comparatively well serviced for their size.

Table 2.2 also considers the extent to which towns are self-contained in terms of employment. The first variable considered is the average distance travelled to work by those working.[6] A key factor explaining the extent of long-distance commuting is the type of employers for the town residents. In those towns where there is a high proportion of residents employed in manufacturing, public administration, and wholesale and retail, journeys to work were shorter. Exploring the data suggests that this reflects employment in these sectors

Table 2.2 Regression models explaining market town characteristics

Variables	Unemployed (%)	In-migrating from inside the UK (%)	At retirement age (%)	Ln (average distance travelled to work) (%)	Self-employed (%)
Constant	6.92 (8.70)	4.88 (4.43)	23.32 (16.84)	2.13 (4.09)	14.99 (7.872)
Population		-0.00006 (-3.50)			
Change in population (1991–2001) (%)		0.0001 (2.80)			
Mean age of the town residents	-0.06 (-3.54)				
Change in over 75-year-olds (1991–2001) (%)		-0.17 (-2.75)			
In-migrating from inside the UK (%)	-0.18 (6.15)				0.20 (3.42)
Unemployed (%)		-0.52 (-3.71)			-0.82 (-6.84)
Self-employed (%)		0.16 (3.00)			
Work mostly at home (%)					0.34 (7.24)
Walk to work (%)				-0.01 (-4.52)	
Drive to work (%)					-0.06 (3.35)
Change in house price (2000–4) (%)	-0.02 (-3.21)	0.02 (2.57)			
Time to drive to a large urban area	0.01 (6.16)	0.02 (4.66)	0.04 (4.35)		
Within 25 km of large urban area		-0.19 (-2.85)		-0.15 (-5.38)	
Number of urban areas within 10 km radius					
Seaside town (1 yes, 0 no)	0.54 (3.20)	-0.59 (-2.62)			
Seaside town or National Park (1 yes, 0 no)					
Employed in wholesale and retail (%)				-0.03 (-5.58)	-0.13 (-3.66)
Employed in hotels and catering (%)					0.09 (2.68)
Employed in public administration (%)		0.21 (10.02)	-0.35 (-5.94)	-0.01 (-4.74)	-0.23 (-8.72)
Employed in manufacturing (%)			-0.29 (-5.73)	-0.02 (-7.90)	-0.10 (-4.96)
Employed in finance (%)				0.02 (2.10)	
Number of services/town population			1077.37 (3.25)		
Isle of Wight				-0.45 (-5.23)	
British white (%)				0.02 (3.24)	
R^2	0.39	0.59	0.37	0.44	0.73
Sample size	202	202	202	202	202

Notes:
1 The t-test statistics are provided in brackets, with all variables being significant at the 5 per cent level.
2 R^2 represents the proportion of the variation in the variable explained by the model. For example, 0.50 indicates that 50 per cent of the variation is explained.

Table 2.3 Economic and service roles of the towns

Variables	Employed in public administration (%)	Employed in manufacturing (%)	Employed in hotels and catering (%)	Number of tourist attractions	Number of services/town population	Number of services
Constant	50.0 (5.08)	55.82 (11.36)	4.27 (10.03)	0.65 (3.38)	0.0007 (-0.99)	-6.60 (-2.35)
population			-0.0002 (-4.32)		-0.00000002 (-2.17)	0.00092 (13.89)
Mean age of the town residents	-0.64 (7.36)	-0.50 (-4.41)			0.00006 (3.34)	
In-migrating from inside the UK (%)	0.91 (6.45)	-1.16 (6.79)				
Change in unemployment (1991–2001) (%)						0.016 (3.02)
Change in house price (2000–4) (%)	-0.06 (-2.57)					
Time to drive to a large urban area			0.02 (3.28)			
Number of urban areas within 10 km radius					-0.0002 (-5.32)	
Seaside town (1 yes, 0 no)		-2.68 (-2.60)	1.81 (3.09)	0.86 (2.79)	-0.0007 (4.11)	
National Park (1 within or close to, 0 not)			2.62 (4.42)	0.72 (2.17)		
Employed in hotels and catering (%)					0.00006 (3.63)	
Employed in wholesale and retail (%)	-0.58 (-6.32)			0.14 (4.22)		0.65 (4.31)
Employed in manufacturing (%)	-0.30 (5.87)					
Number of tourist attractions			0.36 (2.86)			5.04 (5.04)
Number of campsites			0.93 (4.80)			
Number of ladies' clothing shops			0.21 (3.67)	0.12 (4.68)		
Average distance to work	-0.09 (-2.00)	-0.77 (-4.75)				
Average distance to work squared		0.008 (4.13)				
R^2	0.54	0.36	0.52	0.31	0.35	0.59
Sample size	202	202	202	202	202	202

within the towns themselves and this is likely to affect the location of work. The second self-containment variable relates to the percentage of people that are self-employed. The model provides strong evidence that such work tends to be home-based. Those towns where there is a comparatively low proportion of manufacturing, public administration, and whole-sale and retail are more likely to have self-employed people; the models suggest a link between hotels and catering, and self-employment.

Turning to Table 2.3, it considers the economic and service roles of market towns. The relationship between high levels of employment in public administration and a younger age profile, high in-migration and higher degrees of self-containment is often indicative of the presence of defence establishments. Towns with higher levels of manufacturing employment tended to have a lower average age profile, shorter journeys to work and lower levels of in-migration.

Towns with a higher reliance on tourism (percentage employed in hotels and catering) were likely to be smaller than average and be located further away from large urban areas. They were also more likely to be located close to or within National Parks, or to be coastal towns. Interestingly, in terms of services, the number of ladies' clothes shops was also related to tourism, suggesting that those visiting the area are supporting this form of comparison shopping, which can also benefit local residents.

The final two models in Table 2.3 consider the service role of towns. Those towns that were comparatively well serviced for their size were more likely to have an older population, to be remote from other towns, were less likely to be seaside towns, more likely to be tourist towns and likely to be smaller than average in terms of population. Of these characteristics, remoteness from large urban areas is particularly interesting. Although this is to be expected on grounds of competition, the time to drive to a large urban area is not significant, suggesting perhaps a different market in terms of town and large urban centre retail.

The co-existence of tourism and better services may have important implications in terms of the maintenance of town services, but whether this means that the range of services better matches the needs of the resident population is unclear. The second model merely considers the factors affecting the number of services in towns. Interestingly, location with respect to towns and larger urban areas does not significantly affect trade. However, there are positive associations with population, falling unemployment and the presence of tourist attractions.

Classification of towns

As stated in the introduction to this chapter it is important that we not only understand the nature of market towns, but also are able to classify them in terms of their characteristics, in order to be better able to develop and evaluate policy. There have been three main approaches to town classification – criteria/threshold, cluster analysis, and idealised types – each of which use a combination of data and expert judgement.

The criteria or threshold approach has been recently used by SERRL (reported in Countryside Agency, 2004a – results noted above), to determine whether towns are acting as service hubs. On a more regional scale, KPMG (2000a) categorised 17 market towns in the West Midlands of England into the following functional categories:

- *large towns* – over 30,000 population and not small rural towns;
- *tourist towns* – defined by numbers of visitors, level of tourist-related employment and range of facilities;
- *commuter towns* – complementing data on movement with a range of geographical information;
- *rural towns* – essentially a geographical definition supplemented by information on economic functions;

- *service and governance centres* – notable for their social assets and level of public sector employment.

Scores against objective criteria such as is yielded by demographic and economic data was supplemented by a degree of subjective judgement (KPMG 2000b) to arrive at this classification. Clearly, towns might fit into more than one of these categories – indeed four of the sample of 17 'could not be easily put into a single category' (KPMG 2000b: 18), emphasising the difficulty of achieving a simple form of categorisation that has significant analytical value.

Another example of a threshold type classification is provided by Gray (2004), where, using a combination of experience and data, market towns were classified in terms of their transport problems, reflecting location in relation to large urban centres and the degree of dispersal of users in the rural hinterland.

The two most in-depth studies of town classification are provided by Shepherd and Congdon (1990) and the National Assembly for Wales (2002), who used cluster analysis to provide a classification of small- to medium-sized urban areas (see Box 2.1 for an explanation of cluster analysis). Using a list of 39 variables, Shepherd and Congdon (1990) identified 12 clusters mostly reflecting issues of employment, location and growth. The National Assembly for Wales (2002) classified wards in Wales in terms of small town units and rural resident units, and using these spatial areas, generated twelve components in terms of the economic factors and nine in terms of social and housing.

Given the words of caution in Box 2.1, any attempt to provide such a classification of market towns needs to be thoroughly tested. A less ambitious, though equally valid approach, is reported by the Countryside Agency (2004a), where a cluster analysis is performed of the employment structure of market towns. Simplifying the analysis to the consideration of employment structure provides a greater chance of providing robust results.

Box 2.1 Cluster analysis

Cluster analysis is a data reduction and classification technique, to enable us to identify 'clusters' with similar characteristics within a large group of examples for which we have a large amount of descriptive data. For example, you may start with 200 towns and on the basis of an algorithm the data is reduced to a small number of clusters. Cluster analysis is good for exploring data structure and identifying relevant groups for further consideration. For a particular group you can look to see the range and average values for other relevant variables and how they differ from the sample as a whole: this can identify trends. The analysis is achieved either by starting off with having each observation in its own group and then repeatedly fusing the groups together (hierarchical approach) or by pre-specifying the number of groups and allowing the computer to choose the best clusters to fit that pattern (optimisation approach) (Rogerson 2001). It was this latter approach that was used by Shepherd and Congdon (1990) and also within this chapter. The output from these models will be sensitive to arbitrary parameters of the model setup (Fotheringham *et al.* 2000) and the range of variables used. Furthermore, these modules will always produce clusters but it is the responsibility of the researcher to determine whether they have meaning (Bailey and Gatrell 1995). This suggests care should be taken when using cluster analysis that the outputs are not overly sensitive to model choices and expert judgement is used within the interpretation of cluster meaning.

The third approach to classification develops idealised types. This approach uses typical characteristics to provide a description of fictional, though typical, neighbourhoods that are illustrative of a similarity of problems or likely shared future trends. This approach has been used by Scase and Scales (2002) to classify types of neighbourhood. Although no methodological justification was given by Scase and Scales (2002) for the approach taken, the classification followed a very detailed discussion of housing trends in England; indeed, the authors point out that the neighbourhoods identified 'are not representative of present day neighbourhood realities but, rather, represent abstract critical cases against which particular and specific neighbourhoods can be compared' (78). Such an approach can be used to illustrate the results of a more formal and quantitative analysis but with some added immediacy, and can provide a basis for analysis and comparison.

Classifying our sample towns

Through a number of attempts at building 'clusters' we found that the most robust classification of towns in our sample was one that was essentially simple and based on a restricted list of variables; such a classification was found to be robust to changes in parameters. The characteristics used were: level of services, extent of tourism, specialised employment, commuting, characteristics of town residents and affluence or deprivation. Hence, in agreement with the Countryside Agency (2004a), we have found that there is no such thing as a stereotypical town; they are just too varied and complex.

More specifically, the cluster analysis was undertaken using an optimisation approach (see Box 2.1), where the researcher is required to choose the number of groups. Given this responsibility, the number of groups was chosen with consideration to their plausibility and sensitivity to changes in the model parameters. Choice of variables was difficult and great care was taken with selection. In a similar way to regression analysis, bivariate correlation was undertaken. If two variables were highly correlated then the variable with the strongest contribution was included and the other dropped. All variables available to the model were used when interpreting the results. Table 2.4 provides a list of variables, groups and typical towns.

These analyses have established that, while there are no simple sets of categories into which all market towns easily and obviously fit, there are a number of key variables which help define their function. Each town will sit somewhere along a continuum, from high to low levels of association with a particular characteristic. The cluster analysis enables us to identify what is a 'typical' town for each characteristic – that is, a town at a mid-point along the continuum. As most towns can be satisfactorily fitted into this classification system, they can be described by reference to the six variables in a way which allows them to be identified and compared with other towns of a similar nature.

Tables 2.5 and 2.6 provide illustrative examples for the North East and East of England regions respectively. [7] In terms of individual towns, the analysis allows us to think about how they might be characterised by picking out a number of defining features that can be explored with reference to each town. By identifying dominant features – where these exist – we can characterise towns according to a number of functional roles. So, for example, a town might be characterised as a 'tourist town' as providing for tourists as its key defining feature, but this would not mean that it did not perform, to a lesser extent, a number of other functions. In Tables 2.5 and 2.6 Hexham in Northumberland and Burnham-on-Crouch in Essex might be said to have such a characteristic.

The results also enable towns within a region to be characterised. Table 2.5 lists the results for the North East towns, suggesting them to have a strong visitor attraction role, varied employment but a particular specialism in public administration (due partly to a major Royal Air Force base). The towns would also seem to attract commuters, but are also comparatively less affluent than averages for England. Despite the larger number of towns

Table 2.4 Cluster analysis results

Town characteristics	Variables used	Groups identified
Level of services	Number of banks and building societies Number of ladies' clothing shops Services as a proportion of population	Well-serviced towns (9) Medium-to-large towns with good services (60) Towns with good services for their size (25) Below average serviced towns (108)
Tourism	Number of campsites % employed in hotel and catering Number of tourist attractions	Visitor attractions (25) Day-tripper locations (59) Not key visitor attractions (118)
Economic structure	% employed in manufacturing % wholesale and retail % hotel and catering % public administration	Hotel and catering (14) Public administration (12) Slightly more wholesale and retail (68) Average values (108)
Commuting	Time to drive to a large urban area Average distance to work	Close to urban (106) Remote (short distance) (6) Remote (30) Long-distance commuter (60)
Characteristics of town residents	Mean age Moving to the area from elsewhere in UK (%)	Older population (38) More in-migrants (30) Less in-migration (72) Average values (59) Others (3)
Affluence or deprivation	Change in house price (2000–4) Change in unemployment (1991–2001) Unemployment rate	High unemployment (33) Slow improvers (49) Improvers (68) Getting worse (5) House price increase (42) Other (5)

in the East of England MTI, it is still possible to give a flavour of their general characteristics. Compared to the North East towns, East of England towns seem to be more affluent but poorly serviced. Reflecting growth in population within the region and its locality near London, there would appear to be significant pressures on house prices. As with the North East, commuting seems to be very common, with the remoter towns tending to be labelled in terms of long-distance commuting rather than their location. This could be used as basis for further interpretation through policy analysis and other methods. See Chapter 8 for a more detailed consideration of the regional differences between the North East and East of England regions.

The results have illustrated the multifunctional nature of most towns – a feature they have always exhibited since the role of providing a marketplace began to be complemented by functions such as service provision and manufacturing. In line with the range of classification systems discussed earlier, a number of key roles can be developed from a combination of descriptive, regression and cluster analysis. The following functional roles emerged for market towns:

- *Service centres* – these towns were divided into 'rural service centres' and 'service centres'. Rural service centres are comparatively well serviced for their size and represent perhaps the 'classic' market town role. These towns tend to have older populations, to be remote from other towns, are less likely to be seaside towns and more likely to

Table 2.5 Illustration for towns in the North East region

	County	Level of services	Tourism	Specialised employment	Commuting	Characteristics of town residents	Affluence or deprivation
Barnard Castle	Durham	Medium-to-large town with good services	Day-tripper location	Average values (manufacturing)	Remote	More in-migrants	Slow improving (unemployment)
Crook	Durham	Medium-to-large town with good services	Not a visitor attraction	Average values	Long-distance commuter	Below-average in-migrants	High unemployment
Stanhope	Durham	Town with good services for its size	Key visitor attraction	Average values	Long-distance commuter	Older population	High unemployment
Alnwick	Northumberland	Town with good services for its size	Day-tripper location	Public administration	Long-distance commuter	Average values	High unemployment
Amble	Northumberland	Below-average services	Day-tripper location	Public administration	Long-distance commuter	Less in-migration	High unemployment
Berwick-upon-Tweed	Northumberland	Well-serviced town	Key visitor attraction	Slightly more wholesale and retail	Remote	Less in-migration	High unemployment
Haltwhistle	Northumberland	Below-average services	Not a visitor attraction	Average values	Long-distance commuter	Less in-migration	High unemployment
Hexham	Northumberland	Medium-to-large town with good services	Key visitor attraction	Slightly more wholesale and retail	Long-distance commuter	Average values	Slow improving (unemployment)
Morpeth	Northumberland	Medium-to-large town with good services	Day-tripper location	Public administration	Long-distance commuter	Less in-migration	Getting worse (unemployment)
Prudhoe	Northumberland	Below-average services	Day-tripper location	Average values	Close to urban	Less in-migration	Slow improving (unemployment)
Rothbury	Northumberland	Town with good services for its size	Day-tripper location	Average values	Long-distance commuter	Older population	Slow improving (unemployment)
Wooler	Northumberland	Town with good services for its size	Key visitor attraction	Slightly more wholesale and retail	Long-distance commuter	Older population	Slow improving (unemployment)
Guisborough	Redcar and Cleveland	Medium-to-large town with good services	Day-tripper location	Slightly more wholesale and retail	Long-distance commuter	Older population	High unemployment

Table 2.6 Illustration for towns in the East of England region

	County	Level of services	Tourism	Specialised employment	Commuting	Characteristics of town residents	Affluence or deprivation
Chatteris	Cambridgeshire	Below-average services	Not a key visitor attraction	Slightly more wholesale and retail	Long-distance commuter	Average values	Improver (unemployment)
Ely	Cambridgeshire	Medium-to-large town with good services	Day-tripper location	Average values	Long-distance commuter	More in-migrants	Slow improver (unemployment)
Littleport	Cambridgeshire	Below-average services	Not a key visitor attraction	Slightly more wholesale and retail	Long-distance commuter	Average values	Improver (unemployment)
March	Cambridgeshire	Medium-to-large town with good services	Not a key visitor attraction	Slightly more wholesale and retail	Long-distance commuter	Average values	Improver (unemployment)
Whittlesey	Cambridgeshire	Below-average services	Not a key visitor attraction	Average values	Close to urban	Less in-migration	Improver (unemployment)
Wisbech	Cambridgeshire	Medium-to-large town with good services	Day-tripper location	Slightly more wholesale and retail	Close to urban	Less in-migration	Improver (unemployment)
Brightlingsea	Essex	Below-average services	Not a key visitor attraction	Slightly more wholesale and retail	Close to urban	Less in-migration	Improver (unemployment)
Burnham-on-Crouch	Essex	Below-average services	Key visitor attraction	Average values	Long-distance commuter	Less in-migration	House price increase
Manningtree	Essex	Below-average services	Day-tripper location	Average values	Long-distance commuter	Average values	House price increase
Saffron Walden	Essex	Medium-to-large town with good services	Day-tripper location	Average values	Long-distance commuter	Average values	House price increase
Walton-on-the-Naze (and Walton census)	Essex	Below-average services	Not a key visitor attraction	Slightly more wholesale and retail	Long-distance commuter	Older population	Data not available
Berkhamsted	Hertfordshire	Medium-to-large town with good services	Not a key visitor attraction	Average values	Long-distance commuter	Average values	House price increase
Tring	Hertfordshire	Below-average services	Not a key visitor attraction	Average values	Long-distance commuter	Average values	House price increase

Table 2.6 Illustration for towns in the East of England region (continued)

	County	Level of services	Tourism	Specialised employment	Commuting	Characteristics of town residents	Affluence or deprivation
Aylsham	Norfolk	Below-average services	Not a key visitor attraction	Slightly more wholesale and retail	Close to urban	Older population	Improver (unemployment)
Dereham	Norfolk	Medium-to-large town with good services	Day-tripper location	Slightly more wholesale and retail	Long-distance commuter	Average values	Slow improver (unemployment)
Diss	Norfolk	Town with good services for its size	Not a key visitor attraction	Slightly more wholesale and retail	Close to urban	Older population	Slow improver (unemployment)
Downham Market	Norfolk	Below-average services	Day-tripper location	Slightly more wholesale and retail	Long-distance commuter	Older population	Improver (unemployment)
Harleston	Norfolk	Below-average services	Not a key visitor attraction	Slightly more wholesale and retail	Long-distance commuter	Older population	Slow improver (unemployment)
Watton	Norfolk	Below-average services	Not a key visitor attraction	Slightly more wholesale and retail	Long-distance commuter	Average values	Improver (unemployment)
Wymondham	Norfolk	Medium-to-large town with good services	Day-tripper location	Average values	Close to urban	Average values	Improver (unemployment)
Beccles	Suffolk	Medium-to-large town with good services	Not a key visitor attraction	Average values (manufacturing)	Close to urban	Average values	Slow improver (unemployment)
Brandon	Suffolk	Below-average services	Day-tripper location	Average values	Remote	More in-migrants	Improver (unemployment)
Debenham	Suffolk	Below-average services	Not a key visitor attraction	Average values	Long-distance commuter	Average values	House price increase
Haverhill	Suffolk	Medium-to-large town with good services	Not a key visitor attraction	Average values (manufacturing)	Close to urban	Less in-migration	Improver (unemployment)
Mildenhall	Suffolk	Below-average services	Not a key visitor attraction	Average values	Close to urban	Less in-migration	House price increase
Newmarket	Suffolk	Medium-to-large town with good services	Not a key visitor attraction	Average values	Close to urban	More in-migrants	Improver (unemployment)
Wickham Market	Suffolk	Below-average services	Not a key visitor attraction	Average values	Long-distance commuter	Older population	Slow improver (unemployment)
Woodbridge	Suffolk	Medium-to-large town with good services	Day-tripper location	Average values	Close to urban	Older population	Improver (unemployment)

be tourist destinations, and be smaller in terms of population (12 per cent of towns). Service centres (which may or may not have sizeable hinterland linkages) are medium-to-large towns that are well serviced (30 per cent of towns).

- *Visitor attractions* – these are divided in terms of tourist towns and day-tripper locations. Visitor attractions tend to be remote from other urban areas and often located near the coast or National Parks (12 per cent of towns). They are also identifiable by their higher-than-average level of services. Day-tripper visitor towns are often without campsites or a high proportion of employment in hotels and catering, but consistently have a higher-than-average number of visitor attractions. For such towns, day-trippers are likely to be important to retailing (29 per cent of towns).
- *Locations for specialised employment* – towns that have one dominant employer or sector of employment are harder to identify, but public administration and manufacturing were identified. The dominance of public administration in some towns is due in the main to the presence of Ministry of Defence establishments (6 per cent of towns). Towns with key employment within manufacturing were also identified (at least 11 per cent of towns). Both 'public administration' and 'manufacturing' towns have younger populations and more contained work patterns. However, they also have differences, including rates of in-migration and location.
- *Housing commuters* – perhaps reflecting market forces, attitudes towards 'countryside' living and mobility patterns, rather than a deliberate policy, a number of towns are becoming commuter towns. Some towns were identified as potential commuter towns in terms of their close location to large urban areas (53 per cent), whereas other towns were identified in terms of high average distance to work statistics (30 per cent). Only a small proportion of towns were not considered to be commuter towns. A key problem with commuter towns is increasing the engagement of its residents in town activities and in making a contribution to the local economy.
- *Housing the retired* – Also reflecting current attitudes towards 'countryside' living and mobility patterns, attractive market towns are becoming popular locations for retirement. Such towns tend to have more in-migrants, have more of a focus on tourism, be more remote from urban areas, have a smaller population and be more likely to be located near the sea or national parks (19 per cent of towns).

These five functional roles are illustrative rather than exhaustive and, as is pointed out above, are not mutually exclusive; for example, there is often an important link between tourism and levels of service. Based on the analysis above, an indication of how typical these towns are in our sample of English market towns is provided within the brackets.

Conclusion

As well as increasing our understanding of small towns, this chapter has provided tools that can be used to improve decision making and act as a framework for the consideration of case studies. While the analysis is based on 202 towns from the 1,274 in the size band, these towns cover a representative selection of towns. The regression analysis has illustrated the degree of commonality occurring between diversely characterised towns, with very respectable proportions of the variation being explained by the models. This illustrates that although no typical town exists, small towns do share similar characteristics. The cluster analysis enabled towns to be grouped on the basis of six key characteristics important to our understanding. This provides a useful method of assessing the generality of the findings and assessing their degree of transferability. It has also contributed to the development of a set of functional roles that can be used to characterise towns and which will be used as a basis for further analysis in the book.

The development of policy for small rural towns, seeking to address a mixture of social and economic issues in a sustainable manner, has taken place within a relatively short space of time and has been applied to a relatively large number of towns. We are approaching a time when an evaluation of these initiatives could usefully be undertaken, but evaluation would be greatly assisted by the development of classifications, particularly if the transfer of 'best practice' is to be made between comparable locations and circumstances. The development of a town classification will be an essential element in addressing the fundamental evaluation question – 'what works best, where and why?'. It is felt that the approach developed here provides a valuable contribution towards the achievement of this goal, and the following chapter develops this analysis further by reference to some of our case study examples.

Notes

1   See for example Social Exclusion Unit (2004a; 2004b); Cabinet Office (2005); Glennerster *et al.* (1999) and Lupton (2001).
2   Countryside Agency (2004a) described the 1,274 towns as market towns. This is inconsistent with their earlier definition reported within Countryside Agency (2000). Indeed, as will be shown later the designation of towns for the MTI did not require that the towns were necessarily acting as trade and services focal points for their hinterland.
3   The State of the Countryside 2005 (CRC 2005a) provides further data but it is broken down into: hamlet and isolated dwellings; village; town and fringe; and urban (greater than 10,000). This data has not been included as it does not indicate what is happening in towns 2,000 to 30,000 in size. Within their district analysis the 'larger market towns' are taken into consideration, but data was not provided on this basis.
4   However, caution is required when interpreting this data as census boundary changes make comparison difficult.
5   The 45–75 age group is particularly large as in the 1991 Population Census the statistics were provided on the basis of retired where 60 was the retirement age for women and 65 for men. The data was presented in such a way that no disaggregation was possible.
6   The natural log of this variable was taken in order to account for non-linearities in the model.
7   The authors are happy to provide a full list of all towns upon request.

Chapter 3
Exploring contemporary functional roles

Neil Powe, Trevor Hart and Tim Shaw

Introduction

The last chapter suggested a classification of towns through the functions they provide. These functions offer a basis for analysis, explanation, policy development and evaluation. As such, knowledge of these functions is of value to regional and local agencies when they are deciding where to focus interventions and what types of interventions to offer; such knowledge can also be of value in the development of planning policies for localities and can help establish an understanding of the roles of different settlements in an area, both in terms of how they function now and how they might function in future. When evaluating policy, a classification can be helpful in identifying benchmarks against which performance can be judged and in seeking to transfer 'best practice' to appropriate contexts – towns with similar roles in similar circumstances. Through a review of the evidence and building on the classification proposed in the previous chapter, this chapter explores the contemporary functional roles of market towns and the challenges they face.

This chapter begins with an overview of the functional roles to be considered and the common challenges facing most towns. Each functional role will then be singled out for specific consideration, drawing on both the evidence assembled for the analysis in the previous chapter and from academic and policy literature. This chapter then goes on to introduce 11 case study towns (see Chapter 1 for details of methods), which are characterised in terms of their contemporary roles. For ease of reading, boxes are provided throughout the chapter to illustrate the characteristics of and challenges faced by case study towns.

Town characteristics by function

When considering the part market towns play in the rural economy and society, a key role has been that of rural service centre. Although, to varying extents, all towns still perform this service role, in response to challenge and change, roles have developed and diversified. So, where they are located near other larger towns and/or larger urban areas, the service role may have diminished with time and new roles may have developed, such as becoming a base for commuters who get most of their services elsewhere. For other towns where the role of rural service centre remains, this may be supported by the spending of tourists or day visitors. In other cases, they may be home to an ageing population less able or willing to 'out shop' to other more distant locations, and they will maintain a significant but possibly skewed representation of services. Other towns might have other historical roles such as providing a base for a significantly sized defence establishment and its distinct population, or a centre for manufacturing of a particular type of product. Although each town is likely to perform multiple roles, understanding their nature and importance helps characterise the towns, provide a basis for comparison and sharing of good practice, as well as a focus for policy development.

By considering the empirical data described and analysed in the last chapter the following functional roles were identified for market towns:

- *Service centres* – service centres are comparatively well serviced for their size and represent perhaps the 'classic' market town role, with the offering of services to the rural hinterland being the principal raison d'etre.
- *Visitor attractions* – these tend to be remote from other urban areas and often located near the coast or National Parks. They rely on the spending of visitors to support and extend the services on offer to an above-average level.
- *Locations for specialised employment* – towns that have one dominant employer or sector of employment – such as defence or manufacturing – are a distinct group, with typically younger populations and more contained work patterns.
- *Housing commuters* – with increased mobility and people able to make 'lifestyle' rather than functional decisions about where they live, a number of towns are becoming commuter towns. The more limited attachment of residents to the towns poses a challenge to the viability of services and can affect their future pattern of development.
- *Housing the retired* – attractive market towns are becoming popular locations for retirement, with consequent impacts across a range of areas including house prices and service provision.

These five functional roles are used in the remainder of this chapter to explore the issues facing market towns and the way they function. But, before giving each of these roles separate consideration, it is important to explore a number of common trends affecting most market towns.

Common trends affecting market towns

First, it is frequently stated that accessibility is a determining factor in the functioning of rural areas, so it should be little surprise that perhaps the most fundamental trend relates to mobility. While approximately 50 per cent of the towns sampled in the last chapter have a railway station, the vast majority of commuting and shopping trips are by car (Banister and Gallent 1998; Powe and Shaw 2003); therefore motoring costs are crucial to understanding current trends in the way people access services and the resulting pattern of use and development. With high levels of car ownership, and motoring costs falling as a proportion of disposable income[1] (DfT 2005), many new threats and opportunities have arisen for market towns. In terms of those living in market towns and their hinterlands, the falling cost of travel as a proportion of income has encouraged residents to look further afield for shopping and employment. For those considering a move to rural areas, this has increased the feasibility of commuting from or retiring to market towns. Increased mobility has also increased the potential for market towns to attract visitors from larger urban areas, both for day trips and holidays. These trends are reflected in a marked increase in rural road usage.[2]

A second key issue, facilitated by falling transport costs and increased mobility, is the wide-scale migration into market towns. Market towns are viewed by many as desirable places to live and, as is the case in other developed countries such as the US (Paradis 2000; Johnson and Beale 1995), considerable housing expansion has occurred in market towns in the UK and particularly in their peripheral areas. The results of the analysis in the last chapter showed that in-migration to market towns was more likely to occur in towns with lower unemployment, a higher percentage increase in house prices and located further away from large urban areas. The consequences of this added pressure on rural housing markets are ones that have both caused significant debate and prompted developments in policy.[3]

Since the first studies describing a change from the long-term process of concentrating in urban areas (Berry 1976), many studies have considered the motivations for moving from urban to rural areas (Champion 1989; Boyle and Halfacree 1998; Dahms and McComb 1999; Mitchell 2004). Evidence of the increased importance of quality-of-life factors in people's decision to move has been observed in a number of studies (Williams and Jobes 1990; Halliday and Coombes 1995). Perhaps the most relevant and detailed exploration of motivations is provided by Halfacree (1994), who used both questionnaires and more in-depth interviews for in-migrants within two English rural areas. For urban-to-rural movers, the physical and social qualities of the environment are key motivations. Although important for long-distance urban-to-rural movers, the social quality of the environment was a lesser concern than the physical quality. Physical environmental issues that were of significance included the openness, quietness and cleanliness of the areas, as well as the views and natural environment. Social environmental issues related to the slower pace of life, the nature of the community, social quietude, and generally the escape from the urban 'rush'.

Life in a market town may be different from that of the village environment considered by Halfacree (1994), but some of these issues are still relevant. For example, although not as attractive as living in a village, country town residents are still likely to be closer to the countryside than those living in larger urban areas, and some of the social elements may still apply within market towns. As such, the pull factors to market towns may represent a second-best situation for in-migrants, perhaps reflecting house prices,[4] availability of new houses and access to services, providing the closest realist approximation to the rural idyll. Given the local distinctiveness of market towns (history, tradition, architecture), they are also likely to be chosen for their own merit. In exploring the potential motivations for in-migration in market towns, it is useful to understand urban attitudes towards market towns. In the survey of urban residents presented in the last chapter, the reasons for visiting these settlements related to the experience being 'different from the city'. This difference equates to more than the smaller size of market towns, but also their particular characteristics in terms of history, heritage and countryside locations, with the diversity of the shopping experience also being commonly mentioned. Other reasons for visiting noted were the peacefulness and friendliness of the towns. For urban residents considering a move to country towns, this is likely to represent their image of the towns and could represent part of the motivation for moving.

Service centres

Central to the definition of market towns is their role as rural hubs for the provision of services. In Chapter 2 it was explained that there are estimated to be 1,274 small towns in England with populations between 2,000 and 30,000 (Countryside Agency 2004a) of which 499 were categorised as service hubs. Given the importance of the service role it has been the subject of much research. This section will draw from the detailed surveys of SERRL (2004),[5] Powe and Shaw (2003; 2004)[6] and Courtney *et al.* (2006)[7], which illustrate the market town function for a range of settlements.

Despite recent improvements in mobility providing the opportunity for rural residents to shop elsewhere, Powe and Shaw (2003) found town and hinterland residents to be the key visitors to market towns in the North East of England, with town residents making up between 25 and 45 per cent of the visitors and rural hinterland residents between 42 and

45 per cent. For these towns there exists a mutual dependence, whereby the viability of the town services are dependent upon trade from hinterland residents, and many of these hinterland residents also depend on such services being provided within their nearest town (see Box 3.1 for the example of Alnwick in the North East of England). Although this traditional linkage still exists, SERRL (2004) found that town and hinterland residents made use of a variety of services in different locations and that the 'functional attachment' to market towns was greater for their residents than those living in villages. This suggests that, for the majority of towns, market town services are more dependent on their hinterland residents than vice-versa.[8] Looking to the future, SERRL (2004) suggests that market towns are in a phase of transition with a declining employment role, and with residents using local services more selectively.

In terms of specific services, SERRL (2004) found market towns performed most strongly for main food, top-up and convenience shopping, but less so for non-food (comparison) shopping. The market town of Alnwick provides an example of this (see Box 3.1), where Powe and Shaw (2004) found 63 per cent of hinterland respondents still doing their main food shopping in the town but, in terms of non-food retail, 'out-shopping' was much greater, with 67 per cent of respondents not conducting their main non-food shopping in Alnwick. However, SERRL (2004) found that the provision of banking, finance and professional services was very much focused in the market towns.

Powe and Shaw (2003) considered current use and the possibility of increased use of the town centre in the evening. As perhaps is to be expected, use and frequency of use of the centre in the evening was greatest among town centre residents (between 40 and 80 per cent).[9] However, a sizeable minority of hinterland residents visited the towns in the evenings (between 31 and 41 per cent). Of those who potentially would use the market towns' services in the evening, there was generally a request for variety beyond pubs, illustrating potential for future improvement; though whether such extensions would prove viable is open to question.

SERRL (2004) suggested that, to a significant extent, town and village residents lead different work and service lives, with work journeys longer than journeys to access services. A small minority work in the towns, but the remainder travel far and wide to work (Chapter 9 illustrates how this varies considerably between towns). This trend is more pronounced for village residents. Overall, SERRL (2004) and Powe and Shaw (2003) found that the car was the dominant means of travel to work and to access services. Bus use was minimal and related to the level of affluence of the residents, and Courtney *et al.* (2006) found access to private transport to affect levels of out-shopping. Walking was the only other popular means of transport and was observed by Powe and Shaw (2003) to be common only for market town residents. For example, in terms of accessing market town centres, the majority of town residents walked (between 51 and 68 per cent), with the car coming a clear second (between 27 and 36 per cent). So, it seems that attempts to achieve greater levels of sustainability by concentrating development in settlements such as market towns is more likely to work for residents of the town than residents of the hinterland.

The evidence presented suggests that the 'market town' service function is very much still present within many market towns, but a number of factors are leading residents to be diverted elsewhere to shop and for employment (Pinkerton *et al.* 1995; Robertson 1997; Collis *et al.* 2000; Thomas and Bromley 2002). However, insofar as the desires to live in market towns can be translated into patronage of shops and services by new arrivals, there is cause for optimism. The overall principle will be to compete better by providing what visitors want from their market towns, within the confines of their size and potential. The issue remains of how and where to encourage new growth to develop. Chapter 4 considers the relevant policy frameworks attempting to manage growth, and Chapters 7 and 8 consider the role of new housing in town regeneration.

Box 3.1 Rural service use in Alnwick

Alnwick (see Plate 1), with a population of approximately 8,000, serves a predominantly rural hinterland (it is the largest town in a district of 31,000 population) and holds sway in a sub-region between the other market towns and the city of Newcastle upon Tyne, which is within an hour's drive. Typical of many other rural areas in England, Alnwick District has an ageing population and has a higher proportion of car ownership when compared to national figures (Population Census 2001). Tourism is important to the local economy, with Alnwick Castle (now of Harry Potter fame) and water gardens being key visitor magnets. Reflecting tourism trends, retailing within the town has seen a marked change over the last twenty years, moving away from the provision of comparison goods, for example electrical, furniture and clothing, to shops more reflecting the needs of the tourists.

Based on town centre visitor and hinterland resident surveys, a mutual dependence was identified between the town and its hinterland: the prosperity of the town is dependent on the patronage of its hinterland residents, many of whom depend on services being in the town. It was suggested that the future of market town services and their provision, particularly for less mobile people, depends on the continuation of such a relationship. More specifically, the town was found to be visited for a wide range of services including: supermarkets; other food shops; non-food shops; pubs; general services (e.g. district council, health, insurance, solicitor, travel agent or bank); post office; market; cinema; theatre; and cafes and restaurants. Although non-food products are usually purchased elsewhere, usually in larger urban areas, hinterland residents still make extensive use of their market town for their main food shopping. The results also showed that those using the supermarkets in Alnwick for their main food shopping were more likely to visit other services in the town. This demonstrates the potential of good supermarkets (price and range of products) located close to town centres to support the viability of the centre as a whole. For residents commuting to work elsewhere, those commuting furthest were found to be least likely to do their non-food shopping in the market town.

The town is visited in the evening by hinterland residents of all ages. Although pub use was found to be related to distance from home, the use of the cinema/theatre was not, suggesting a wider catchment area and greater potential for such evening entertainment facilities.

The results of focus groups of hinterland residents suggested that the participants did not feel there was anything 'special' about visiting their town. Rather than having a sense of affinity and/or loyalty towards the town, their relationship with it was purely instrumental. In contrast, village-level services were held dearly and seen to provide an added value in terms of an informal meeting place and to play an important role in community cohesion, but there was no evidence that this perception was matched by patronage. This suggests that if market towns are going to compete with the better quality and/or lower prices within larger urban areas, they may need to provide an added value beyond their current services.

Source: Powe and Shaw (2004)

Visitor attractions

There is little evidence available in terms of the current importance of urban visitors to country towns, with perhaps the only study available suggesting urban visitors make up as much as 16 per cent of those interviewed (on a next-to-pass basis) within market town centres (Powe and Shaw 2003). For some towns the dependence on tourism is greater, and this was demonstrated during the foot and mouth crisis,[10] with Williams and Ferguson (2005) providing evidence for the town of Keswick in Cumbria, Northern England (see Box 3.2 for a description of the town and issues faced). This crisis illustrated the importance of the hinterland as a source of trade to market towns which are tourist attractions. In spite of there being no restrictions on access to the town itself, sizeable losses in trade were reported, emphasising the importance of considering the town in the context of its hinterland. Despite the importance of urban residents as visitors to market towns, little is known about how they view the towns and what they find attractive (see Chapter 9 for survey results considering this issue).

The cluster analysis in the last chapter identified that about four in ten market towns were attractions for staying and day visitors. Towns that were visitor attractions tended to be typical in the English counties of East Sussex, Worcestershire, Northumberland, Cumbria, County Durham, Herefordshire and Devon, suggesting that visitor attractions are very important for the rural economy in these counties. These data also suggest that most of the towns have a tourist information centre (45 per cent open all year and 11 per cent seasonally open) and 71 per cent have at least one identifiable visitor attraction. 14 per cent of all towns have a castle and 48 per cent a museum, underlining the role of 'heritage' in acting as a visitor attraction. Six towns had racecourses, making their names better known than otherwise. Location was also important, with 12 per cent being seaside towns and a further 18 per cent located within 5 km of a National Park. A further 12 towns are associated with nearby large lakes that have been used to attract tourism to the area.

Box 3.2 Keswick: a major visitor attraction

Keswick is a relatively remote market town located within the Lake District National Park in North West England, with a wonderful mountainous backdrop (see Plates 4 and 5). The area attracts a large number of visitors each year and tourism is a major contributor to the local economy. Keswick is characterised by an ageing population and house prices much greater than the average for English market towns, with 10 per cent of the housing being second homes (Keswick Area Partnership 2006). The tight planning controls of a National Park mean that there is little new housing being built and, with the market prices being so high, there is little incentive for the provision of private rented properties.

Given the remote location of the town, approximately 70 per cent of residents working work in the town, which compares favourably with the towns considered within Chapter 8. With a great deal of the indigenous employment being based in the tourism industry, noted for seasonal work and low wages, there are particular problems with housing affordability (CRC 2005b). Indeed, local actors suggested there to be considerable commuting into the town from elsewhere, particularly from the more deprived west of the county. CRC (2005b) demonstrated the extent of this affordability problem, where there is a need to enable young families, particularly, to continue to live and work in the town and maintain the pool of labour for local businesses. Indeed, given the wage/house cost imbalance it is often necessary for local businesses to provide accommodation for their employees.

Box 3.3 Minehead: a coastal tourist town

Minehead is located in a rural area with relatively poor access. It is the largest town in West Somerset District, and is home to around a third of the district's 35,000 population. The town has a strong dependence on tourism, with other large employers – a laundry and a catering equipment business – being related to its tourism role. Minehead has adapted rather better to the changing fortunes of English seaside towns than some others, possibly because of the presence of a major investor committed to the town (Butlins) and because of its links, manufactured or real, to a growing segment of the market, the countryside holiday. While it describes itself as the 'gateway to Exmoor' many of its visitors will stay at – and inside – the Butlins holiday camp at the eastern end of the town. It has a capacity of just over 9,000 visitors and hosts about 400,000 staying visitors each year. It also employs 200 full-time and 1,400 seasonal staff.

In terms of retail, the town has a representation of some key multiples and there is a good-sized supermarket (and another under consideration), but the range of shops has the difficult task of satisfying a number of separate markets:

- local people looking to meet their daily needs;
- 'incomers'/lifestyle choice people, who perhaps have higher-order needs;
- visitors to Butlins, who are looking particularly for one range of essentially 'holiday' goods; and
- 'Exmoor gateway types' who have a different range of sometimes higher-order needs.

Comparing the visitor attraction to that of the rural service role, both have implications for town centre retail. The extent to which there are synergies and inconsistencies between these roles is explored in detail in Chapter 10. Box 3.3 provides an illustration of the retail challenges in the town of Minehead in the South West of England.

Locations for specialised employment

Historically, and in policy terms, a key function of market towns may be seen as acting as a location for employment. The two roles previously considered – service centres and visitor attractions – clearly have an employment dimension but here we are considering the distinct contribution of roles as centres for public administration (see Box 3.4) and manufacturing as sources of employment. Evidence cited in the last chapter highlights the importance of this specialisation (public administration: 6 per cent of towns; and manufacturing: at least 11 per cent of towns). Such towns tend to have younger populations and more contained work patterns, such that the average distance travelled to work is less than in other towns. Those towns with high levels of 'public administration' tend to have high rates of in-migration, whereas the opposite is true for manufacturing towns. An important factor affecting employment in public administration and, to a lesser extent, manufacturing towns is government support and spending. Employment in public administration and policies for public sector management and service delivery have a direct impact on public sector employment, both in scale and location. While public sector support for manufacturing is now very limited, various forms of regional and sectoral policy can have an impact on the location of business and employment growth.

Box 3.4 Richmond: the effect of being located near a large defence establishment

Richmond is a town with a population of just over 8,000, located in North Yorkshire in Northern England. It is noted for its castle, large marketplace (see Plate 3) and Georgian theatre. The town centre is blessed with a number of attractive buildings and is designated as a conservation area.

Although Richmond provides an administrative centre for Richmondshire District Council, this is unlikely to be the key reason for the high level of public sector employment in the town. Three miles away from the town centre is Catterick Garrison, a large Ministry of Defence establishment with a population of about 12,000. Catterick Garrison is almost a separate settlement and it gained a large supermarket and retail park in 2000, outside the barracks and open to the general public. Under plans released in 2005, the Ministry of Defence is looking to expand the population of the garrison to 25,000 by 2020.

With most of the solders living within the barracks, it is unlikely to have had a huge effect on the local housing market, although officers and civilian employees are likely to live off-site. The new supermarket and retail park (Richmondshire Walk) would appear to have reduced trade for some of Richmond town centre's shops, but it also provides a successful shopping area of a different character for local residents to use, and to some extent reduces their need to travel to distant urban centres to shop. With the barracks increasing in size, this shopping area can be expected to grow.

Richmond's marketing focuses very much on its heritage, emphasising that it provides an attractive place to live and visit. Richmond is 'off limits' as a drinking place for the soldiers, but the town's restaurants and theatre attract patronage from a wide area. With the comparatively high house prices in Richmond, the occasional release of housing for private sale by the Ministry of Defence is seen to be providing much-needed affordable housing: for example, a number of Richmond shop workers live in Catterick. Indeed, our research suggested that shops in Richmond struggle to recruit staff. Casual visitors to Richmond would not be likely to be aware of the presence and impact of the garrison, but its effects on the town are considerable, in an economic and social sense.

While there are sustainability benefits of these types of local employment, there are also likely to be economic benefits to the local economy. The importance of encouraging employment that minimises leakages from the local economy was explored by Courtney and Errington (2000), who compared a 'remote' (Kingsbridge) and an 'accessible' market town (Olney). Generally, they concluded that these towns acted more as a source of sales than a source of inputs for the local rural firms, but linkages all along the supply chain were greater for the more 'remote' market town. Yarwood (1996) presents some comparable findings for the remote town of Leominster, where most of the firms on an industrial estate had been founded within the county and most of the workforce was locally sourced. However, such employment is unlikely to provide sufficiently attractive opportunities to stop the out-migration of young educated rural residents. More promising results are provided by Bolton and Chalkley (1990) and Renkow and Hoover (2000), who have illustrated how economic growth within an area can attract in-migrants for employment. The research suggests that such in-migrants will tend to be older than the existing population, but more highly qualified (also see Dean *et al.* 1984).

Housing commuters

Considerable changes have been occurring in working patterns with people travelling increased distances to find suitable employment, increasing the length of the working day; at the same time, the numbers of households where both partners work full-time are rising. According to Green (1997), dual career migrants tend to prefer 'accessible semi-rural areas, with good access to transport infrastructure, especially motorways' (635). Market towns often fit these criteria, where the desire for improved quality of life can be achieved whilst maintaining the level of income associated with the job opportunities in large urban areas.

Towns located sufficiently close to, or with good transport links to, larger urban areas, may take on the role of commuter towns. As noted above, 53 per cent of the towns that were within the MTI are located close to larger urban areas and a further 29 per cent (of varying distance from large urban areas) are characterised in terms of long-distance commuting. The extent to which towns are locations from which to commute will depend partly on whether the towns are considered as desirable places to live, and the quality and quantity of their indigenous employment. Furthermore, as the results in Chapter 9 suggest, remote towns such as Downham Market can also provide important locations for the housing for rural employment located mostly outside the town.

The extent to which people are moving into rural areas to commute has been the subject of much research. The 'quality of life' attraction of rural areas has been described above, and commuters must be willing to bear the financial and time costs of travel in order to gain their desired residential location. For example, considering commuting in North Carolina, USA, Renkow and Hoover (2000) found the cost of travel to be an important factor within their models, where a threshold of 35 miles determined whether in-migration and commuting were occurring together. Within this distance the relationship was statistically significant, but outside it was not. The link between in-migration and place of work was also found to be statistically significant by Findlay *et al.* (2001) for both England and Scotland. The analysis reported in Chapter 2 found some relationship between sector of employment and commuting behaviour, with work in the financial services sector being significantly related to the propensity to travel to work outside the area of residence.

While 50 per cent of the MTI sample of towns (see Chapter 2) has a railway station, in most cases rail travel is not an important means of commuting. For example, in Crediton in Devon, where the station is part of the Countryside Agency's 'Gateway Stations' scheme aimed at developing integrated transport networks, only 3.5 per cent of journeys to the nearby city of Exeter were made by train. As is common in most towns, the vast majority (71 per cent, in the case of Crediton) make their journey to work by car. The dominance of the car is mainly a reflection of the low density of public transport services of all sorts. Something of an exception to this is Todmorden, where its location between the major urban areas of Leeds/Bradford and Greater Manchester means that it benefits from services that are both regular and operating throughout the day, early and late. A further case is provided in Box 3.5, where the market town of Wymondham illustrates travel to work patterns for a town planned for further expansion.

A key challenge for towns performing the commuter function is encouraging these residents to engage with the town, in terms of using retail and service facilities, and contributing to the development of social capital (see Chapter 8 for a more detailed consideration). As commuters are likely to have higher incomes (reflecting their ability to pay for the extra cost of transport and increasingly higher costs of housing), there is potential for the prosperity of the towns to benefit.

Although increased in-migration is likely to lead to more commuting, the long-term effect may be more positive. Renkow and Hoover (2000) suggest it to be unlikely that in-migrants will both move into rural areas and simultaneously change employment. They suggested instead that this may come later. Indeed, the regression results from Chapter 2 suggest high

---

Box 3.5 Wymondham: a commuter town planned for further expansion

Wymondham (population 11,500) is situated only 9 miles from the city of Norwich in the East of England. The town is steeped in history (Plate 6), with an attractive market cross (Plate 2) and abbey near its centre, as well as an award-winning railway station. As such, it represents an attractive place to live. As will be discussed in more detail in Chapter 8, the town is seen as an important part of the Norwich sub-region for housing development. Plate 7 illustrates a major housing estate isolated from the town by a main road and located near to the A11 convenient for 'out-shopping' and 'out-working'. Our resident survey illustrates that only 26 per cent of town residents currently employed work in the town. This compares with 61 per cent for the more remote town of Alnwick. Of those out-working, the use of the car dominated. Despite the central location of the train station, only 6 per cent used this facility to travel to work beyond the town. Use of the bus service was also minimal (8 per cent of those out-working). These figures compare dramatically with figures relating to those respondents living in the town, of which approximately half did not use the car to get to work (54 per cent). This illustrates the extent of out-commuting occurring within a town close to a larger urban area. Other issues associated with housing development are discussed in detail in Chapter 8.

---

rates of in-migration and self-employment to co-exist. Using surveys of in-migrants in Scotland, Findlay *et al.* (2000) found that 22 per cent of the sample to be self-employed and nearly all of them (85 per cent) had based their business locally (within less than 20 km of home).

Housing the retired

Freed of the need for employment, retired people are likely to have more freedom to choose where to live. Although house prices and services may still be important constraints, lifestyle factors in residential location choice are likely to be more important for the retired. Dean *et al.* (1984) noted that a substantial proportion (40 per cent of non-return in-migrants over the age of 59) of in-migrants were older than the general population in Cornwall in South West England. Although the majority of in-migrants were employed, those retired made up a sizeable proportion. Likewise, Halliday and Coombes (1995) found retired in-migrants to be moving into the more remote and attractive areas of Devon, and this was seen to be occurring simultaneously with the movement of younger families into larger settlements. Similarly, in the US, Frey (1993) suggests elderly residents were likely to select attractive non-metropolitan areas. Other studies, which have considered rural areas of comparatively high rates of economic growth, found a much smaller proportion of in-migrants to be retired (Bolton and Chalkley 1990; Williams and Jobes 1990).

These results from previous empirical work suggest that in-migration will vary between the types of rural area. Indeed, Smith and Phillips (2001) found that remote housing attracted people of higher socio-economic groups from those living in villages in West Yorkshire. Likewise, differences in house preference were observed by Bolton and Chalkley (1990), where those in North Devon moving to remoter rural areas preferred older, more traditional properties, but those moving into the nearby market town were observed to tend to buy recently built modern properties. However, this may be an effect of availability of different types of property in different localities.

Little is known about the preferences of retired residents towards market towns. As most rural house building is occurring in market towns, this creates the potential for in-migration. With market towns having a higher level of services than their surrounding rural areas this may have great appeal for those retired. Indeed, such concerns may lead to a movement from hinterlands to towns as residents get older and less mobile (see Chapter 6). The results of the regression analysis in the last chapter showed that those towns with a higher percentage of people of retirement age were more likely to be remote from larger urban areas. Given that needs for health and social care are likely to increase with age, this can give rise to a number of consequences. This is particularly the case for the over-seventies, where Joseph and Cloutier (1991) illustrate how their need for health and social services increases and, with the increase in widowhood, dependency increases. For those in-migrants who are less likely to have the social networks, Joseph and Cloutier (1991) suggest that they will have a greater dependence on the state for support.

Despite possible difficulties caused by the requirement for extra public services, retired residents may actually represent potential for market towns, in terms of trade for town centre shops and in terms of acting as contributors to the generation of social capital. Indeed, Powe and Shaw (2004) found that older hinterland residents are more inclined to purchase food locally. Furthermore, Findlay *et al.* (2001) found the relationship between those retired and 'out-shopping' to be present only for incomers, who are more likely to have links with urban areas. Such in-migrants from urban areas may also bring with them greater expectations of the services they require and place new demands on their market towns, the fulfilment of which may benefit the local economy, or may be beyond its capacity to satisfy. Indeed, with the simultaneous out-migration of the young, the net effect on town centre shops may be quite marked. Backing for the link between retired residents and town centre usage is provided by the regression results in the last chapter, where towns with a higher percentage of people of retirement age tended to be comparatively well-serviced for their size.

In terms of the survey towns (Alnwick, Morpeth, Downham Market and Wymondham), retired residents are clearly less likely to contribute paid labour to the towns and they are also statistically less likely to contribute to the evening economy, but they were found to be just as likely to shop in the towns (food and non-food) and be more likely to engage with local community activities. As such, retired residents provide an important contribution to the towns. Indeed, the voluntary labour of retired residents was found to be very important within the running of local organisations (see Chapters 8, 9 and 10 for other results from these surveys).

Comparing their results to those of Dean *et al.* (1984), Bolton and Chalkley (1990) suggest in-migration for retirement is more likely to occur in coastal and/or areas of high landscape amenity. Considering the regression analysis in Chapter 2, variables reflecting coastal towns and those located in or near National Parks were not statistically significant at the 10 per cent level. This suggests the link between these town attributes and retirement to be more complex. Box 3.6 illustrates a retirement town located on the coast, with external demand for retirement putting pressure on house prices, but simultaneously the local tourist industry depends on there being a supply of low-paid workers who are likely to have problems finding affordable housing.

Case study towns

As part of this research visits were made to the following towns: Crediton and Minehead in the South West; Haslemere in the South East; Downham Market and Wymondham in the East of England; Oswestry in the West Midlands; Keswick in the North West; Richmond and Todmorden in Yorkshire and Humber; and Alnwick and Morpeth in the North East. The towns were selected as examples of the five functional roles of towns identified

---

Box 3.6 Hunstanton: a remote coastal town in Norfolk

Hunstanton is a remote town located on the north Norfolk coast. It has a high percentage of retired residents and high levels of in-migration (32 per cent and 13 per cent respectively in the year prior to the Population Census 2001). Hunstanton also has a relatively high proportion of second homes. The results of a survey of residents within the town (Powe 2007) suggest that the beach and countryside location of Hunstanton is the key motivating factor for moving to that town. When asked about housing issues, affordability was a key issue for local, particularly young, residents, with some of the respondents noting personal hardship. Indeed, house prices are 25 per cent higher than the county average (Land Registry 2006), and have risen by 116 per cent over the period 2000–5 compared to a 106 per cent average for Norfolk as a whole. Further to the town's role as an attractive location for housing, 13 per cent of residents are employed in the hotel and catering sector, putting Hunstanton in the top 5 per cent of towns in terms of this form of employment. In a similar way to Keswick, the dual roles of retirement town and visitor attraction cause many difficulties in terms of finding low-paid workers in an area challenged in terms of affordability of housing.

---

in Chapter 2, as well as attempting to cover a range of locations and contexts. Using the cluster analysis results a summary of the characteristics of the case study towns is provided in Table 3.1.

Having considered the literature, the case study towns are described to gain a better understanding of the roles market towns play. Considering services initially, all the towns considered do, to some extent, support a rural hinterland, though this varies between towns, with Oswestry servicing perhaps the most extensive hinterland (see Box 3.7) and, because of the topography of the area, Todmorden the least. Of those more remotely located it would seem important that the towns are key centres for their districts. For example, Alnwick is the dominant town within the district and as such provides the important roles of service and employment centre, whereas Downham Market is dominated by the nearby large town of King's Lynn and provides a lesser employment and service role, but is a very important rural location for provision of housing. Alternatively, Minehead's location on the coast means that the hinterland is in some way limited.

Towns located near larger urban areas, such as Wymondham and Morpeth, come under more intensive competition for retail trade and many residents travel out to their employment. Although Haslemere is relatively distant from large urban areas, the draw of the London job market is great (50 minutes by train). Indeed, Haslemere has one of the highest average distances for travel to work in the sample over of 200 towns (22 miles) and the second highest percentage of people using the train to go to work (13 per cent).

Keswick's role as a service provider is much enhanced by its popularity for tourists (see Box 3.2), having a wider range of shops than would be expected for a town of 5,000 people. Although some shops are specifically targeted at the tourist, a number are also popular with local residents. The town performs a very strong local employment role, although there are severe difficulties with housing affordability.

As might be expected, the two remote tourist towns (Keswick and Minehead) have an older population and to an extent perform the role of retirement locations. Downham Market also performs this role by providing relatively cheap rural housing for people retiring from London. Less in-migration was observed in two types of towns – those towns suffering

Table 3.1 Characteristics of case study towns

	County	Level of services	Tourism	Specialised employment	Commuting	Characteristics of town residents	Affluence or deprivation
Alnwick	Northumberland, North East	Town with good services for its size	Day-tripper location	Public administration	Long-distance commuter	Average values	High unemployment
Morpeth	Northumberland, North East	Medium-to-large town with good services	Day-tripper location	Public administration	Long-distance commuter	Less in-migration	Getting worse (unemployment)
Keswick	Cumbria, North West	Well-serviced town	Key visitor attraction	Hotels and catering	Remote	Older Population	Slow improver (unemployment)
Oswestry	Shropshire, West Midlands	Well-serviced town	Not visitor attraction	Slightly more wholesale and retailing	Remote	Less in-migration	High unemployment
Todmorden	Calderdale, Yorkshire and Humber	Below-average services	Not visitor attraction	Average values	Close to urban	Less in-migration	High unemployment
Richmond	North Yorkshire, Yorkshire and Humber	Below-average services	Day-tripper location	Public administration	Long-distance commuter	Average values	Improver (unemployment)
Downham Market	Norfolk, East of England	Below-average services	Not visitor attraction	Slightly more wholesale and retail	Long-distance commuter	Older population	Improver (unemployment)
Wymondham	Norfolk, East of England	Medium-to-large town with good services	Day-tripper location	Average values	Close to urban	Average values	Improver (unemployment)
Haslemere	Surrey, South East	Medium-to-large town with good services	Not visitor attraction	Average values	Long-distance commuter	Average values	House price increases
Crediton	Devon, South West	Below-average services	Not visitor attraction	Slightly more wholesale and retail	Close to urban	Average values	Slow improver (unemployment)
Minehead	Somerset, South West	Medium-to large-town with good services	Key visitor attraction	Hotels and catering	Remote	Older population	Slow improver (unemployment)

Box 3.7 Oswestry: a traditional market town

Oswestry is a remote market town situated in the 'Marches' close to the Welsh border. Arguably, the defining characteristic of the town is its weekly livestock market where the main trade is in Welsh sheep. It has a population of approximately 15,000 people, and 47,000 live within its catchment area. Agriculture remains important to the economy of Oswestry, with agri-business having a major presence in the town and the surrounding area. In terms of hinterland linkages, initiatives such as 'Local to Oswestry' offer opportunities for farmers to 'brand' their produce, as does the growing interest in the development of high-quality restaurants in the town. Also related to agriculture, haulage companies continue to thrive and there are also some substantial storage businesses in Oswestry.

Location works against Oswestry's competitive position and this may remain a lasting problem. However, there are clearly some sectors of industrial activity that are showing signs of overcoming these locational difficulties. These include medical research, haulage and storage, agriculture and agriculture-related industries. The tourism potential of the town is uncertain. The visitor centre on the bypass highlights the major problem. It regularly logs 80,000 visitors a year but the majority of these are flowing into Wales and not looking to visit or stay in the town. Nearby in Wales, Llangollen has major attractions to offer national and international visitors. Although Oswestry has a great deal to offer, bed spaces, cafes and restaurants will have to be expanded and improved if tourism is ever to play a major role in the future economy of the town.

---

from unemployment (Oswestry and Todmorden) and those with some constraints on housing (Morpeth).

The three 'specialised employment' towns (Alnwick, Morpeth and Richmond (see Box 3.5)), are characterised by a mixture of local authority and Ministry of Defence establishments providing employment. Todmorden has a history of manufacturing employment, although this has declined over a long period and a brief description of the challenges facing this town is provided in Box 3.8. Keswick and Minehead both have a concentration of employment in or related to the tourist industry, particularly in hotels and catering, with Minehead being the location of a long-established Butlins holiday camp (see Box 3.3). With its favourable location close to Norwich, on the soon-to-be-further-improved A11 and with a train route to London and Cambridge, it was reported that new businesses have been moving to Wymondham, which adds to employment created in the town by the opening of the Norfolk Constabulary's Operations and Communications Centre in 2002.

Fuelled by external demand, high house prices are a problem for a number of towns. Box 3.2 provides an illustration of the difficulties in Keswick and the results in Chapter 8 illustrate the problems encountered in Alnwick in particular. In discussion with key actors it was suggested that relatively high house prices in Richmond and a lack of affordable housing has led to difficulties in getting workers for the town shops, and there seemed to be little prospect of new housing being provided in the town.

The results in Table 3.1 suggest that the problem of affordability is particularly challenging in Haslemere. The town is situated on the main railway line from London (50 minutes) to Portsmouth (45 minutes) and close to the A3 trunk road (London 44 miles and Portsmouth 26 miles). With commuter demand for housing high and with severe planning (green belt and Area of Oustanding Natural Beauty – AONB) and environmental restrictions (water and

---

Box 3.8 Todmorden: a town looking for a new role

In common with many Pennine textile towns, Todmorden has suffered a loss of employment and population during the twentieth century. Its role as a producer of cotton goods has all but disappeared and its population has halved from a peak of 30,000 in the 1920s to around 15,000 today. These and other closures have left a legacy of empty buildings that are becoming partly occupied by a range of small businesses. Indeed, proportions of self-employed are a little higher than local and national averages, but so too are skill levels. Unemployment – numbers claiming Jobseeker's Allowance – for both males and females is above local and national levels. There are also a number of indicators suggesting that pay is low in the area. House prices in the town are lower than in the surrounding countryside and in the wider district.

The economy of the town is in a state of flux. There is a gradually emerging commuter function, facilitated by good public transport links to the nearby metro-politan areas of Manchester and West Yorkshire. Indeed, it was described as 'the last town to be found in the Calder Valley' and commuter in-migration is now starting to affect house prices. There are also signs of a developing media industry. The predominant working class culture is gradually being overwritten by a middle class veneer. Commuters or 'newcomers' are not felt to engage fully with the life of the town.

Clearly the town faces many challenges and its future is unclear. It is one of a number of towns with a similar history in the Upper Calder Valley, of which Hebden Bridge is probably the best known. They are the collective subject of Yorkshire Forward's (RDA for the region) latest take on the MTI. Hebden Bridge was perhaps first in the group of towns to make steps towards regeneration, and it has developed as both a commuter base, perhaps initially for Manchester but also for West Yorkshire, and as a centre for tourism with a certain 1960s feel.

---

sewage) on development there is little prospect of new housing easing this problem. Private housing in Haslemere is expensive, with the common problem of a mismatch between house prices and local wage levels, even though the latter compare favourably with national averages. Indeed, Waverley Borough Council's website suggests that, if you had a 10 per cent deposit and a mortgage three-and-a-half times your income, you would need a salary of £70,000 to buy the average-priced property in Waverley and a salary of £39,000 in order to buy a flat/maisonette. 37 per cent of Waverley residents, however, earn less than £23,000 (Waverley Borough Council 2006). The eastern part of Haslemere does have housing for rent, some of which was initially designed and built as council housing. It is unlikely that there will be any significant expansion of this part of the town for the reasons noted above. However, it does bring into sharp focus the difficulties, which are particularly pronounced in the town, of younger people accessing the housing market. Many key workers have to commute into the area.

Relatively high house prices are not, however, a universal finding. Indeed, in Crediton, house prices were not high compared with Exeter and some of the surrounding villages, but affordability was still seen as an issue, particularly in the rural parishes. Crediton itself was seen as 'well served' with a choice of housing, including social housing, and there was felt to be 'no great shortages'. However, there was some resistance to further development until transport improvements were forthcoming, but these seemed a distant prospect.

Conclusion

The evidence presented suggests that, while all market towns are, to a greater or lesser extent, multi-purpose entities, many possess clear functional identities. These functions drive and shape the development of the towns. For example, if the market for the town centre's retail is primarily from residents of the town and its hinterland, it can be expected to provide a range of services, which meet day-to-day needs and also some comparison shopping needs. If its market is skewed towards meeting the needs of visitors, then the range of shops and services is likely to be extended or be skewed towards that market.

Illustrated through case studies, the synergies and inconsistencies between town functions have been considered. For retail, these may be in terms of balancing a range of customers. The effects of external demand on local house prices have also been seen to pose a challenge for low-paying tourist industries, where it is important to ensure that sufficient affordable housing is provided to house employees and maintain the local economy. Pursuing one of these functions will not be sufficient for a market town to succeed, requiring action to ensure a balancing of needs.

More generally the results have shown that, while a simple and categorical classification is not possible, a slightly looser and more flexible form of characterisation can provide valuable insights into the working of market towns and a basis for making comparisons between towns and the policies applied to them.

Notes

1 See Chapter 5 for a detailed consideration of this issue.
2 Indeed, in recent years (1993–2003) there has been a 21 per cent increase in traffic flow on rural 'A' roads (only 5 per cent for urban), with traffic on rural minor roads staying much the same (DfT 2005).
3 See Chapter 8 for further details.
4 Exploring the relevant data, it is suggested in Chapter 7 that market towns are the most affordable places to live in rural England.
5 Using household surveys SERRL (2004), summarised by Shorten (2004), considered the rural service centre role for eight English market towns distributed throughout England (Balsall (Warwickshire); Haltwhistle (Northumberland); Marlborough (Wiltshire); Maltby (South Yorkshire); Okehampton (Devon); Ripon (North Yorkshire); Sheringham (Norfolk); and Whitchurch (Shropshire)).
6 Using visitor surveys of three market towns in the North East of England (Alnwick (Northumberland); Bishop Auckland (County Durham); and Hexham (Northumberland)), Powe and Shaw (2003) explored town centre usage. Powe and Shaw (2004) extended this analysis using house surveys and focus groups, considering specifically Alnwick's rural hinterland.
7 Courtney et al. (2006) compared the surveys of town and hinterland residents from six English (Leominster, Tiverton, Swanage, Burnham-on-Sea, Towcester and Saffron Walden) and six Dutch towns (Dalfsen, Schagen, Bolsward, Nunspeet, Oudewater and Gemert).
8 Note, however, that SERRL (2004) was based on house surveys and as such does not give an indication of the importance of hinterland residents to market town services but instead only the importance of market town services to hinterland residents. For this reason, Powe and Shaw (2004) explored the mutual dependence using a combination of town and house surveys.
9 The wide percentage range reflects the difference in evening entertainments available within the towns.
10 Foot and mouth is a non-fatal disease which affects cloven-hoofed animals. With the outbreak of the disease, the UK government restricted access to some areas of the countryside as a measure to prevent further spread of the disease. Access to market towns was not restricted.

Chapter 4
Policies for market towns

Trevor Hart

Introduction

Market towns have only recently become a focus of interest and intervention for policy makers. They first emerged in the UK as a theme in the Rural White Paper in 1995 (DoE and MAFF 1995) and this area of policy was further developed in the second Rural White Paper in 2000 (MAFF and DETR 2000). One reason for this interest could be found in the changing economic roles and fortunes of market towns and the threat posed to the economic and social fabric of the settlements. Another significant but related reason concerns the role of market towns as rural service centres, and their ability to continue to perform this role in the face of changes in patterns of retailing and the centralisation of professional and other services. Policy was developed with a concern for the fortunes of the towns in their own right, but also because of their perceived role as service and employment centres for their rural hinterlands. Policy was thus seen as a means of sustaining the quality of life for rural communities, by maintaining access to services and employment in market towns, but more recently market towns have also been seen as the logical centres in which to focus regeneration initiatives for rural areas.

The underlying logic for this policy – that market towns act as service hubs for rural areas and they are the types of settlement in which development should be focused – echoes a much longer tradition to be found in land use planning policy and in the approaches adopted to the distribution of development between settlements, or 'settlement policy'. While terminology has changed over time and has varied between different localities, a consistent thread in rural settlement policy has been the classification of rural settlements into a hierarchy defined by capacity and potential to accommodate future development; typically, development is concentrated into a proportion of larger and better-serviced settlements which, in turn, can help provide for the needs of surrounding and usually smaller rural communities. This has been seen as meeting a number of environmental, social, economic and public finance objectives, although the relative importance of each of these components has varied over time and, in the view of Cloke (1983: 72), the dominant driver is better described as 'economic and administrative expediency'.

In its earliest manifestation, settlements selected for development were known as 'key settlements', but this has subsequently been supplanted by other terms such as 'local service centres', 'rural service centres', or something similar. In some early strategic planning documents, market towns were identified as performing the role of key settlements – Cloke (1983: 145–8) cites the examples of Cornwall, Herefordshire and West Wiltshire – and, to the extent that an element of the current market towns policy is that the selected towns are seen as playing a role as a focus for rural regeneration, the terms 'market town' and 'key settlement' continue to share some similar objectives. While most market towns are likely to fit the pattern of what would be recognised as key settlements (or a more recent terminological equivalent), not all key settlements will be market towns. However, the recent MTI continues the 'resource concentration' strategy of hierarchical 'key settlement' policy, albeit with an emphasis on regeneration and implementation that was not common in earlier planning debates and strategies.

The focus of this book is on market towns, but there is also a recognition of the extent to which 'market towns' are absorbing the mantle of 'key settlements' in strategy and policy, and the extent to which the underlying logic of policy also relies on the same assumptions that have underpinned settlement policy in land use planning. Therefore, this chapter reviews the essence and nature of rural settlement planning and relates this to some more recent research on the function of market towns/key settlements. This links quite clearly to the assessment of possible classifications of market towns considered in earlier chapters. It also considers the nature of more recent regeneration policy for market towns, as a means of examining some of the assumptions underpinning market towns policy. Given the dominance of the partnership paradigm in policy design and implementation, the chapter also considers the key partners/stakeholders in the development and roll-out of policy measures.

Rural settlement policy and planning – a history

While a heightened interest in market towns is a relatively recent phenomenon, the idea of 'key settlements' or 'rural service centres' is long established at the heart of rural planning policy – in the view of Cloke (1979), it was the dominant approach to rural planning in Britain and had been so since the early 1950s. Indeed, as will be shown later, the approach of seeking to concentrate development in a small number of selected settlements still continues to hold sway and is promoted in recent policy documents such as the Rural White Paper (MAFF and DETR 2000) and Planning Policy Statement 7 (PPS7) (ODPM 2004a).

This history of hierarchical settlement policy provides the backcloth against which current policies for rural settlements have developed and been deployed. Cloke (1979) suggests the emergence of key settlement policies can be traced to the Scott Report of 1942 and the Town and Country Planning Act of 1947. These favoured the concentration of new development in larger settlements possessing an endowment of basic services. At that time, the (imputed) objectives of the planning system of countryside protection and the presumption against building on good agricultural land (Hall 1973) coincided with a continuing decline in the rural population. So, the objectives of settlement policy included the maintenance of the status and position of rural communities – or, in some cases, their managed decline – and achieving an efficient use of resources, particularly in the sense that the economic provision of services could only be brought about by the selection of certain villages for expansion.

Key settlement policies began to emerge in county development plans from the 1950s, and grew into the cornerstone of rural planning policy. They aimed to confine the growth of housing, services and employment to a small number of settlements. These settlements were selected by reference to their role and function within the rural area under consideration, as well as by reference to a range of broader strategic objectives for the rural area as a whole. The rationale for the policy was by no means uniformly articulated in development plans, but reasons given for its adoption included 'restraining the pressure for development on agricultural land, reducing the costs of services, maintaining the quality of the environment and improving the quality of rural life' (Martin and Voorhees Associates 1980: 1).

However, the assumptions underpinning key settlement policies were by no means unchallenged. Cloke (1979), citing the work of Gruer on the economics of hospital outpatient services, questions whether the concentration of services provides the least expensive solution when all costs – personal as well as public – are taken into account. Similarly, Gilder's (1984) study of the costs of provision of services in West Suffolk found that 'there is no clear-cut relationship between the costs of services and the size of settlement' (Gilder 1984: 245), partly because economies of scale were only realised for a small number of services. Second, Cloke (1979) also points out that the original idea underpinning key settlements – that facilities would be shared by a surrounding rural population – would not take place automatically, and that attention is also needed to be paid to the means by which this sharing might be encouraged to take place.

Some more recent work (for example Ladd 1992; Powe and Whitby 1994) has produced further support for the proposition that there is a definable relationship between settlement size and the cost of providing public services, and Powe and Whitby assert that 'the cost of providing services should be an important element in rural settlement planning' (432). However, the same authors also point out that other factors – economic and non-economic – have an important part to play in developing settlement policy. It is the inclusion of these 'other factors' which contributes to contestability of decisions in rural settlement planning. That the planning of rural settlements and associated service delivery is a complex and challenging task is neatly summed up by Moseley's (2003) 'dilemma of rural service delivery'. This states that it is not possible to achieve more than two of the three goals for service provision at any one time, with the goals being low per capita cost, high quality of service and wide geographical dispersal.

So, from the outset, the pursuit of key settlement policies was not without its critics, being accused of worsening conditions in more remote villages, changing the character of settlements and disturbing the social balance of rural areas. The view of Cloke is that while such planning policies are 'not necessarily the cause of rural social problems, the planning process has to a large extent allowed them to develop' (Cloke 1983: 112). This may be seen as reflecting the rather narrower perspective of planning at the time, and the greater priority and influence given to countryside interests over socio-economic factors in determining patterns of development.

The advantages and disadvantages of key settlement policies were reviewed in 1980 (Martin and Voorhees Associates 1980). The study found that such policies were more effective in dealing with physical development issues than with the wider range of factors of concern to rural communities, and that they had little impact in diverting the path of market forces. They were generally unsuccessful in promoting rural services, in encouraging economic development, or in addressing social problems, principally because the planning policy was – at the time – not accompanied by the powers necessary to ensure the implementation of the broader policy objectives. The study concluded by arguing that 'the uniqueness of rural areas defies the adoption of a single type of settlement policy for all rural areas . . . rural planning should always be a problem-solving exercise' (Martin and Voorhees Associates 1980: 223).

Since the 1980s, there has been little by way of systematic study of rural settlement policy – either its approach or its effects. Some of the structure plans that started to emerge in the 1980s began to reflect a wider interest in socio-economic issues, partly prompted by guidance and partly by changing circumstances and responses to them. So, from 1973 we saw a rise in unemployment that prompted more local authorities to develop interests and activities in local economic development, including local authorities in rural areas, which were not among the most seriously affected by worsening national economic conditions. The emergence of a more active involvement in rural regeneration by the Rural Development Commission, first with its 'advance factories' programme and then with the Rural Development Programmes, helped develop a different emphasis to the planning activities, by pushing economic factors up the agenda of those rural planning authorities involved with these initiatives and programmes. The launch of the 'right to buy' policy for council houses in

1980 also acted to intensify interest in the supply of affordable rural housing and through it was added a further imperative for widening the range of issues considered by planning policy makers. At the same time, rural services continued to be under threat from market and public policy pressures, with the future of key services such as petrol filling stations, post offices, schools and medical services at various times becoming uncertain.

However, while the focus of interest may have been widening, there is little evidence that the espousal of hierarchical settlement policies was weakening. So, for example, the recently published (2004) *Draft Structure Plan* for Lincolnshire identifies a 'settlement hierarchy which will be used to direct the largest proportion of new development' to a number of main settlements (23). While these settlements may have been selected on the basis of a more sophisticated appraisal of facilities – present or planned – the selection of a number of 'key' settlements for development remains a dominant paradigm.

Rural settlement policy and planning: current components[1]

Current policy for rural development in England and Wales was set out in the Rural White Paper (MAFF and DETR 2000) and is followed in the most recent planning guidance for rural areas, PPS7 (ODPM 2004a). This closely adheres to the hierarchical settlement policy paradigm, stating that 'planning authorities should focus most new development in or near to local service centres, where employment, housing (including affordable housing), services and other facilities can be provided close together' (ODPM 2004a: 6).

Both the 2000 Rural White Paper and PPS7 develop policy within the overriding objective of the achievement of sustainable development and sustainable rural communities. Guidance issued on the nature of Sustainable Communities (ODPM 2003a) highlights economic, social, environmental and political features that are key requirements. Some emphasis is given to issues of scale – 'sufficient size, scale and density . . . to support basic amenities' (ODPM 2003a: 4) – perhaps implicitly supporting a quest for more self-contained rural communities with functionally linked surrounding areas and a generally reduced need to travel. A reading of adopted development plans prepared under pre-2004 Planning and Compulsory Purchase Act guidance frequently reveals an approach to spatial strategy that equates to concentrating development in (often a small number of) main settlements, with the objective of providing services and facilities in a way that will have minimum adverse impact on the environment, from dispersed development or non-sustainable patterns of movement: 'it is an implicit assumption of national policy that massing of new development in larger settlements with better accessibility and a fuller range of local services will produce more sustainable outcomes, chiefly reducing travel by private car' (Shorten *et al.* 2001: 39).

Such approaches still need to have regard to a matter that was part of the underpinning of key settlement policies – the economics of service provision. Resource constraints continue to affect the provision of public services, and these pressures are exacerbated by considerations of quality management and modes of delivery that are part of the debate on 'modernising' public services. Competitiveness and profitability are also issues impacting on individual providers of private services, as well as having an impact on settlements as a whole. In the retail sector, competition from out-of-town shopping and the dominant position of the major supermarkets affects rural settlements as much as or more than town centres. Loss of one or two key facilities can see the start of a spiral of decline affecting a much broader range of services and posing a threat to the ability of a settlement to perform its designated role in the hierarchy.

The 2000 Rural White Paper was also the vehicle which launched the MTI, which, in itself, can be seen as reflecting the ideas underpinning hierarchical settlement strategies, as well as embracing the principles of sustainable development, in a nominalistic or principled manner. In that they are now arguably one of the more significant vehicles for rural regeneration, they are just the sort of initiative that PPS12 suggests should be among the 'other policies and programmes which influence the nature of places and how they function' that local development framework documents should take into account in their preparation (ODPM 2004b: 13).

Sustainability issues

While there are great swathes of literature on sustainable development, there is little that tackles the task of interpreting the doctrine for planning practitioners in a way that will guide their work on matters such as settlement policy planning. Owen (1996) advances an 'argument against simplistic thinking and for the application of balanced and considered judgement' in seeking to achieve sustainability in rural settlement planning (46). This may be seen as axiomatic, given the complex nature of the planning process in urban or rural contexts. There can be no simple 'set of rules' to smooth a path through the collaborative processes that planning has been identified as involving (Healey 1997), nor managing the political process that rationalising into planning policy the multiple strands of sustainability demands (Haughton and Counsell 2004). While policy needs to be developed to meet local circum-stances and reflect the outcomes of participation, pursuit of dominant paradigms – such as concentration – can lead to the simplistic solutions that Owen eschews. However, if, as their study of the process of preparing regional planning policies reveals, 'different people interpret sustainable development in different ways' (Haughton and Counsell 2004: 214), is there a clear pattern within which we can expect planning for market towns to fall?

The elusive nature of some of the principles underpinning sustainable development – environmental capacity, environmental capital, economic benefits and distribution of environmental or social costs – have to be translated into more concrete terms when they are related to particular localities and to particular issues with a local expression. This thrusts land use planning into the difficult position between theory and practice where many of the issues and conflicts that are able to be concealed by the very generality of the principles become exposed. This dilemma is well summed up by Susan Owens:

> Because land-use is so closely bound up with environmental change, land-use planning demands the translation of abstract principles of sustainability into operational policies and decisions. Paradoxically, this process is likely to expose the very conflicts that 'sustainable development' was meant to reconcile . . . The planning system is likely to remain a focus of attention because it is frequently the forum in which these conflicts are first exposed.
>
> (Owens 1995: 8)

So, in the absence of a Luther or Loyola emerging from within Whitehall to show the one true path to following the doctrine, we can expect the development of a sustainable planning context for market towns to involve much debate.

Current experience of the policy

Given the nature of the economic and social changes that have taken place since 'key settlements' emerged as a defining element of rural planning policy, it should not be surprising that their original logic continues to be questioned. Most recently, a study for the Countryside Agency by Land Use Consultants (SERRL 2004) examined the nature of the service and employment roles performed by eight key settlements for their surrounding villages. Using a combination of secondary data and primary surveys, the study concluded that there were a number of weaknesses in the assumed relationship between key settlements and their surrounding villages.

First, it was found that there is a far from uniform pattern in the way that different centres function, with the extent to which a key settlement provides for local needs in surrounding villages varying greatly between settlements. This reflects the fact that different centres have several differentiated (albeit linked) service roles – shopping, education, leisure, professional services – and may not be equally strong in all of them. Second, the extent to which key settlements act as employment centres is seen to be much less than has traditionally been assumed. This is seen as a reflection of greatly increased personal mobility and the extent to which this has enabled choices of workplace and home to be made separately. The extent to which increased personal mobility has allowed in-migrants in particular to select their home location on a 'lifestyle' rather than a functional basis has had the most marked effect on people living in villages. By and large, they are no longer so closely linked to the designated key settlement for work and services as was assumed to be the case. There is also evidence of 'leakage' of patronage for local services from the residents of the key settlements themselves, particularly for the purchase of comparison goods and leisure services.

The overall conclusion from this recent study of the role of rural settlements is that 'no two rural towns are likely to be exactly the same' (SERRL 2004: 135). This is seen to be a reflection of a complex range of factors affecting an individual town's functionality, including:

- the nature of the town;
- the nature of its close context, including infrastructure, the open countryside and villages; and
- relationships with close and more distant urban neighbours.

Some of the findings – and particularly those concerning increased mobility and weakened local functional linkages between key settlements and surrounding villages – suggest that recent patterns of living are running counter to those needed for the achievement of aspects of rural sustainability. The report argues for a more sophisticated approach to establishing local settlement hierarchies, based on a detailed, evidence-based understanding of functions and relationships, in some respects echoing the conclusions of the work by Martin and Voorhees Associates. It is contended that this improved understanding of how people live and how settlements function can then form the basis for a more effective policy framework for the achievement of rural sustainable development. So, while market towns are seen as likely to continue in their role as local service centres, the way they perform this role will vary from town to town. But the study concedes that there will be degrees of similarity in some dimensions that will allow lessons to be transferred between towns, implying some scope for categorisation between what is perceived to be a collection of unique entities.

This recent research thus casts doubt on the way that settlement hierarchies have been defined in development plans, but does not suggest that the essence of hierarchical approaches should be replaced. Some of the criticism of past policies is based on the fact that concentration of development has not produced Sustainable Communities, as 'public and private services in the countryside have been in steady decline for years' (Shorten, 2004: 186). If lessons are to be transferred between policy makers in different areas, and if an evaluation of the effectiveness of policy is to be carried out, then some form of categorisation of towns has to be attempted. This is the essence of the justification for the approaches to constructing such a characterisation considered in the previous chapters.

Regenerating market towns: key issues for policy

While market towns policy, exemplified by the MTI, has a primary focus of regeneration, planning settlement policy, reviewed above, has a broader focus. In policy terms, the regional and local planning strategies provide a spatial framework within which regeneration policy development and implementation takes place, but – particularly within the context provided by the 2004 Planning and Compulsory Purchase Act – the existence of town regeneration initiatives will form an important input to planning policy review or development. Both policy areas draw on similar analytical frameworks and seek to address, from their own perspectives, factors affecting the success of the towns in performing their role as rural service centres. How are the challenges faced by planning policy interpreted and addressed by regeneration policy?

As with planning, policy can be viewed as the means of managing or engineering change, and market towns have undergone change for many years. So, for example, in reviewing the fortunes of market towns in the East Riding of Yorkshire between 1600 and 1850, Noble (1979) points to a failure to develop a wider economic role, an administrative function, up-to-date communications links and a 'social' function – to generally remain 'competitive' – as the roots of decline.

Problems faced by market towns today are articulated in different terms but many are, in essence, similar to those of earlier times. The first Rural White Paper (MAFF and DoE 1995) identified a number of pressures for change including changes in agriculture, central-isation of professions and services, changing patterns of leisure activity, and competition from out-of-town shopping centres. The second White Paper (MAFF and DETR 2000) largely echoed this list, adding the threat from Internet-based services. It goes on to identify that the 'businesses and communities in these towns need to respond to their changing circum-stances to maintain their physical fabric, economic vitality and a good quality of life' (MAFF and DETR 2000: 74).

In the last ten years particularly, several market towns have undertaken various forms of 'audit' of their facilities, strengths and weaknesses: a study of market towns in the West Midlands (KPMG 2000a) provides a useful overview of common issues:

- Data and knowledge about the market towns is generally weak.
- Retail provision is a very important element of market towns' economies and service provision; however, it is often in need of re-invigoration.
- Access to affordable accommodation for local people is becoming more of an issue as house prices are driven up by incoming residents.
- Although public transport linkages between large settlements can be of good quality, linkages between market towns and their hinterlands are often poor.
- Market towns tend to have older populations than the national average. This will affect the size of the working-age population and the demand for services.
- The availability of high-quality land for commercial and industrial development is diminished as more land is developed for residential uses.
- The demand for local services is changing as the populations of market towns change.
- Social exclusion is often a present, if not visible, problem.

It also goes on to point out that 'high-capacity ICT infrastructure will be an essential requirement if market towns are to remain competitive in the future and effectively overcome the restrictions of geography' (KPMG 2000a: 1).

This presents a formidable list of issues to be addressed, involving national and regional responsibilities as well as local analysis, diagnosis and leadership. Of course, a key part of the planning process is the resolution of conflicting aspirations, so planning should be expected to be an integral part of a sub-regional market towns strategy. While it does provide an important element of context, it is not always visible – or referred to – as an explicit driver of policy. However, the *Assessment of the Market Towns Initiative* (Countryside Agency 2004b) found that local market towns partnerships saw development plans as their second most important source of guiding policies (after the Community Strategy/Plan).

A number of national agendas offer important contextual elements to the definition of approaches. The need for 'sustainable' solutions is frequently emphasised, both in the sense of the broad conceptualisation of sustainable development outlined above, and in the sense of needing to develop approaches that will give an assured future as opposed to some temporary palliative for current problems. In the context of current actions, the additional drive and priority provided by the impact of the outbreaks of foot and mouth disease and BSE at the start of the twenty-first century should not be overlooked. This helped place market towns at the centre of rural regeneration for affected rural areas and to place them centrally on the agenda of the RDAs, effectively reinforcing the guidance given to them at their inception by the Government. However, echoing the findings of the research on the function of rural settlements, a study for the National Assembly for Wales (NAW 2002) found no evidence that small towns acted as drivers of prosperity for their surrounding rural areas.

Regenerating market towns: a brief history

The current approach to regeneration in market towns is often felt to have developed from the Civic Trust's work in Wirksworth in the Derbyshire Peak District. There had been work focused on 'town improvement' before, and the number and condition of historic buildings in Wirksworth that were thought to be empty, neglected or in need of repair (Eardley 1999) was a significant prompt for action. However, the comprehensive approach exemplified by the Wirksworth initiative, marrying work on social and economic issues to action to address threats to the physical fabric, is seen as a significant step forward (Gwilliam 1998). This type of approach was developed by the Civic Trust Regeneration Unit and applied to more towns throughout England.

The key agency in rural regeneration at this time, the Rural Development Commission, in partnership with the Civic Trust, developed an involvement with market town regeneration, through its activities in its Rural Development Areas. From the time of the first Rural White Paper (MAFF and DoE 1995), a wider set action began to develop, including the development of a 'Market Town Forum', and the diffusion of best practice in regeneration.

More recently, a sharper focus on the retail future of market towns began to emerge. Lessons here were learned from the USA National Trust for Historic Preservation's Main Street programme, which has been in existence since the early 1980s. As the 'National Trust' link suggests, it also has a concern, as early UK programmes did, with the physical environment, but it added other elements, including an enhanced element of 'commercial awareness':

> The Main Street Approach is a community-driven, comprehensive methodology used to revitalize older, traditional business districts throughout the United States. It is a common-sense way to address the variety of issues and problems that face traditional business districts. The underlying premise of the Main Street approach is to encourage economic development within the context of historic preservation in ways appropriate to today's marketplace. The Main Street Approach advocates a return to community self-reliance, local empowerment, and the rebuilding of traditional commercial districts based on their unique assets: distinctive architecture, a pedestrian-friendly environment, personal service, local ownership, and a sense of community.
>
> (Main Street 2005:1)

Assisted by the Rural Development Commission and as trailed in the 1995 Rural White Paper, Action for Market Towns was launched in 1997 as a mechanism to support activities in market towns, along with the 'community' or 'grass roots' element that is part of the Main Street approach and is now a key component of the MTI. Action for Market Towns has spawned or assisted a range of local initiatives that have worked with and alongside the national and regional regeneration programmes, developing local approaches to what are often shared problems.

While such activities assisted in the development of an understanding of 'what works' in attempting to boost the fortunes of market towns, from the 1990s, research was also being undertaken into how market towns functioned. This also helped to emphasise the need for a comprehensive approach to the future of the towns, but through an analysis of the functions and linkages that towns possessed. Examples can be found in studies of Bude and Liskeard in Cornwall undertaken by the Market Towns Research Group at the University of Plymouth. The focus of this work was described in the report on Bude:

> This means looking at much more than just the physical appearance of the town centre, the availability of parking or the number of shops which are now closed. It involves looking at the underlying demographic profile of the population; where the resident population work and how they get to work; the use they currently make of local facilities and what they think of those facilities. And it involves finding out more about local businesses – what they do, who they employ and how they see the town, its future and their own.
>
> (Dawson and Errington 1998: 2)

This focus on a comprehensive approach to understanding issues for particular places and developing policy responses is carried through in some respects to much of current policy.

Regenerating market towns: current policies

The immediate origins of current policy are perhaps to be found in the report *Rural Economies* (PIU 1999), which stated that 'there is a case for government making a "New Commitment" to Market Towns, which would recognise the critical role they play in economic and social life as well as the maintenance of rural economies, and bolster their position' (118). This was followed in the Rural White Paper (MAFF and DETR 2000) by a 'new commitment to market towns', aimed at a number of objectives:

- help market towns manage the process of change affecting them;
- strengthen their role of service provision to surrounding rural areas;
- help regenerate the most deprived; and
- ensure that central and local government recognises the role of market towns in their strategies.

The latter objective was to be addressed through shaping RDA strategies and planning guidance, but in addition, extra resources of £37 million were included in RDA and Country-side Agency budgets over a three-year period to support market town regeneration; with matching funds, from EU programmes and partners' budgets, the total budget was expected to amount £100 million. This was to be devoted to around 100 towns, selected on the basis of:

- their potential to act as a focus for growth in priority areas;
- their potential to act as service centres for the surrounding area;
- the ability of local partners to commit resources; and
- the extent to which they have already benefited from regeneration funding.

The role identified for such towns as 'rural service centres', and their role in acting as a focus for meeting the needs of a wider rural area, re-emphasise a commonality with a central element of hierarchical settlement policy.

The Market Towns Initiative, as it was rolled out in 2001, consisted of a number of elements:

- A web-based toolkit available to communities in all market towns, giving advice on a number of areas including:

  - carrying out a 'Health Check';
  - preparing an 'Action Plan'; and
  - seeking sources of funding and advice.

  Health Checks and Action Plans are an essential element of the process, and help to provide a common understanding of issues facing a market town and its surrounding area, and a vision for the future to which all can contribute. They are also elements which echo the advice and guidance that has been a central part of national planning policy guidance, most recently in PPS6.

- Support for coordinators (who help communities carry out Health Checks) and project managers (who help deliver Action Plans). Towns were selected by regional partnerships of the Countryside Agency and RDAs, and much (but not all) of the work on Health Checks and Action Plans was undertaken by independent consultants on behalf of the partnerships guiding the processes at a local level.
- A monitoring and evaluation programme.
- Testing out solutions to the issues that affect market towns through research and a programme of Beacon Towns.
  The Beacon Town network consists of towns that have been chosen for their potential to contribute to learning and to the development of best practice that can be used to help other towns.
- An electronic learning network for market town professionals interested in exchanging information.
- Support for Action for Market Towns.

Effective responsibility for the implementation of the MTI gradually moved from the Countryside Agency to the RDAs, while the approaches of RDAs developed as their understanding of issues advanced and their methods of managing funding evolved towards the 'single pot' approach.[2] The change was followed or paralleled by the development of changed approaches to market towns funding by RDAs. The approach to market towns is not uniform across the nine English RDAs but the idea of action planning remains at the core, with some of the detail undergoing subtle alteration. An example of how one RDA – Yorkshire Forward – is implementing its programme is set out in Box 4.1, but it is interesting to note that one of its areas of action focuses on a group of market towns in the Calder Valley in West Yorkshire and seeks to address the issues that face them through collective action. However, RDAs are gradually developing a differentiated approach to market towns, to reflect differing regional needs and priorities. So, for example, the South West RDA (SWRDA) has 'outsourced' its responsibility for operating the MTI to a semi-independent 'Market and Coastal Towns Association', which has taken on a responsibility for supporting the efforts of individual towns.

This process of transfer of functions was cemented by the Haskins review of rural delivery and its subsequent adoption by government in 2004 (DEFRA 2004a). This led to there being a number of changes in responsibilities and a promise of rationalisation in the hundred or so funding schemes available to assist rural projects. The functions performed by the Countryside Agency would change in that its responsibility for developing policy would pass to the Department for Environment, Food and Rural Affairs and resources for policy implementation would pass in their entirety to RDAs, leaving it with a role as 'watchdog and advocate for rural people and communities' (DEFRA 2004a: 77).

Box 4.1 Yorkshire Forward's approach to market town regeneration

Renaissance Market Towns Initiative

Sufficient lessons have been gained from the MTI coupled with the experiences from the Urban Renaissance approach to enable the roll out of the Renaissance Market Towns Programme (RMT) in the Yorkshire region. There was a clear need to move from a funding-driven to a strategy-led approach, coupled with a need to bring about a step change in aspirational thinking in market towns: RMT was born.

Launched in January 2003, RMT is a pioneering 10-year plan to support sustainable small towns in Yorkshire and Humber. As one of Yorkshire Forward's flagship projects, RMT aims to ensure that the region's 'rural capitals' are places where people want to and are able to live, work, invest and visit.

'Strategy-led not funding fed' – the objective of RMT is to generate sustainable development through:

- The development of a fully operational and sustainable 'Town Team' whose role it is to drive the RMT process forward. Each team is comprised primarily of local people with an interest in creating and delivering a vision for the renaissance of their town over the next 25 years.
- The development of ambitious yet achievable town visions or charters that are translated into action plans for implementation.
- A portfolio of prioritised projects with defined delivery mechanisms.

The first round of RMTs, launched in 2003, are well on the way to completion of their town charters, which is a testament to effective partnership building within each of their Town Teams.

The second round of towns is about to be launched, and the team at Yorkshire Forward, supported by the RMT Consultant Panel, are looking forward to working with them to help them establish a renaissance strategy and delivery plan that really will make a difference.

Source: Yorkshire Forward (RDA for the region)

Policy for market towns perhaps also needs to be seen in the broader context of the full range of mechanisms to guide planning and regeneration in a local area. It has always been the case that the role of the local authorities has been of some significance in shaping policy and in providing resources for implementation, but the introduction of both Local Strategic Partnerships (LSPs), Community Strategies and Local Area Agreements (LAAs) can impact significantly upon market towns. LSPs are intended to play a key role in bringing together public, private, community and voluntary sectors and all the activities of agencies and service providers in an area to coordinate activity and ensure a strategic and coherent approach at the local level. They also play a key role in drawing up Community Strategies through consultation with local communities with the aim of improving everyone's quality of life. The LAA is effectively the delivery plan for the Community Strategy and a basis for partnership and performance management. At the time of writing, it is hard to identify the level of impact that LSPs, Community Strategies and LAAs are having on the policy community in general and market towns in particular, although some of our case study interviews suggested that market towns were struggling to register a strong interest with the LSP process.

An assessment of the MTI was commissioned by the Countryside Agency in early 2004 and it reported in September 2004 (Countryside Agency 2004b). Maybe because the initiative was at a relatively early stage – too early to be able to identify transformative impacts on the towns and their performance – the focus of the evaluation was more on process than outcome. The report emphasised the value of the Health Check process and the value of an effectively functioning partnership to guide work. Generally, the work of MTI partnerships complemented the work of other key actors in the region, but there was felt to be more scope for the development of effective relationships with LSPs.

Regenerating market towns: managing the key actors

From what has been set out above, it is clear that a wide range of people need to be involved in designing and implementing policy. Caffyn (2004) makes a useful distinction between the range of stakeholders in a vertical hierarchy, from national government to neighbourhood, and particularly focusing on how local interests can shape the delivery of top-down policies; and interests at a variety of spatial scales, spanning interests within a town to its relationships within its region. The task of managing these complex relationships is one which demands significant levels of capacity that are only infrequently available to the local communities who hope to drive the market town's agenda.

The emergence of more complex institutional frameworks and the development of power and resource-sharing networks and alliances in place of more rigid hierarchical structures can be traced back to the 1980s and 1990s. Changes in structures and practices included the creation of a number of dedicated agencies that plan and deliver services, and the compartmentalisation of functions within government and beyond through the emergence of the 'contract culture'. This was paralleled by the emergence of interest in a broader debate about the relationship between state, market and civil society encapsulated in the growth of interest in the concept of 'governance' (Maidment and Thompson 1993; Rhodes 1995). These types of changes have continued and have recently seemed to accelerate in the rural context, with the changes of roles and responsibilities associated with the shifts in functions between the Countryside Agency, DEFRA and RDAs. Partnership approaches are inevitably necessary to manage these complex networks of policies and actors, and Woods (2006a: 151) has identified that these 'new rural governance arrangements inevitably has had [*sic*] implications for the transparency of governance and for the resource demands on those involved'. A critical question is then who has what power and how is it exercised, and perhaps particularly how is power exercised within the partnership? (see Box 4.2 for a list of key actors.)

The average MTI partnership consists of 25 people (Countryside Agency 2004b: 12) and is, as in most UK partnerships, dominated by political rather than business elites (Davies 2003). The role of the local authority is very evident but the role of the RDA can be expected to be significant, exercised perhaps principally through its control over funding. The evaluation of the MTI points out that 'public bodies such as district or town/community councils are perceived to have most influence. Many market town partnerships have to work hard at inclusiveness' (Countryside Agency 2004b: 18). How some organisations become involved and others do not is not always clear, and similarly there is no transparent route into influence and decision making within the partnerships. Inevitably, managing activities in such a complex arena requires specific skills and resources. Woods (2006: 152) has identified the existence of 'a growing cadre of local governance professionals' concerned with this task. Clearly, access to such a skill and resource can do much to shape progress in a market town.

Box 4.2 Key actors in market towns partnerships

District/Unitary Authority	Key roles in preparation of Community Strategies and Development Plans and service delivery; often play a proactive role in MTI
County Council	Planning/delivery of services; support for MTI
Town/Parish Council	Local representative body; limited service role
Regional Development Agency	Source of funding and MTI programme planning
Countryside Agency	MTI programme planning (lost under new arrangements)
Other Public Sector	Vary from area to area but could include local Business Link – responsible for small business support
Private Sector	Local businesses and property owners
Voluntary Sector	May be significant service providers locally
Community Groups	Representing local interests
Members of the public	Numbers may be significant if the partnership is a 'membership' organisation, but role less so

---

Conclusions

Market towns policy has been considered by this chapter in the context of the longer-term perspective provided by a review of land use planning settlement policy, on the basis that they represent an element of a broad concern with the provision of services to rural communities and the management of development. Settlement policies in their various hierarchical forms have been criticised for a failure to consider and reflect the full range of issues affecting rural communities and for failing to deliver social benefits. More recently they have been criticised for being out of touch with the reality of how people live in rural areas – how they arrange their lives and how they use the facilities that are provided. While the patterns of planning and provision remain broadly hierarchical, their behaviour apparently isn't. This does not deny the legitimacy of the hierarchical model of settlement planning and the normative element of policy making it includes; rather it points to the difficulty of influencing individual and corporate behaviour.

This difficulty of managing delivery may be a challenge that market towns policy will face. While it has a greater emphasis on implementation than is the case with settlement policy, it does not control or strongly influence many of the factors it seeks to manage, such as the economic and market context. It is too early to say how far the MTI will achieve the sustainable transformational change that it seeks. Such evaluation as has taken place has been concerned with the process by which the initiative has been implemented, but this itself may yield some useful lessons for the factors shaping levels of success with policies aimed at influencing the fortunes of rural settlements, from whichever policy community they originate.

Notes

1 A brief review of the present planning system can be found in Appendix 2.
2 Single pot funding refers to the process whereby several RDA funding streams – such as single regeneration budgets – ceased to be ring-fenced, giving greater flexibility for the RDA in allocating its funds, perhaps allowing RDAs to argue that funding is becoming more 'strategy driven'.

Part 2
Issues and challenges

The second section provides greater detail on a number of topics raised within Part 1, all of which contribute to our understanding of the likely issues and challenges faced by market towns. Part 2 begins with a chapter on transport (Chapter 5), which is a key factor shaping the future of market towns. Another important rural trend, ageing of population, is then considered in Chapter 6, which explores the evidence of ageing in Britain's rural places and the implications for market towns. Chapter 7 provides an overview of housing and regeneration in market towns, considering trends in house prices, the delivery of affordable housing and the role of regeneration funding in meeting the needs of housing renewal. Given the importance of the housing role of market towns, Chapter 8 goes on to explore regional differences in housing provision in market towns. Chapter 9 then considers the scope for market towns to act as centres for employment and the contribution of employment development to the fortunes and futures of the towns in a number of related dimensions. The last chapter in this section (Chapter 10) explores the retail futures of market towns in terms of their roles as rural service centres and visitor attractions, where the synergies and inconsistencies of pursuing both these roles are considered.

Chapter 5

Transport and mobility in the English market town

Geoff Vigar

Introduction

This chapter has two focuses. First, it scopes existing travel patterns within market towns. Travel data shows such towns to be car-dependent and thus to be environmentally and socially less sustainable than they might be, with little to suggest that this situation is changing. Possible reasons for this are explored. Second, policy and service delivery mechanisms are investigated through literature review. This analysis highlights the problems facing market towns, such as road vehicle traffic and its external costs, and the potential for initiatives in public transport, such as on-demand services and innovations in promoting green modes of transport. It is argued that smaller urban centres are under-researched and rarely given specific attention in the literature. Policy and service delivery mechanisms for market towns, however, vary significantly partly due to their scale. For instance: most services available within a town could be accessed using the green modes of cycling and walking; and a lack of significant congestion implies running reliable public transport is a real possibility, often to link market towns to their hinterlands. This notion of market towns as hubs for public transport is historically prominent in debates on transport in such places but progress in this regard has not been systematically reviewed despite increases in rural bus services in recent years. Practical conclusions are then drawn as to how more sustainable transport planning in market towns might be realised.

Travel trends in market towns

National trends

The background to any discussion of transport issues in the UK is provided by the large increases in car ownership and usage over the last few decades (see Figure 5.1). Parallel to this has been a decline in cycling, walking and bus usage for all area types outside London. These changes have no doubt enabled most, but not all, people to access a range of opportunities previously unavailable when relationships between home, work and services were spatially more confined. However, there has been a range of consequences that leads many to question whether continuing increases in car use are sustainable in economic, ecological or social terms. For example, many market towns have lobbied for improved road access to larger urban settlements on economic grounds, but have found that economic opportunity can flow out as well as in, often leaving them worse off (SACTRA 1999).

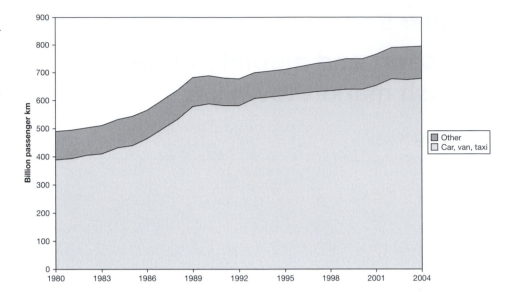

Figure 5.1
Passenger travel by car
and other modes,
1980–2004: Great
Britain

Source: data from DfT
(2006a)

Bypasses can similarly deprive a town of economic activity. The resultant reductions in travel times arising from road construction can also shape local housing markets in ways that deny local people access to them as the town becomes a focus for commuters.

In ecological terms the arguments against private vehicle use are well rehearsed. Given existing technologies, private vehicle use, with typically low occupancy rates, is environmentally more damaging than other surface modes. Other aspects of the impacts of prevailing transport trends on sustainable development are more prosaic – the atomisation of individuals and societies caused by breaking the links between home, work and leisure, for example.

Thus, and returning to transport trends specifically, the distances travelled by an 'average' person in the UK increased by 5 per cent in the period 1990 to 2005 (DfT 2006a). Journey numbers, however, have fallen slightly, implying that people are accessing similar levels of opportunities but travelling further to do so, typically by car. This can be seen as positive in that people may be making active choices, to access services that they see as better but that may be more distant. However, this choice may be forced in that it could arise from the closure of a local service. And this in turn may have resulted from many people in the past making this active choice and undermining the local provision of that service. There are of course, in addition, important issues for those without access to a car who no longer have a local service and may find accessing a more distant one difficult.

In understanding why car use has increased it is not just a matter of individual choices; technological improvements and costs are important too. It is partly improvements in road and vehicle technologies that enable the greater distances referred to above to be attained. And, as Figure 5.2 demonstrates, rises in disposable income outstrip cost increases in all modes, but motoring costs have actually fallen. These general trends do, however, mask variations for individuals and households, and remoteness in rural areas is one pertinent issue that distorts these relative cost differentials. Thus, although efficiency savings make annual rural travel costs little different from those for urban dwellers (CfIT 2001), fuel price increases do hit very remote rural residents harder than others (Gray 2004).

Market towns and rural areas

Rural areas and market towns exhibit a continuing growth in car ownership and use so that 85 per cent of rural and market town households have access to a car (Countryside Agency

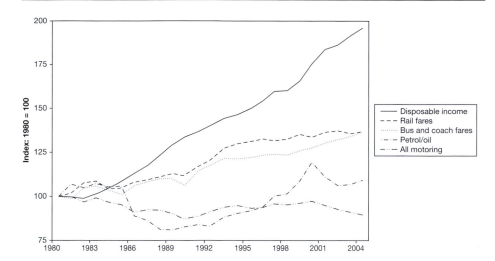

Figure 5.2
Changes in the costs of
travel and disposable
income, 1980–2004:
Great Britain

Source: data from DfT
(2006a)

2003). But not only does this mean that there remain some 15 per cent of households without car access at all, it also implies that around 30 per cent of individuals in a given household may not have access to one at particular times (Williams and White 2001). Thus the provision of other ways of accessing services becomes an important public policy consideration for those suffering a 'poverty of access' (Farrington *et al.* 2004). A long-standing aim of rural transport policy has thus been to maintain mobility opportunities for those disadvantaged by limited or no access to a private vehicle. Some population groups, such as women, the elderly and younger household members, are over-represented in this regard. Through maintaining mobility opportunities for such individuals, social inclusion and labour market objectives can be met. Creating such opportunity may also prevent households 'having' to own more than one vehicle, with knock-on environmental and social benefits. It also helps maintain a virtuous cycle whereby rural public transport services are supported. In addition, such non-car movement can help maintain and create street life and critical mass on cycling and walking networks. In this vein it should be noted that car ownership is often a necessity and not a choice, and can be a drain on the budget of low-income households.

Car ownership increases within rural areas and market towns, but also in nearby conurbations, have fuelled particularly strong traffic growth on rural networks in recent years, on 'A' roads in particular. Market towns are often the destinations for this traffic and thus traffic levels within such places have also, almost universally, increased. This increase has contributed to problems of accommodating such traffic and of balancing local environmental conditions and the accessibility of car users and the perceived consequences of tackling the latter through restrictions.

There are peculiarities to market town road traffic 'congestion' that bear further examination. Unlike in major conurbations, where in-commuting is the primary cause of inner urban traffic problems, the diversity of reasons to travel to market towns implies that peak times are highly variable in such places. Tourism and shopping opportunities create their own demands such that a peak time for 'congestion' in a market town might be a summer Sunday lunchtime. That said, congestion in such places is limited in relation to that in conurbations, often to very small delays at very specific points in space and time. It should thus be understood as a social construct linked to expectations of a free-flowing network in such places built up over years where traffic flowed easily.

Gray (2004) notes that transport problems for places such as market towns are as varied as the towns themselves. Thus a thriving market town may face problems of traffic levels and their attendant issues and parking problems, whereas a market town with a less viable retail centre, bypassed by shoppers using other retail opportunities, would face rather different transport challenges. That said, dealing with road traffic, in the form of both private and heavy goods vehicles, is typically the major focus of public and policy maker attention in market towns.

While the car is of primary importance to most individuals and households other modes are significant. Within towns themselves, walking is very important and within smaller towns around half of journeys to town centres by town residents are on foot with Powe and Shaw (2003) putting it at over 50 per cent and Shorten (2004) putting it at 43 per cent for access to services (almost equal with car use). Walking is often the glue in accessing longer-distance modes too, with rail travel particularly dependent on people walking to stations (e.g. Higginson 2005). Lift giving is also an important element of people's mobility in rural areas, but this can be precarious (Williams and White 2001). This leads to a search for a greater structure to informal means of accessing services.

While often derided for their limitations, public transport services, whether traditional or demand-responsive, can play a vital role with the market town often being the hub for services to the surrounding hinterland as well as providing a means to get around larger towns. Cycling is one mode that is often neglected in such places however. Everywhere in a market town is accessible on a bike for most residents and yet census data shows little use being made of this mode.

Thus, policy choices and improvements in transport technology, particularly in road infrastructure and private vehicles, have broken traditional, spatially close, relationships between home, work and leisure opportunities. In relation to market towns, this has led to many becoming places for commuters to live and out-commute, typically to nearby larger urban areas, alongside a more traditional role as a source for in-commuting from their hinterlands. There is thus a balancing act facing policy-makers in market towns, as in other places, primarily around accommodating a desire for easy access to market towns by car while preserving the environments that people want when they move around such places on foot. This balance varies depending on whether the primary focus of the town is as a 'tourist town', a 'commuter town' or a 'remote town', etc. (see Chapter 2). But, whatever the town's primary role, traffic has become a major problem for many market towns. But the context for such debates over policy direction is different to that in larger urban areas, or remoter rural parts. This is discussed further later after a consideration of the policy framework for transport in market towns and the relative roles market towns perform in relation specifically to transport issues but also in relation to issues that have knock-on consequences for mobility and accessibility in such places.

The policy framework

The above discussion helps illuminate the context, the opportunities and threats for transport planning in market towns. But transport trends do not simply happen. Past policies, such as the closure of rural rail branch lines in the 1950s and 60s for example, have major long-lasting effects on issues such as individuals' modal choice but also on more long-term decisions such as where to live and where to site businesses. An exploration of the macro-policy framework is therefore important.

In England the Rural White Paper (MAFF and DETR 2000) is important to understanding the policy context, and has five priorities in relation to transport:

- Bringing services closer to people;
- Improving personal mobility through car access and car clubs;
- Use of rural grant schemes to encourage mobility;
- Tackling traffic problems; and
- Encouraging cycling and walking.

It is difficult to form an assessment of how these elements are being delivered, but a preliminary appraisal is possible and each of these five issues are discussed in turn. First, people are generally reporting it easier to access services in England as a whole, with the exception of post offices (see Figure 5.3). The closure of bank branches is also reported to be a continuing problem for all but the banks themselves. How this works out spatially is a moot point however. Many argue that a continuing centralisation of services has meant that access has been made more difficult for many residents of market towns (Caffyn 2004). Banister's (1999) call for an auditing of social costs associated with the closure of local facilities might help tackle the drift of services to higher-order centres, but this seems unlikely in the current era of the private finance initiative and the restrictions placed on those charged with such developments. It is possible to imagine that the shift from a land-use planning system to a spatial planning focus, which in theory brings policy agendas such as health and education closer to planning, might help in tackling this issue, but as yet there is limited evidence of the co-aligning of these agendas (Counsell *et al.* 2006).

Second, car clubs are increasing in numbers nationally, although how far this is a rural phenomenon is difficult to determine. Car sharing, or at least less formal lift-giving, similarly appears to be on the increase and has been a hidden, but important, feature of mobility in rural areas for many years (Williams and White 2001; Farrington *et al.* 2004).

Third, rural grant schemes such as the Rural Bus Subsidy Grant, the Rural Bus Challenge Scheme, the Rural Transport Partnership Scheme, the Gateway Stations Initiative and the Parish Transport Fund have been important in recent years, particularly in relation to rural bus services. The government has thus met its target of 50 per cent of rural households to be within 13 minutes of an hourly bus service (see Figure 5.4). This doesn't imply that the service is convenient or well used and usage statistics are hard to come by (and due to practices and information being slow to change and disseminate, it is only in the long-term that we should judge the success or otherwise of these initiatives). In market towns more specifically, in 2005 in England 89 per cent of households in settlements with populations between 3,000 and 10,000 had an hourly serviced bus stop within 13 minutes' walk and 92 per cent in towns with population 10,000 to 25,000 (DfT 2006b). Initiatives such as 'Wheels to Work' that typically provide mopeds for young unemployed to find and access work are also significant.

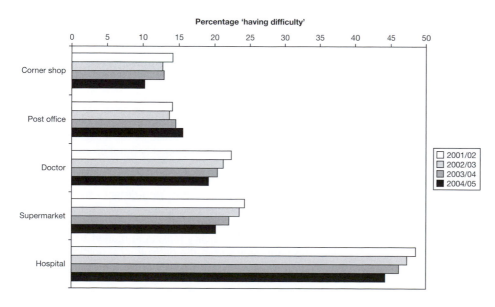

Figure 5.3 *Difficulties of accessing services in households with no access to a car: England Source: data from DfT (2006a)*

Figure 5.4 Households
within 13 minutes of an
hourly bus service by
area type: Great Britain
Source: data from DfT
(2006b)

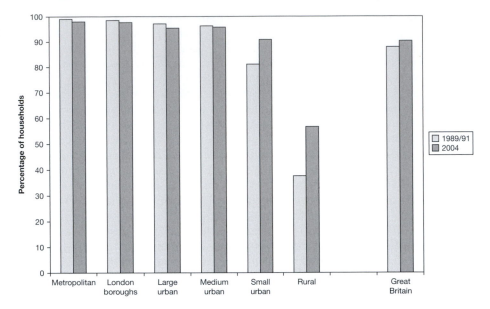

Figure 5.4 Households within 13 minutes of an hourly bus service by area type: Great Britain Source: data from DfT (2006b)

However, there can be conflict between developing mobility tools such as these and promoting mainstream public transport services as one can take the market from the other.

Other grant schemes such as the Rural Transport Partnership programme have been important in relation to rail and cross-mode integration. Although here changes in the institutional environment led to discontinuities of funding and, more generally, an on-going institutional fragmentation in the rail and bus industries does not help such partnerships to succeed. And while these initiatives are significant, the low absolute levels of many local authority transport budgets, and public transport budgets in particular, means that revenue funds to maintain services is often lacking. The UK policy environment in this regard is littered with pilot schemes and one-off initiatives but in on-going revenue support terms the UK fares badly in comparison with our European neighbours (CfIT 2001).

The fourth Rural White Paper objective refers to the tackling of vehicle traffic. This is probably the single biggest issue for market towns, especially the larger ones. Many feel that unregulated vehicle access to town centres is vital for economies. Equally many feel that the retail and leisure environments of such places are often undermined by the traffic taking advantage of such access. Many towns have lobbied or continue to lobby for bypasses and yet sometimes this can undermine local economies, taking away passing trade. Similarly, heavy vehicle traffic can be a large problem, creating danger for people and buildings. There have been some useful attempts to moderate vehicle use, particularly into tourist towns, and the deployment and marketing of public transport services have been important in this regard. But, to paraphrase Colin Clark, traffic can be the maker and breaker of places, and performing the delicate balancing act of accessibility is not an easy challenge for many policy makers in market towns.

Finally, with some notable exceptions, there is little evidence that much investment is occurring in cycling and walking networks in towns beyond long-distance tourist-centred programmes. While these long-distance networks can be important for local transport too as well as being a vital economic boost in some places, such provision is not a substitute for a systematic provision for local needs and few policy makers in market towns appear willing to grasp the nettle here. This partly stems from the difficult local politics of taming vehicle numbers and speed referred to above, which is often essential for cycling initiatives to succeed.

Market town as service hub

Market towns have a range of 'roles' but a key one is their position as places where, due to their population level and that of the surrounding hinterland, a range of services can be maintained. This can prevent 'leakage' of trade to other towns and, in transport terms, reduce the number of miles travelled to access services. Such a role creates opportunities and threats.

In relation to opportunities, market towns can act as hubs for transport services. It is often reported that rural areas cannot support much in the way of public transport services due to low densities and high levels of car ownership. However, partly for the reasons cited in the first section of this chapter, there is a market for rural public transport. The composition of market town hinterlands is important in understanding the extent to which market towns can support a number of services. Gray (2004) notes that where hinterland populations are dispersed, public transport is harder to deliver and an absence of services results. Car dependence in such places is, therefore, not surprising. However, even in such potentially infertile policy ground, market towns have acted as the focus for a wide range of innovative solutions in recent years.

Innovation in transport provision

In the past, conventional public transport services alongside various social economy actions such as lift-giving and para-transit provided the safety net for those unable to access services using other modes. However, with conventional public transport more and more difficult to provide and the effects of car dependency and large-scale car use on town environments increasingly acknowledged, other solutions have been pursued. The new menu of initiatives involves a patchwork of ideas adapted to individual places. For example, many places have started community bus schemes and shared taxi services as a way of overcoming the difficulties of living in remoter areas. In the former case, communities use volunteers to run a minibus to enable residents to access certain facilities. Typically such services run from villages into market towns for shopping and leisure purposes. They thus usually perform something of the safety net function for those without regular use of a car. Similarly, community car schemes use a more structured form of lift-giving, or may entail the purchase of vehicles for community use. Some local authorities are also exploring using public sector vehicles, such as school buses, for public transportation of some kind when not in use.

Demand-responsive transport refers to a range of initiatives that differ from more conventional public transport by their flexibility. Some may operate to approximate timetables or routes but allow for deviations within given areas on demand from passengers; others operate on a more flexible 'ring and ride' approach. All attempt to link towns and their hinterlands to overcome problems of isolation. In some instances a small number of users are found to have the alternative of a car but choose to use the service (Wigglybus 2006).

These initiatives are generally viewed as positive developments but there are issues for policy makers in their deployment. The first is that while the running of a community scheme is a positive contribution to local social capital, settlements differ in their ability to mobilise existing levels of social capital to develop such mobility opportunity (Farrington *et al.* 2004; Williams and White 2001). The second potential difficulty is that new initiatives may adversely affect the market for mainstream public transport provision and disadvantage those poorly served by the new schemes.

Private vehicles

Arguably, the largest immediate threat to market towns in the transport arena comes from the growing numbers of road vehicles accessing market towns. Such increases create a range of difficulties chiefly concerning the loss of public amenity arising from the space they occupy and the danger and intimidation they inflict on humans and other species.

Market towns are often historic environments where space is at a premium and local heritage concerns prevent some solutions that may be appropriate to other areas, such as road widening and multi-story car parking. Continued pressure in many towns from in-commuting and retail provision, when combined with car, use creates pressure on parking. While the desire to price the scarce good that is parking may be there for local authorities, not least as a revenue raiser, this can be a delicate balancing act where neighbouring towns in different boroughs apply different charging regimes. The problems of inter-town competition and that from edge urban retail parks where parking may be free is a major issue in such instances, coupled as it often is by resistance to charges from residents who may be used to having free parking in a range of centres.

The sustainable market town?

A sustainable town is clearly an accessible town and yet, as noted earlier, traffic can be both the maker and breaker of a place. Thus, perhaps the key transport challenges for towns are retaining a level of accessibility for those without access to a car and managing the town in such a way that cars do not damage the environments that people, whether residents or visitors, value. The sustainable market town may then be one that has accessibility at its core, but is not necessarily characterised by high levels of mobility, especially auto-mobility.

However, beyond this general assertion things get more complicated! Gray's (2004) assertion of the diversity of market towns is backed up by our data on travel patterns. Thus, while nationally 'rural areas' and 'smaller urban centres' exhibit certain trends, there are significant variations around these aggregated statements. Thus, while only 15 per cent of 'rural households' have no car nationally, in Sheerness (Kent, South East) it is over 40 per cent. Comparing other market towns, less than 5 per cent of households in Broughton Astley (Leicestershire, East Midlands) walk to work, which can be contrasted with over one-third of residents in Barnard Castle (Durham, North East) and Keswick (Cumbria, North West).

Much of these variations are due to a variety of factors such as the economic opportunities available in a given place. Providing a degree of employment opportunities in a place has long been a feature of policy in market towns. Such policies aim for a degree of self-containment, keeping a relative balance between housing levels and employment opportunities in a place. Two towns illustrate this well, Broughton Astley and Carterton (Oxfordshire, South East). Both towns have similar demographic profiles with similar population levels, low levels of older age residents, very low levels of unemployment (less than 2 per cent) and high levels of car ownership, and neither has a train or bus station. They are less than 50 miles apart. And yet each exhibits very different travel characteristics. In Broughton Astley few residents walk to work, cycling levels are low, and 73 per cent of residents drive to work. By contrast, Carterton has over 11 per cent of residents cycling to work, a fairly substantial 6.5 per cent commuting by bus and as a consequence less reliance on the car to get to work.

Table 5.1 Two towns' travel patterns compared

	Population	% over 65	No car	Drive to work	Cycle to work	Walk to work	Bus to work
Broughton Astley	8,290	7.9	7.3	72.9	2.0	4.9	2.9
Carterton	12,958	8.1	10.8	57.8	11.2	10.3	6.5
MTI Median	8,633	16.3	21.1	59.5	2.5	13.4	2.4

Source: Population Census 2001

So, why might there be such marked differences in travel patterns? Carterton is close to RAF Brize Norton and nearly 30 per cent of the town's population is employed at the base. Carterton is thus chosen as a place to live due to its proximity to the base and the potential to cycle and walk to work. Broughton Astley by contrast is close to a number of urban centres and also motorways – a high proportion of people work in retail warehousing, which is typically located at motorway junctions with poor access by public transport. The town may thus become a good choice for double-income households looking for 'centrality' to two places of work, but in a rural setting.

So, the specifics of any town are going to determine to a great extent the travel patterns of residents. And yet policy can make a difference to such patterns. So, the challenge for all towns is to examine existing travel profiles and try to slowly shape patterns in the right direction of travel, as it were, i.e. to make travel patterns more sustainable into the future, not less. Those making the 'right' choices should be encouraged to continue to do so. Other groups, through travel planning initiatives for example, could be targeted to change some of their behavioural patterns. This does not imply that suddenly a dependence on the car is going to change, merely that small incremental changes can add up to large-scale behavioural changes over time.

Transport futures for market towns

One of the concerns for market towns is that there is very little systematic analysis of the transport opportunities and threats within them. Policy approaches and tools tend to cascade to such places from higher-order centres, but are not necessarily applicable.

That said, certain principles can be readily transferred. There is evidence that many English market towns are suffering the same problems as larger urban areas, chiefly in managing the demand for private travel and providing attractive alternatives in the face of increasing levels of car ownership and traffic. There is much innovation going on but there are also questions about whether the resources, financial and intellectual, widely exist. The financial difficulties are well rehearsed, although here there appears to be much 'path dependency' in funding with a historic emphasis on roads continuing and an over-emphasis on capital projects at the expense of revenue funding. But, related to this, there may well be questions of institutional capacity on the part of policy makers too (see also Shorten 2004). How much do local planners know of and understand the complexities of transport provision in market towns? Are they aware of the range of tools at their disposal and about the relationships between what they do in land-use planning arenas and its potential effects on transport conditions? Can and are they building institutional links to other policy communities to co-align planning goals with those of others? There are also particular political difficulties in attempts to restrict car use given the history of unfettered car access to such places. Local traders in particular typically vociferously oppose restrictions on car access and parking. And yet the overwhelming evidence is that such restrictions can improve local business conditions (Hass-Klau 1986).

Some nettles are not being grasped locally and much emphasis in UK policy neglects the realities of travel in market towns. Although there may be an aim for an efficient, integrated public transport system that provides links to services and facilities, this ignores the fact that for residents of market towns cars (driving, lift getting, taxis), and walking are the primary modes. Access for these, particularly the latter, needs to be emphasised. In all transport policy there seems an emphasis on 'boys' toys' and in rural planning an emphasis on counting things such as services in parishes. But what could be done instead to systematise lift sharing, develop cycling networks and create better walking networks that encourage people to walk into towns? As others have noted (Transport 2000 and CAB 2003), provision for cycling to and in market towns is poor in the UK relative to European counterparts with little segregation offered to cyclists on busy roads and little done to calm traffic and reduce motor vehicle traffic speed on routes potentially important to cycling. It is of little surprise, therefore, that cycling levels in and to market towns are very low in the UK compared with much of Europe.

What then is on the horizon? One key trend explored elsewhere in this book concerns the ageing population. There are two points to note here. First, the increase in the number of elderly drivers is significant in a number of ways not least in adding to a growing problem of vehicular traffic trying to access town centres and causing damage to neighbourhood environments. And yet, market towns are often retirement destinations for those from remoter areas who may be unwilling or unable to drive, and for them the policy focus should be on good walking conditions and easy-access public transport (Age Concern 2003a). And perhaps of primary importance, somewhat ironically, is the issue of traffic, as the elderly are much more likely to be hit by cars than other parts of the population (Age Concern 2003a). This is a social justice issue that is largely hidden and increasing; it shouldn't be ghettoised as a transport issue. Children are similarly disadvantaged by an emphasis on motor vehicles at the expense of other modes.

A further question lies in the implications of environmental conditions in market towns arising from national road pricing. This has tentative support from all political parties despite apparent public opposition and could affect the 'threat' posed by road traffic in town centres and neighbourhoods depending on the scheme's implementation. Research tends to indicate that rural areas will experience an increase in road traffic under a revenue-neutral scheme, but that small urban areas (of below 25,000 people) would experience little change (Glaister and Graham 2006). Much of this does of course depend on other policies, both within the transport sector and beyond. It is reasonable to assume, despite these conclusions, that traffic arising on rural roads may start and/or finish in market towns unless action is taken to discourage it and provide alternatives.

Finally in looking to the future much has been made of the role of information and communication technologies (ICTs) in overcoming distance to services, through online shopping and banking for example. Rural development initiatives over the last two decades have been pursuing policies of connecting up market towns and their hinterlands to ICT networks. The relationships between physical travel and virtual communications possibilities are, however, very complex. There is no doubt that in some instances ICT use can substitute for physical travel, and can potentially overcome some of the exclusionary tendencies described above. However, more typically, ICT and travel may have a complementary relationship (Stead and Banister 2006). For example, information broadcast through ICT may encourage travel to a market town. Again, however, there is little information on the relationships between ICT usage and transport specifically in relation to market towns.

So in conclusion we can say that the immediate transport challenges are likely to remain the same. On one hand accessibility has to be maintained and promoted for those who have difficulty accessing services. The ageing population of market towns puts this into greater focus. Second, how can market towns, particularly those with a strong retail core and/or those with a strong tourist focus, retain and enhance the features that make them attractive without being destroyed by traffic? This is no easy challenge, there are likely to be unintended consequences of any action and there is a paucity of data for policy makers to base their decisions upon. Perhaps this is the main challenge, to improve our understanding of the dynamics of travel in and to market towns, and then to mobilise this knowledge effectively to shape town futures in positive, sustainable, ways. In turn this is likely to require packages of measures that go beyond single initiatives such as a bypass, or a cycle network, and careful attention to bring local populations on board with policies to ensure effective implementation.

Chapter 6

Ready or not

The ageing of the market towns' population

Rose Gilroy, Liz Brooks and Tim Shaw

Introduction

In this chapter we take up the issue of demographic change, specifically the ageing of rural Britain and the emergence of some market towns as retirement destinations. The Rural White Paper (MAFF and DETR 2000: 73) saw market towns as 'service centres and hubs for surrounding hinterlands' with the potential to exploit their attractiveness as places 'to live, work and spend leisure time'. While this sounds like a package that might prove attractive to older people, detailed discussion of how this revival might serve their interests or how older people might bolster such a vision was lacking.

The chapter begins by considering the evidence of ageing in Britain's rural places and the implications for market towns. It moves on to analyse the policies of New Labour, examining the extent to which there is a robust framework to meet the specific needs and aspirations of older people in market towns and their rural hinterlands. The chapter then turns to consider how demographic change, policies and market forces play out in Northumberland. Drawing on in-depth interviews with older people we focus on the market town of Hexham, then, taking a service provider perspective, we explore the viability of delivering services in the market town and beyond before drawing conclusions.

Retiring to the countryside?

Demographers have been forecasting the ageing of the population in Britain (and Western Europe) since the 1880s, when birth rates were first observed to be falling (Warnes and McInerney 2004). This decrease has continued throughout the twentieth century, resulting in greater proportions of older people in the population. Greater advances in medical science and changed lifestyles have added years to life – currently rising at the rate of 5 hours per day – with the result that more people are living into their ninth and tenth decades (Kirkwood 2006). This picture of fewer babies and longer lives is the demographic challenge facing all societies (Ermisch 1990; Harper 2006). In Britain these issues are becoming more important as the two baby boomer cohorts of the 1940s and the mid-1960s work through to create a bulge of people in their early sixties and a further group set to retire in the next 20 years.

While all places are, therefore, to some extent retirement communities, it has been clear to census analysts that strong regional differences have been created by retired people, freed-up from the work-based commute, relocating to more climatically advantaged parts of the UK. Law and Warnes (1976), commenting on the censuses of 1951, 1961 and 1971, were talking of the concentration of older people in the coastal parts of southern Britain. Analysing the 1981 census, Warnes and Law (1984) observed that migrating retirees were seeking out a greater diversity of locations:

> Favoured rural areas peripheral to long standing retirement towns were joined during the 1970s by others with similar environmental attractions in inland areas of East Anglia, Lincolnshire, North Yorkshire, the southern Lake District, the Scottish and Welsh Borders and the Cotswolds as the areas with the most rapid increase of their pensionable population.
>
> (Warnes and Law 1984: 44)

While retirement to the countryside is still significant (about 10 per cent of in-migrants according to the Countryside Agency 2004a) it is not the main driver of rural ageing. More significant has been the ageing of the long-term rural population and the ageing of working incomers. Champion (1989; 1998: see also Champion and Shepherd 2006) has written extensively on the issue of counter-urbanisation revealing the diversity of this group, which includes families with school-age children and the late-stage-worker accepting a brief period of long-distance commuting before retiring from work. While the latter group clearly add to the ageing of the countryside, the combined pull of university and the push of fewer economic opportunities lead to an out-migration of rural-based young people leaving behind older people. Work in the United States suggests that the mid-life migrant may be followed by their older parents seeking the benefits of familial co-location. Around one-third of older in-migrants in Glasgow and Brown's study (2006: 186) had adult children living near to their new location.

Some of the diversity of the geography of ageing in the UK is captured by the Mosaic database (Experian 2003). Mosaic classifies postcodes in the UK by allocating them to one of 11 groups such as 'Symbols of Success' or 'Suburban Comfort' (see Table 6.1 for a description of these terms) and then further sub-divides each group into 61 types such as 'Maturing Mortgagers' or 'Settled Minorities' based on more than 400 data variables from Census data, electoral records, commercial credit information and other marketing information.

Table 6.1 Mosaic UK group and type descriptions

Group	Symbols of success	Suburban comfort
Type	Semi-rural seclusion	Small-time business
Demography	Older, less well-paid locals and newcomers who are mature; well-paid professionals who commute longer distances to work	Professionals in mature working phase from 45 until retirement
Environment	Detached houses built in last 20 years in cul-de-sacs off village streets or off routes out of small market towns leading to open countryside. Local convenience stores but major shopping trips require a car. Poor public transport	New estates in market towns set in areas of average landscape value. Walking distance of town centre and shops
Comments	People are well integrated in their communities	Local networks are important, groups such as Rotarians are well supported, as are local charities

Source: Experian (2003)

In some localities ageing is largely due to out-migration of young people while in others – characterised by high-quality environments – in-migration of better-off, older people contribute to price escalation that may take home ownership out of the reach of younger locals. Some places are attracting mature workers with a view to retirement who are building social networks in the good times as it were, while in others it is post-retirement moves that dominate. The relationship of these groups to the market town is also different, some choosing to move there echoing Leather's (1997) prediction that footloose affluent retirees would seek rural towns and larger villages with services rather than deeper and more remote rural places. For others, in settlements with minimal or no local services, the market town may be the nearest destination for food shopping and other everyday needs. The Mosaic database records that in some market towns more dwellings have been created through the conversion of former agricultural or commercial buildings and also from the building of small estates on the edge of existing settlements. Market towns, then, have a growth in service users that creates potential for new restaurant, leisure and retail development as well as housing (see Chapter 8). However, this is only likely to happen where older people are viewed as an opportunity to be built upon rather than a threat to vibrancy and economic viability (Butler *et al.* 2003). Phillips *et al.* (1987), commenting on the restrictive planning policies of Blackpool, Eastbourne and Bournemouth, judged their policies to stem from an assumption that older people are a 'burden on local taxation'. These issues come to the fore again with the debates over planning permission for continuing care communities, which are judged by planners in the UK to be classed as C3 (housing applications) or C2 (institutional care applications). Planners often struggle to see that C class developments for older people are likely to create local employment beyond the construction phase (Tetlow 2006). As well as the arguments that older people may need domestic help or care, research demonstrates that older people are a powerful group of consumers who may support local businesses (Baker and Speakman 2006) and, as Green (2006) asserts, are more likely than younger people to be self-employed and thus creating jobs for others.

From statistics to policy response

While demographic trends have been under discussion for some time, it was only with the 1997 election of the Labour government that a policy response to ageing began to proliferate. We might ask what, apart from a possible normative idea of social justice, could account for this awakening. The bulge in the 60-to-70 age group, caused by the 1940s baby boom working through, has added pressure (Evandrou 1997). There is a perceptible shift in the 'culture of ageing' caused by this generation – the iconoclasts of the 1960s – used to protest, and now largely with the affluence to get what they want. There is greater political confidence among older people evidenced by Jack Jones and the Pensioners Convention's successful campaign against the imposition of higher VAT on fuel and, more recently, older people ready to risk imprisonment for non-payment of Council Tax as a protest against their steep increases (Seniors Network 2006; Farquharson 2006). People over 50 represent 25 per cent of all voters, and among the over 65s, 75 per cent exercise their right to vote (Age Concern 2006). All this may add to a realisation among politicians that increasingly it is older people who vote governments in (and out). This does not equate to an 'age interest' vote but it sends a clear message to political parties that the broad concerns of older people, namely personal and national security, quality services, financial security and health care, need to be addressed (Vincent 2003; Age Concern 2003b; Audit Commission 2004).

The greater policy focus on older people has been matched by a conscious listening to their experiences. The Benefits Agency (Croden *et al.* 1999) and the NHS (DoH 1998; 1999) have developed new ways of delivering services partly as a result of working with older people's reference groups. The publication in 2001 of *Quality and Choice for Older People's*

Housing: A Strategic Framework (DETR and DoH 2001), the Green Paper 'Independence, Wellbeing and Choice' (DoH 2005) and the introduction of the 'choose and book' appointment system for accessing hospital consultations (DoH 2003) have contributed to a policy framework that increasingly sees older people as choice makers, not passive beneficiaries.

At the same time as older people's concerns have been rising up the policy agenda, there has been increasing focus on rural issues. Labour, traditionally the party of the town and city, has paid significantly more attention to rural matters in the last few years than, for example, the neo-liberal administration of Margaret Thatcher who, in defiance of the association between Conservatives and rural England, saw her political battleground as winning the hearts and minds of urban working class populations.

The major rural policy document of the Labour government has been the Rural White Paper of 2000 (MAFF and DETR), which envisioned a role for some market towns as service hubs. Ironically, the scant discussion of older people is confined to seeing them as 'at risk' from poor access to services. To address this issue, the White Paper proposed to support very local services and strengthen links between small settlements and the larger service hub. This was to be achieved by supporting the retention of rural post offices and creating a new fund for parish council transport projects. This transport fund, administered by the (then) Countryside Agency,[1] would divert existing mainstream bus services through smaller settlements to link people to their nearest larger settlement and promote flexible solutions such as community buses as well as taxi vouchers for older people (see Bevan and Croucher (2006) for discussion of the restrictions placed on older people's use of taxi vouchers). In the past, similar transport schemes have not survived through a lack of sustained funding, and this initiative itself is under threat as resources for community transport are diverted from the defunct Countryside Agency to the RDAs, with their primarily economic agenda.

The subsequent review of the Rural White Paper (DEFRA 2004a) amended the Rural Services Standard, which was introduced in 2000, to include for the first time an 'older people' indicator, though this is weakly expressed as the need to keep older people living independently at home. However, the Rural Services Review 2006 (DEFRA 2006a) showed that many of the government departments concerned with delivering generic services and therefore responsible for delivering the Rural Services Standard still did not disaggregate rural data. Without adequate statistics their potential to format or deliver policies that target young or old in rural communities is very limited. In short, the commitment to rural proof policy made in the White Paper is not being carried out (CRC 2006a). Of equal or greater concern is the lack of response to the Countryside Agency's finding that the allocation of resources to local authorities fails to acknowledge the difficulties of service delivery in rural areas (Countryside Agency 2004c; CRC 2005c). It remains to be seen whether the 2007 Comprehensive Spending Review will embrace a review of the grant distribution formula. The impact of the current allocation system is seen in the Northumberland case study.

If rural policies have been slow to recognise older peoples' concerns and have fastened on a view of older people as 'needy', this is matched by age-focused policies that, in waking up to rural issues, have come to the same conclusions. It was not till the publication of *Opportunity Age* (DWP 2005), intended to be the central plank of the government's ageing strategy, that there was any acknowledgement of a distinctive agenda for the older rural population. Access to services is again seen as the nub of the problem exacerbated by remoteness of dwellings and settlements, all of which echo the discussion of the Rural White Paper some five years before (MAFF and DETR 2000). While the White Paper put forward the service hub as a role for some market towns, here the centralisation of services is seen as problematic since the transport linkages that deliver people to these hubs are still lacking. Just as the White Paper hoped to improve the situation through community transport, so *Opportunity Age* introduced free off-peak bus travel within the district of residence (April 2006) as a major plank in the strategy to aid access. In practice, however, the travel pass is of more limited value to rural elders because to access major services such as hospitals, they need to cross district boundaries, and because the more remote routes are regularly reduced or cut on the grounds of low usage. The Social Exclusion Unit's report *Sure Start in Later Life* published in 2006 repeats that there are difficulties in preventing exclusion and promoting well-being in later life in rural Britain with 'effective joined up services at key times'. Echoing the Countryside Agency (2004c), it also concludes that access to services is part of the problem, as are limitations on local authority funding that stifle the provision of services and preventative work by social services.

In 2006 then, two separate policy strands have reached the same conclusions: first, older people need some local services and transport connections to get to service hubs; second, there is a need for properly funded rural local authorities to deliver support services to those who need them. In spite of the great diversity of older people in the market towns and rural hinterland, which includes the economically active, the potential entrepreneurs and volunteers, the dominant vision of rural older people in the policy is the frail needy person in a remote location. While we may criticise this narrow view, our greater concern must be that adequate funding will not follow policy, and that poorly resourced solutions cannot counter market forces.

How do these issues play out in a county like Northumberland, with market towns and remote settlements? Do older people find the market town a satisfying place to live that meets their diverse needs? Focusing on the market town of Hexham, we look first through the eyes of an older couple, Peter and Jane, at the provision for the newly retired incomers and, through Margaret's, at provision for the older long-term resident who has to contend with disability. Then taking a service provider's perspective we explore the opportunities and difficulties involved in delivering older people's services in and beyond the market town.

Ageing in Northumberland

While Northumberland is the sixth largest of all English counties, covering almost 2,000 square miles, it has one of the lowest populations, with just over 309,000 people of whom almost a quarter are 60 years or older. Over 50 per cent of the population live in less than 5 per cent of the land area, giving an urban concentration in the south-east corner of the county in the districts of Castle Morpeth, Wansbeck and Blyth, and a very low population density in the rural districts of Berwick, Alnwick and Tynedale in the north and west (Northumberland County Council 2006).Within the county there are the large markets towns of Berwick, Alnwick, Haltwhistle, Hexham and Morpeth, offering a wide range of services, and the smaller market towns of Rothbury and Wooler located in more remote areas (see Chapter 2 for a description of market towns in the North East of England).

Hexham is one of the three main market towns in the Tynedale district of Northumberland and is situated more or less centrally between the metropolitan settlements of Carlisle and Newcastle in the Tyne valley. In terms of acreage, Tynedale is the largest local authority district in England, and Hexham is at a transport hub at the heart of a thin and widely dispersed rural population. While the majority of Tynedale's larger villages include specialised housing for older people, Hexham has a particularly high density of specialised and supported accommodation, and it is not uncommon for people to move into the town centre from the outlying rural hinterland when their circumstances change – for example, following a bereavement or cessation of driving.

Hexham town centre is well supplied with property of most sizes and periods, from terraces with a small back yard and long front garden and Victorian villas set in sizeable grounds, to modern bungalows and estate houses mainly at the town's perimeter. As planning sustainability criteria set a limit to edge-of-town estates, there is increasing infill with modern purpose-built flats dotted throughout the town. There are also more than 330 units of accommodation designed for older people, close to or within its centre, including unsupported flats and sheltered housing.

Ageing in the market town: older people's perspective

Jane and Peter present a picture of life in a market town from the viewpoint of the newly retired. They recently moved to Hexham in good health to enjoy an active retirement and more contact with their children and grandchildren. Both had enjoyed fulfilling working lives in Newcastle and were, financially, in a position to plan ahead and buy their property over two years in advance of the move. Both the property and location were selected against a carefully considered checklist of attributes.

Two factors in particular led them to settle in Hexham. They were looking for an old, good-sized stone-built property with a garden and with good transport connections, both internally and to more distant centres:

> [. . .] my parents, when they got older, lived in the middle of Northamptonshire which you could not reach by public transport, and when my father was ill, getting down to see him every weekend was an absolute hell and we were determined that we were going to be somewhere that was accessible as we get older, because we do have trains. That was something that we thought about, which was why we didn't go out into the middle of Northumberland . . .

While Hexham is not threatened as a railway town, as recently as 2006, Tyne Valley communities had to fight proposals to reduce the number of the stations on the Newcastle to Carlisle Tyne Valley line, which links a number of villages to Hexham and also to the regional capital, Newcastle. Rail links in this part of Northumberland provide a vital link for those older people who live in villages with few local services.

Jane and Peter also noted a 'push' factor, in the street drinking and anti-social behaviour of young people in their suburb of Newcastle:

> [. . .] we've walked home – it wasn't very late, about 10 – we didn't see any youngsters hanging around at all in Hexham, but if we had been doing the same thing in [Newcastle suburb], it would have been hordes of them. Not just the students, which you expect in [Newcastle suburb], but younger people and something we used to suffer from in [Newcastle suburb] was that you would see parents come and drop their young teenagers off to have a good time, much to the detriment of everyone else.

There is no shortage of activities for older people in Hexham. It has at least three educational establishments running a range of practical and leisure activities. The University of the Third Age offers over 40 different groups, with more than 350 members. Hexham also has a community centre and an arts centre, running subsidised activities, as well as an independent cinema. After a year, Peter and Jane's time is increasingly structured by these activities and, in spite of having no existing social links with Hexham, they are building a social life through their neighbours and activities. This year they expect to be included in Christmas invitations for drinks and parties.

The only privation that the move has entailed – an apparently voluntary one – is forgoing one of the household's two cars. Jane goes on foot to Hexham town centre to use the specialist food shops such as the butchers and fish shop, but for the weekly grocery shop, drives to the edge-of-town supermarkets. Peter mentioned the efficiency and speed of the local independent bookseller, and his grandson's enjoyment of the specialist model shop. The couple expressed some concern that the convenience of the edge-of-town stores for working people could be reducing the sustainability of the town centre shops. Already they have noticed some decline since they bought their property three years ago. Currently most journeys are made on foot or in the car; the couple only rarely use public transport – they might take the train to Newcastle on occasion, but continue to drive into the city if they are seeing a friend in one of the city's less well-connected suburbs.

Private transport is an even greater factor in quality of life for older people in the hinterland of Hexham. Those communities to the south such as Allendale are well linked to the market town with bus services, while to the north, villages in the Northumberland National Park have much poorer linkages. The concept of the market town as service hub for its hinterland only works if people are able to get there. Currently 27 per cent of those rural residents aged 64 and older have no car. While ageing may not bring infirmity, those aged 70 and over are dependent on their doctor for renewal of their driving licence. In 2001 there were 2 million drivers over 70 and by 2015 it is estimated there will be 4.5 million (DTLR 2001). The loss of cross-subsidy for rural bus services in the 1980s has led to a continued decline in services that is not overcome by uncertainly-funded community transport schemes.

Peter and Jane planned their retirement move to Hexham well in advance and admit that while there might well be the possibility of a further move in Hexham if one or both of them became severely disabled, they have to an extent been able to future-proof. The maisonette they live in could be adjusted for living on ground floor level. The shuttle bus that visits the adjoining road would keep them connected with the town centre and even their space-hungry hobbies of weaving and wood-turning could be maintained by redeploying the dining room space.

Jane has some concern about the organisation of health care in the Tynedale district. In spite of Hexham's new hospital, people must travel to distant towns for particular specialisms such as cancer and heart problems, a considerable obstacle for those without independent private transport. This issue is more acute in the north of the county. The border market town of Berwick's nearest hospital offering cardiac and (limited) cancer care is Ashington (a distance of 54 miles), which entails three bus journeys taking more than 2 hours. As part of their transport plans, local authorities are required to produce accessibility maps demonstrating the time taken to access major services including the nearest GP and hospitals by public and private transport. Recent re-organisation of health services has led to centres of excellence and a move away from a spread of specialists. Hence the nearest hospital may not deal with all medical problems and may not provide accident and emergency services. The impact of policy and practice changes within the NHS is most clearly brought into focus when looking at the spread of dental provision. While there are 43 practices in Northumberland, only 18 serve the three most rural districts. More worrying is the privatisation of dental services such that only two practices in the rural areas are currently accepting new NHS patients; both of these are in Hexham. Only one practice (and again that is in Hexham) offers a service to housebound and otherwise excluded patients.

Margaret, in her late seventies, is at the needy end of the health spectrum. A lifelong Hexham resident and wheelchair user, she has lived in her current accommodation, a one-bedroom flat in a housing association block, for over 14 years. Although she was born with her disability, she had been able to live independently for most of her life, until a serious illness left her unable to move between bed and wheelchair without support. This health crisis caused her to move to her flat where she is assisted to live independently by home care workers who visit three times every day.

Until her illness, Margaret lived an active life in Hexham, attending literature and drama classes. Now she focuses activity on her work with the local disabled people's group, where she sits on the management board. She attends church once a week, goes to a Friday lunch club, and regularly spends time with a friend she has known since childhood.

Margaret has accepted the constraints on her life and expressed satisfaction with the social options open to her, although she feels that these are narrowing as her disability increases. From an outside perspective, however, it is less Margaret's disability that curtails her activities, but rather the physical characteristics of Hexham, and the apparent lack of able-bodied assistants who might help her to try new routes and activities, safe in the knowledge that help is at hand should her electric wheelchair run out of charge, or if she should lose her bearings.

Topographical obstacles are not unusual in traditional settlements like Hexham, sited to enjoy the defensive advantages of an elevated position, and the natural rise from a fertile flood plain once essential for fresh food supplies. The changes in level can create considerable disadvantages for anyone lacking optimum mobility, from parents with pushchairs to older people with walking aids. Hexham is situated on three levels:

- The flood plain of the River Tyne, where the train station and three of Hexham's four edge-of-town supermarkets are found;
- The level plateau of the traditional town centre that is increasingly focused on comparison retail and tourism goods as the supermarkets undercut smaller food retailers; and
- The steep inclines in the residential areas of Hexham, rising from the main street to the moors of the Hexhamshire hinterland, intercut by the deep valleys of the Tyne's tributaries.

Prior to the move into her ground floor flat, Margaret shared a house with her sister on the steep incline above the town centre. When her sister moved to a care home and Margaret's mobility was further affected by illness, she found it difficult to manage at home. Even in an electric buggy, the hill between her front door and the town centre was an ordeal. The flat she has now moved to is level with the traditional town centre.

> I had a different electric wheelchair, but it was similar to the one I've got now. When I went down to do the shopping, by the time I got all the way back up the hill, I used to get tired. But here, you see, I just have to go along the street and it's so much handier.

Another common disadvantage of a traditional town for the mobility impaired is the narrowness of the pavements (Imrie and Hall 2001). Even where pavements are wide enough for a wheelchair, those of less than the recommended 1.8 m may create barriers to wheel-chair users who need to make the turn from the pavement to the street or from the street into a shop (Mitchell 2006). Margaret's nearest shopping street is inaccessible to her along part of its length for this reason. It seems feasible that the council could create a turning place for wheelchair users on this street without causing dangerous obstruction to vehicles. The historical and aesthetic character of the area would be altered, however, with potential conflict between policy objectives and potential loss of appeal to some retirees.

Margaret's experience exemplifies the benefits and disadvantages of market town life for an older person with mobility impairment. People of higher chronological age are statistically more likely to suffer a disability, and as Margaret's story demonstrates these historic environments may be particularly 'disabling' environments for the mobility impaired (Imrie 1996). The narrowness of traditional streets, the unevenness of traditional surfaces such as cobbles and flagstones, and in many towns, several changes of level, may add charm but also present obstacles to the less mobile. The increasing siting of everyday shopping facilities on edge-of-town sites, where large parking facilities may be provided, gives increased choice for the car driver but creates difficulties for the non-car user that might over time become worse if local shop closures result.

Hexham has one pedestrianised shopping street that includes an accessible low-priced grocery and department store. This street is Margaret's mainstay for everyday items although she depends on carers for her main food shopping from the edge-of-town supermarkets. She remarked on the increased difficulty of finding clothes as traditional retailers address younger markets. She also noted the retail trend for cramming more goods and stands in smaller spaces. This has prevented her accessing shelves or, having accessed them, turning safely to access the cash desk. Although this policy of high street stores might be challenged as contravening the Disability Discrimination Act (1995) in the short term, Margaret would be better served by the purpose-built edge-of-town supermarkets, whose large footprint enables generously spaced aisles and lack of obstructions. She might also benefit from the greater choices for clothes available in out-of-town malls, such as that in Gateshead. But in both respects, Margaret's disability puts her at a disadvantage.

Tynedale District Council has made some improvements to facilitate access between the town's levels for those on foot – for example, a handrail runs some of the way up the partly pedestrianised connection between the low-lying supermarket area and main town plateau. At the very top of the road two benches serve as resting places but it would be unlikely that an older person in a wheelchair could be confident of achieving the ascent without the reassurance of back-up assistance. This anxiety has prevented Margaret from visiting the edge-of-town supermarkets for two years:

> the last time I went [. . .] I met Helen on the way and I says, 'I'll have to be careful in case the battery gets low on the chair.' And I went back up, you see, I decided to come up by the Wentworth café – I could tell it [wheelchair] wasn't very happy. Because it's really steep there. Fortunately, somebody's sitting in the café, a lady, she was sitting having a meal or something so she sent her husband . . . out to give a big push for a while until we got onto the flat level.

This puts the train station out of bounds, but the bus station is on the plateau of the town and thus theoretically accessible. But a less technical obstacle has prevented Margaret from trying out the new disabled-friendly buses:

> Well actually they have got a low floor bus. They do use low floor buses, which I think I could get onto, but I've never actually tried. [. . .] Well you see, once you've done things once, it's easier.

In fact, Margaret has not left Hexham for 6 years, except on a weekly trip to a nearby lunch venue with the local older people's luncheon club. In spite of these limitations, Margaret is clearly enjoying life in Hexham and praised many of the interventions to support access to wheelchair users – including ramp access to the local hospital and the post office, and the ramps and lifts available in the local department store. Her requirement for personal support to access buses and shopping outside Hexham may change with the new rehabilitation model of care support about to be introduced by Northumberland Care Trust. This model provides intensive team support to care recipients over a 6-week period, with the aim of restoring lost skills and independence. The model appears to apply particularly well to the recently disabled, and people recovering from hospital treatment, but might also open up new areas of Hexham and Northumberland to the long-term disabled like Margaret. The prospect also raises Margaret's main concerns about her care, which is increasingly expensive, while the range of tasks that the ever-changing carers are permitted to undertake contracts.

Providing services to older people

Hexham provides a good quality of life for older people, though those who are in good health and can drive can enjoy more of the opportunities. If Margaret's health worsens or if Jane or Peter need support from statutory or voluntary services, what can they expect? We turn now to think of service provision for older people from the providers' viewpoint, providing quotes from those responsible for such care in Northumberland. Margaret's concern about her ever-changing care-workers is mirrored by the care providers, conscious that they are offering jobs that pay low wages but demand car ownership in the face of local house prices that demand high incomes.

> Well there's a crisis in home care services nationally, and it's more acute in a rural area. People that can afford housing in Hexham are not willing to do low-paid jobs, particularly in home care, because you need a car . . . the staff are covering 4 or 5 million miles, at 600 miles a week, some do over a 1,000 miles a week, and when you're on a lower wage, everything impacts, doesn't it, it's like the petrol prices in rural areas are above average, Northumberland County Council doesn't get anywhere near the amount of money it needs to run the services.

Those who are willing and able to take on the work are sometimes taking home care as a stop-gap job: 'It only takes Tesco or Asda [large supermarkets] to open up in a town and we lose all our home care. The money's better and it's a more socially acceptable job.'

Statutory services are supplemented by the voluntary sector, which works effectively within towns such as Hexham but struggles to provide in more remote areas:

> In Hexham we have contracts for home care, day care, dementia day care, social day care, luncheon groups, and health groups. But people tend to want it in their own area so we combine Allendale and another area [district councils] – but [Allendale] people only want to go if it's in Allendale. And if it's run by volunteers because it's very very difficult to get volunteers to travel . . . then it has to be in the local area.

An unsung but very clear contribution that older people make is through volunteering. Far from being recipients of care, many older people are using their time and life experience to assist others. Prohibitions placed by insurers prevent the contribution of older volunteers, particularly those who can offer themselves as drivers: 'we have tried getting volunteers, but the trouble is insurance companies wouldn't insure them over the age of 70 and I would say 90 per cent of volunteers are in that category'.

The implications for older people, particularly those in more isolated areas, is that their services are almost perpetually at risk, and for those who lose services there is often only one choice: the move to care coupled with dislocation from the place that they know and are known in.

> I've got no doubt that some people can't deliver a service to certain parts of the county and it's what worries me about people in rural areas, the people in very rural areas. What the Audit Commission said about Northumberland – I think it's all rural counties – where people go into care unnecessarily, and quite often the care isn't anywhere near where they come from.

An interrogation of the care homes database held by Northumberland Social Services demonstrates concentrations in the larger market towns while, for those who might become mentally infirm, the paucity of bed-spaces increases the inevitability of moving out of their locality. Hexham has 236 care home places, sixty-five of which are for dementia sufferers and one place for an older person with learning disabilities. In contrast, Wooler, a small market town in the border country with an increasing retirement population, has only one care home with seventeen places. However, this establishment cannot provide care for those who need nursing support or who have dementia. Someone in either position would need to be placed in Berwick 17 miles away. This analysis does not factor in the critical issue of cost and the greater difficulty for those dependent on social services to meet these. The need to move is not only dislocating for older people themselves but may sever ties between the person and their friends, particularly those without private transport.

Hexham is a market town that is successfully drawing in older people through its combination of quiet and in places, quaint environment, and its range of leisure and learning activities and everyday services. However, it is clear that for those in poorer health, mobility around the town is challenging and the provision of care services far from certain. While policy documents have drawn a picture of frail elders in remote places, it is clear that resources are not flowing to service providers who are struggling even in the market towns to deliver the quantity and quality of care expected by older people. Beyond the market town, service providers are working with low resources to meet greater demands while contending with the fragmented governance framework that embraces county, district and parish councils.

Conclusion

We have seen how the limited government attention to rural ageing focuses on issues of access to services and transport, but fails to deliver effective policies on the ground. We have also seen that for both elders who are resident and those visiting from the rural hinterland, the distinctive qualities of a traditional market town, with its unplanned and irregular roads, its uneven surfaces and levels, could present barriers. The relocating of everyday goods and groceries to edge-of-town sites, which privileges the car user, may also present particular problems for those 27 per cent of elders who do not have access to a private vehicle. While this constitutes less than one-third of elders, clearly the lifetime probability of joining this group will account for the majority of people. Policy that concentrates core services and specialist accommodation for older people in service hub towns, yet does not address difficulties of access within those towns, may fail to serve the increasingly large proportion of the local population made up by older people.

We have seen that older people's participation in the cultural and social life adds richness to the life of a market town, but this contribution is also at risk from lack of attention to mobility needs. Recent statistics suggest that around one-third of people between 75 and 84 years of age use some kind of mobility aid, rising to over 60 per cent of people aged 85+, while permanent mobility difficulties are particularly acute for women (Walker *et al.* 2003). As the case study of Margaret suggests, a person with mobility impairment might well need less support and take more part in the life of the town if the issue of access could be expanded from transport and services issues to questions of physical infrastructure and better links between transport hubs, facilities and shopping areas. If this is the case for residents of the market town, consider how an older person in a more remote location may have added problems. The walk to the bus stop and a possibly long bus journey all sap limited energy before the obstacles of the market town itself are faced. It is common in an urban context for older people to shop on a more frequent basis, partly to increase opportunities for social interaction, but also because carrying large loads may be too much of a strain. For an older person dependent on the bus in the rural hinterland, what are the options? The traditional delivery services such as the milk on the doorstep have all but disappeared. The new services of Internet shopping are out of reach of those 80 per cent of elders who are not home Internet users (Ofcom 2006) and those who live beyond the delivery zones.

A further issue that arises from the case study material is the interconnectedness of the generations in a market town. Jane and Peter are typical of the trend in relocations that are primarily house-, rather than settlement-led (Levett-Therivel 2005). Such moves may be largely dependent on the use of a private vehicle – not only because the residential area of a market town may be poorly connected with its public transport links – but because of the need to access edge-of-town stores for everyday shopping, and to maintain contact with a network of friends and relatives dispersed across the region. The rise in car use has increased the clientele for good-quality, old and new housing in market towns and their rural hinterlands, and this often leads to an increase in prices that excludes the kinds of low-skilled and younger workers who might provide support services to maintain older people in their own homes. A key factor for market towns may be therefore, paradoxically, policies to house younger (and less affluent) generations.

Many market towns are developing as service centres, though this is largely due to the operation of market forces and a car-dependent population than by the intent of the 2000 White Paper. A greater awareness of the lifestyle choices being made by older people could lead to considerable benefits to the economies of these market towns. However, as the populations of many market towns and their rural hinterlands grow older, the problems created by centralisation are shown in sharper relief. Policy discussion continues to acknowledge the need to link people to services but money does not follow policy and there is no guaranteed access to services. A reliance on market forces simply sharpens the divide between those with their own transport and those without. Without sufficient resources and a lack of political will at the national and local levels to address these issues, it would be more realistic to abandon the aim of serving the rural hinterland while persuading older people to move to centres of service provision while they are still able. The market town is not an ideal location in which to age to frailty, but it is more able to sustain older people long term: the rural hinterland is not.

Notes

1   The Countryside Agency was split (unequally) into two in 2006. Its major part (landscape, access and recreation) was merged into Natural England along with English Nature and the Rural Development Service of DEFRA. This is a huge organisation with offices in every region to streamline the delivery of services to its customers (farmers). The smaller part (concerned with social and economic issues of rural communities) became the Commission for Rural Communities (CRC); this has three roles as independent watchdog, expert adviser and rural advocate. The CRC has no regional presence or delivery function but is a national agency. One consequence is that the environmental leg of sustainable development has now been separated from the social and economic legs; another consequence is that far more attention and resources are once again focused on agriculture and environment than on wider rural economies and societies – rather the opposite of what was supposed to happen when DEFRA was established out of the ruins of MAFF.

Chapter 7

Market towns, housing and social inclusion

Stuart Cameron and Mark Shucksmith

Introduction

Two contrasting trends might be distinguished in the evolution of the relationship between market towns and their hinterlands, and with it the characteristics of their housing systems and markets. These raise the question of whether housing in market towns simply takes on the housing market characteristics of the rural region within which they are located, or has a distinctly different character and role from housing in the surrounding rural areas.

Embedded in early post-war planning policies and still underpinning the planning of housing in rural regions was a planning tradition that has emphasised the distinction between the market town and its rural hinterland. This involved the concept – explicit or implicit in the terminology of planning documents – of key settlement policy introduced in Chapter 4. Key settlement policies have sought to focus the provision of services and the accommodation of new housing development and population growth into the more substantial settlements, while restraining development in the smaller settlements and open countryside of their rural hinterlands. This perspective assumed a relatively high degree of homogeneity in the character of rural hinterland areas – underpinned by 'productionist' policies focusing on their government-supported role in agricultural production – and a similar homogeneity in the role of market towns and other higher-order rural settlements as the focus of planned growth and service provision within the rural region in which the protection of agricultural land required development constraints beyond these key settlements.

Conversely, more recent discussion of the rural in contemporary Britain has tended to emphasise regionalisation and differentiation in the economic, demographic and social trends affecting the countryside, suggesting a differentiated countryside with significant variations between rural areas in different regions of the country and between different types of countryside:

> The notion of a differentiated countryside arises from a belief that the national rural space consolidated after the Second World War has now given way to a number of increasingly distinct rural spaces. In the early post-war period, dominant economic processes seemed to be orchestrating a homogenisation of the countryside. In contrast, the main processes currently operating appear to be producing divergent socio-economic formations in rural areas. These formations . . . are best seen as consolidated at the *regional* level.
>
> (Murdoch *et al.* 2003: 31).

From this perspective, market towns are more likely to be viewed as reflecting the characteristics of the specific rural region in which they are set, thereby emphasising the similarities
between market towns and their rural hinterlands and the differences between market towns
in different types of rural region. A variety of classifications of types of rural areas, and
classifications of rural housing markets (Bevan *et al.* 2001), have been developed that suggest
markedly different patterns of housing demand and provision in different types of rural
areas. In general these differentiate three categories of rural area that are of particular
significance for housing and related policy issues. First, the most pressured rural areas within
commuting distance of urban concentrations, second the more remote, 'traditional' rural
areas, and third the 'industrial' countryside typified by coalfield areas:

> Counterurbanisation interacts with the urban-rural shift in employment to reinforce
> a 'regionalisation' of rurality. The economic attractiveness of accessible rural areas
> in southern and eastern England and the Midlands is linked to their social attrac-
> tiveness, and here counterurbanisation is at its most advanced. In contrast, the
> declining former coalfield areas of the north and Midlands attract few migrants.
> Likewise, the remote parts of the South West, East Anglia, the Welsh Borders and
> the north of England have low out commuting rates.
>
> (Murdoch *et al.* 2003: 48)

Murdoch *et al.* (2003) suggest that this regionalisation and differentiation of rural areas
was to be seen in the rural policies of the Conservative government in the 1980s and was
then continued in the policies of the Blair government, and encapsulated in the 2000 Rural
White Paper (MAFF and DETR 2000). This is not, though, to suggest that the evolution of
housing in market towns since the early post-war years has involved a linear progression
of increasing similarity between the market town and its hinterland and increasing contrast
between market towns in different types of rural region. A number of other contemporary
trends must be taken into account. First, overlying differences between rural regions, is the
desire to move to the countryside, which brings pressures on rural housing availability and
affordability in most rural regions. Second, recent planning and affordable housing policies
have if anything reinforced the focus of housing development on major settlements in rural
areas even if the explicit designation of key settlements is now a feature of planning history.
Finally, the Sustainable Communities agenda has created a policy nexus integrating city and
rural, with a strong tendency towards an urban focus in development and regeneration
policies, in which market towns can be said to have an intermediate, or even an ambiguous,
status. These influences on the role of market towns are discussed below.

Housing market pressures

Just under one-fifth of the English population (9.5 million) lives in rural areas, where rural
areas are defined as settlements below 10,000 population (DEFRA 2004b). Of these 4.4
million (47 per cent) live in small rural towns of less than 10,000 people, amongst which
are the 'market towns' considered in this volume. A further 3.5 million (37 per cent) live
in villages, and 1.6 million (16 per cent) live in scattered dwellings and hamlets (CRC 2005a).
Many more of England's households would live in rural locations if they could – opinion
polls consistently show as many as 80 per cent of people from the cities would prefer to
live in a rural area. Between 1991 and 2001 there was an average annual net migration
of 30,000 people into rural areas, consisting of 420,000 people moving into rural areas
and 390,000 moving in the other direction each year. As a result, the population of rural
England grew by 14.4 per cent between 1981 and 2003, while urban areas grew only by
1.9 per cent over the same period. It can readily be seen that England's rural areas are
generally areas of high demand for houses. Those able to realise their aspiration of moving

into rural England tend to be older and wealthier owner-occupiers (notably the professional and managerial classes), while those moving to urban areas by choice or necessity tend to be younger and poorer, containing a disproportionate number of skilled and unskilled working classes. Housing market processes are heavily implicated in this selective migration (Shucksmith 1990; 2000; CRC 2006b).

This strong demand for rural living interacts with planning policies intended to prevent housebuilding and other development in the countryside, so restricting the supply of houses in rural areas and forcing rural house prices ever higher. It is this that led the government to establish the Affordable Rural Housing Commission (ARHC 2006) to recommend practical solutions for meeting affordable housing needs in rural areas, in the context of sustainable rural communities.

The CRC's 2005a State of the Countryside report documented rising demand in rural England alongside a static supply, such that the average cost of a house in rural England is now well above that in urban England. The report's analysis of affordability in different types of rural area is summarised in Table 7.1.

It is apparent that houses are, on average, much less affordable in areas of villages, hamlets and isolated dwellings compared to small towns and larger urban areas. Regional analysis shows that there is also a regional dimension, with this affordability ratio rising to 8.2 and 7.9 in hamlets and isolated dwellings of the South East and South West respectively. From this analysis, one might view market towns (among other towns of under 10,000 population) as the most affordable places to live in rural England and indeed perhaps as the only places where newly forming households in rural areas might be able to afford to buy a small house. However, the more attractive market towns experience strong external demand from commuters and others, so that their housing may also be unaffordable to medium- and lower-income groups.

Research undertaken for the Commission for Rural Communities by Roger Tym & Partners (CRC 2006c) indicated that across all rural England (settlements below 10,000 population) only 55 per cent of newly forming households projected over the next 5 years would be able to afford a house in their own ward, leaving an affordable housing need of 22,800 homes per annum, on top of a backlog of a further 40,000 houses already required to meet existing needs. In the South East, South West and East of England regions the proportion unable to find market solutions to their housing needs is expected to be nearer 70 per cent. Research for DEFRA (ARHC 2006) shows that average rural earnings of £17,400 would only be sufficient to fund the purchase of a home in 28 per cent of rural wards.

Table 7.1 Affordability of rural housing by area and settlement type

Area/settlement type (output areas) by – settlement size – sparsity of population	Mean house price, 2004 £	Median household income, 2004 £	Ratio of mean house price to median household income 2004
Town and fringe, less sparse	180,986	27,169	4.5
Urban settlement of >10k, sparse	141,072	21,093	4.5
Urban settlement of >10k, less sparse	175,662	25,919	4.6
Town and fringe, sparse	168,969	21,898	5.2
Village, sparse	211,865	24,729	5.8
Village, less sparse	262,100	30,512	5.8
Hamlet and isolated dwelling, sparse	254,070	25,349	6.8
Hamlet and isolated dwelling, less sparse	327,015	32,097	6.9

Source: CRC (2005a)

For those who can't afford to buy in the open market, the alternative is to rent. The provision of social housing has historically been far lower in rural areas, both by local authorities and by registered social landlords (RSLs) who are now the main providers (Chaplin *et al.* 1995). The stock of social housing has been depleted further by council tenants being given in 1980 a 'right to buy' their homes, with council stock almost disappearing in some areas as a consequence. Four affordable homes have been sold under the right to buy for every three built by RSLs (ARHC 2006), so that the social housing stock is still diminishing. At present there are some safeguards against the loss of housing association stock in settlements below 3,000 population but not in the towns, where tenants enjoy a 'right to acquire'. CRC (2006b) reported that in 2005 social/local authority housing only represented 7 to 8 per cent of all new housing completions in rural areas, a lower proportion than seen in urban areas over the same period. It is noted, though, that 'the significant majority of new houses built in rural areas will be built in the larger settlements, e.g. the market towns and not in the villages or hamlets' (p33).

The CRC State of the Countryside 2005 report presents 2001 Census data on housing tenure by these same categories of settlement size and population sparsity. Table 7.2 summarises this information.

The most striking feature is how little social housing is available in smaller settlements, such that small towns' social rented housing often has crucial importance in meeting not only the housing needs of their own new households but also of those priced out of the villages and surrounding countryside. Only by seeking social housing in the nearest market towns is it possible for many newly forming households to find housing relatively near to their place of work and to family and friends. Even this may lead to reverse commuting (i.e. from urban to rural areas) and a fracturing of social support networks.

Market towns then, if they are similar to other small towns in rural England, have a dual role in meeting local needs for housing, both as places of cheaper owner-occupied housing and as places where a stock of social rented housing endures. As a result, such small towns may be the only places in large parts of rural England where mixed-income communities remain a possibility.

Housing and settlement policies in market towns

Market towns have been defined and conceptualised mainly in terms of the services they provide to those living in the rural hinterland of the town, and the interaction between market town and hinterland has been envisaged as one involving transport-based mobility through which those resident in the countryside visit the market town in order to utilise its various service functions. It is on this dimension that the discussion of key settlement policies in Chapter 4 mainly concentrates. However, especially during the evolution of spatial planning

Table 7.2 Tenure of rural housing by area and settlement type, 2001 (%)

Sparsity	Settlement type	Owned	Social rented	Private rented
Less sparse	Urban settlements of >10k	67	21	10
	Town and fringe	77	15	7
	Village	78	10	9
	Hamlet and isolated dwelling	78	5	13
Sparse	Urban settlements of >10k	70	16	12
	Town and fringe	68	18	12
	Village	73	11	13
	Hamlet and isolated dwelling	71	5	19

Source: CRC (2005a)

strategies in the early post-war years, an additional dimension was added to the planned role of small towns – including market towns – that they should provide a focus for the concentration of new housing development and consequent population growth, so 'protecting' smaller settlements and scattered communities from new housing developments (Cloke 1983).

Ever since the 1940s, planning for the rural areas of England has given the greatest priority to urban containment. In the immediate post-war period the justification for this was the protection of farmland to ensure food supplies and the prevention of urban sprawl. With 1980s food surpluses persuading the government that too much land was being farmed, the justification for urban containment changed to protection of the countryside 'for its own sake'. Today urban containment is justified on the one hand by a pursuit of 'Sustainable Communities', and on the other by the belief (of urban interests) that this might facilitate an urban renaissance.

Post-war settlement planning

From the beginning, with the establishment of the national system of planning control in the 1947 Town and Country Planning Act, the key objective was, as reflected in the title of Hall's (1973) review of post-war planning, the 'Containment of Urban England', and from the beginning 'a crop of key settlement policies appeared' (Cloke 1979: 55) under the auspices of the 1947 Act, contained in the development plans of predominantly rural counties. At this stage, though, the housing element of these policies was less significant. Key settlement policies were initially developed mainly by more remote, sparsely populated counties and large numbers of larger villages were typically included in the list of key settlements (Cloke 1983).

By the 1960s, when the first generation of development plans was due for review, a new situation had arisen. Under the 1945 Labour government almost all housing construction, as well as service provision, was undertaken by the public sector and development plans were intended essentially as a blueprint for public sector development. During the 1950s the resumption of private housing development, and the effective transfer of development gains back to private landowners, undermined the rationale of the development plan system (Gilg 1996). At the same time, some rural counties faced the beginnings of the flood of commuters into the countryside and the growing demand for private housing there. Cloke (1983) suggested that in response the use of key settlement policies was extended, and that it was at this stage that the emphasis on key settlements as the locations into which housing development pressures would be channelled became an important objective alongside the concentration of services.

At the end of the 1960s, with the advent of the structure plan system to replace development plans, and a more indicative framework for channelling development pressures replacing the blueprint of the development plan, development concentration remained an important feature. Although the (by then rather controversial) reference to 'key settlements' was often omitted from structure plans, in effect settlement hierarchies and constraints on development in non-key settlements were a feature of structure plans in most rural areas. Market towns typically constituted the top of the settlement hierarchy and Cloke (1983: 145) identified a 'significant subset' of counties that explicitly concentrated housing, employment and services into market towns.

While settlement policies in planning have traditionally been presented as neutral, technical solutions to the achievement of an efficient and rational distribution of population and services, it is important to note whose interests are served by such policies. Peter Hall and his colleagues in 1973 saw urban containment deriving from an 'unholy alliance' of urban councils seeking to divert resources to the cities together with the rural middle classes seeking to preserve an exclusive countryside and to enhance their own property values. The major gainers, they identified as wealthy, middle class, ex-urbanite country dwellers and the owners of land designated for development. The principal losers his team identified were non-home-owners in rural England (including future generations) and people forced to live at ever-higher densities in urban areas despite the widespread aspiration to rural, or at least suburban, living. Summarising, they concluded that the effects had been regressive in that 'it is the most fortunate who have gained the benefits from the operation of the system, whilst the less fortunate have gained very little' (Hall *et al.* 1973: 409)

Contemporary urban containment

Today, urban containment is even stronger. In the 1980s, in response to growing household numbers and concerns that insufficient land was allocated for the houses needed to accommodate these, greater emphasis was placed in planning on housing land availability studies, and councils were required to ensure a sufficient supply of land for housing for 5 years ahead, whilst still protecting rural land, and especially green belts (12 per cent of England) and other designated areas. From 1998 to 2005 the emphasis shifted again, with less attention being paid by central or local government to the requirement for sufficient land for housing, and emphasis being placed instead on shifting development even more towards brownfield sites. Central government directed local authorities to apply a sequential test whereby houses could only be built in rural areas if no sites were available first within urban brownfield sites, then urban extensions and finally new development nodes in good public transport corridors. Thus, urban capacity studies somewhat displaced housing land availability studies, there are stronger procedures for controlling greenfield approvals to reinforce a 'sequential testing' approach and there is a general shift in philosophy from 'predict and provide' to 'plan, monitor and manage'. Monitoring focuses on a number of indicators of the sustainability of development, e.g. location, type of land and density, with many authorities ceasing to monitor land availability (Stephens *et al.* 2005). Clearly this tended towards fewer housing developments in rural areas while directing such development as was permitted towards market towns.

Moreover, the overall stance of urban containment and prevention of rural development has been strengthened through becoming linked to new agendas of environmental sustainability. In this approach, found by the Affordable Rural Housing Commission (ARHC) to be widespread throughout rural England, local authorities have been categorising rural settlements into those that they regard as 'sustainable' (and therefore suitable for new housing and investment) or 'unsustainable' (effectively red-lined), on the basis of crude checklists of service availability. This was widely believed to be required by ODPM (Office of the Deputy Prime Minister) guidance on Sustainable Communities. Critics have viewed this dualistic construction of Sustainable Communities as an acceptance in planning policy and practice of a rhetoric of sustainability that privileges the environmental over the social, and of exclusivity over inclusion (Shucksmith and Best 2006; Satsangi and Dunmore 2003).

The planning system is currently undergoing reform, with Regional Spatial Strategies (RSSs) and Local Development Frameworks (LDFs) replacing regional guidance, structure and local plans, in response to criticisms that the previous system was slow, complex, remote and hard to understand, and 'too often perceived to be a set of rules aimed at preventing development rather than making sure good development goes ahead' (DLTR 2001: 5). These are early days, but both the ARHC and the Joseph Rowntree Foundation's Rural Housing Policy Forum found in 2006 that RSSs were reducing the land allocations for houses in rural areas still further in the interests of promoting urban regeneration, without regard to the impacts on affordability of rural housing or economic growth (see also Chapter 8). In turn, LDFs are taking this a stage further by applying sustainability checklists as described above with the effect of preventing any new housing outside the towns. Both the Joseph Rowntree Foundation and the ARHC warned there is a real danger that the powerful role given to regional bodies in the new planning system (and the ascendancy of the 'city-region' agenda) facilitates urban interests' collusion with rural elites to limit the supply of housing in rural areas, so assisting the 'unholy alliance' revealed by Hall *et al.* (1973) and Newby (1980) many years ago, to the detriment of affordability.

The consequence for market towns is that, by and large, towns are the only places identified in LDFs (and local plans) where new housing will be permitted in rural areas, whether market housing or social housing, and often the only places where investment in services or other infrastructure will be countenanced. Strong encouragement is given to using any brownfield land in the towns, even if this leads to 'town cramming', and if extensions to the settlements are to be allowed they are to be constructed at as high a density as possible.

Furthermore it is hoped, at least by the Housing Corporation and housing associations, that any new housing developments permitted in market towns should include a significant proportion of affordable housing, whether social housing or low-cost home ownership, and that the cost of building this affordable housing should be met through cross-subsidy from the development gains made by the developer and landowner on the market housing element of the development. The issue of finance is discussed in detail below, but first we consider planning's role in facilitating affordable housing.

Planning's role in facilitating affordable housing

Three main mechanisms are now available for planning to assist in promoting affordable housing provision in rural areas, though the third is relatively new.

First, the exceptions policy allows local planning authorities 'to grant planning permission for small sites within and adjoining existing villages, which may be subject to policies of restraint, such as Green Belt, and which the local plan would otherwise not release for housing, in order to provide affordable housing to meet local needs in perpetuity' (DETR 2000: Annex B).

Very few houses are actually built on exceptions sites (only 262 dwellings in 2003/04 across all of rural England, rising to 551 in 2004/05). This is partly due to a lack of finance and poor information on local need, but the main factors limiting the contribution of this approach are the limited supply of land, and the potential tension between environmental and social objectives of policy. The process is also very slow and time-consuming, for all those involved, taking anything from 3 to 12 years. The low numbers and slow progress may also reflect the greater tendency of anti-growth interests to mobilise and to engage with the planning process (Shucksmith *et al.* 1993). Very rarely were exceptions sites approved in areas of green belt, AONB or National Park, for example. On the other hand, this was the only social housing provision occurring in villages, hamlets and open countryside. Despite the small numbers, this mechanism is highly valued.

Second, local authorities have also been encouraged in PPG3 (DETR 2000) and the more recent PPS3 (DCLG 2006a) to use mainstream planning policy and Section 106 agreements to provide affordable housing in rural areas, through the use of quotas of affordable housing and related cross-subsidy in private developments. A demonstrated need for affordable housing (through housing needs surveys, etc.) 'is a material planning consideration which should be taken into account in formulating development plan policies' (DETR 2000: para 14). Appropriate thresholds for developments in which quotas of affordable housing may be required are set out in Circular 6/98. In settlements of 3,000 or less, sites smaller than the normal threshold of 1 ha or twenty-five dwellings may be appropriate provided that such a lower threshold is specified in the local plan or LDF. The Rural White Paper goes further, suggesting that 'there is no reason why, in small villages if there is evidence of need and subject to financial viability, [local authorities] should not seek to match every new market house with an affordable home' (MAFF and DETR 2000: 50). Cross-subsidy alone is unlikely to be able to achieve this, as discussed further below. PPS3 allows local authorities to set lower minimum thresholds than the minimum fifteen dwellings set out previously in PPG3, above which a quota of affordable housing will be sought, and furthermore there is provision for local planning authorities in their LDFs to set lower thresholds and higher quotas of affordable housing on each site in their rural areas, where it contributes to mixed and sustainable communities.

By far the majority (85 per cent) of 'affordable dwellings' provided in rural England are built in this way under Section 106 agreements as quotas of large private developments on the edges of market towns as urban extensions or on major brownfield sites (e.g. former hospitals). Few rural councils were found by Crook *et al.* (2001) or ENTEC *et al.* (2002) to be seeking quotas from smaller developments in market towns or villages (though this may have changed subsequently), and those that did ran up against a shortage of Housing Corporation Social Housing Grant funding since such schemes tended to generate less cross-subsidy from profits made on the private houses sold at market value alongside.

Crook *et al.* (2002) found that housing associations could only obtain land in areas of housing pressure at considerable cost, and that Section 106 contributions were essential to the viability of any schemes in these areas by bringing down total development costs to levels within the limits that the Housing Corporation could then fund. Building in these more expensive areas was seen as contributing to the government's mixed communities agenda. This is confirmed by more recent Department of Communities and Local Government Housing Investment Programme data. The number of affordable houses (in both urban and rural areas) provided with Section 106 cross-subsidy has doubled in the last 5 years from 9,173 in 1999/2000 to almost 19,000 in 2003/04, while the overall total of affordable houses completed has fallen. More than half are now built on Section 106 sites. A concomitant is that the need for cross-subsidy is pushing more affordable housing into larger schemes in, or on the edge of, the market towns.

Third, PPS3 (and the final revision to PPG3) also includes policy that allows local planning authorities to allocate sites in their LDFs purely for affordable housing – so-called planned exception sites. This policy is being piloted in Wealden district's Housing Our People (HOPe) project, with support from the CRC. Unlike PPG3, the draft PPS3 suggested such sites should only be allocated in larger villages or market towns, although in practice the HOPe project has allocated sites in Wealden's smaller villages as well. Happily, the final version of PPS3 has omitted this restriction, as well as incorporating many more of the ARHC's recommendations.

In summary, then, in rural England, Section 106 agreements are effective in delivering affordable rural housing, but only in larger settlements such as market towns, while the exceptions policy that operates more in the smaller settlements delivers relatively few houses. The reliance of housing associations on obtaining land through Section 106 agreements is increasing, and this is allowing affordable housing to be provided in the larger settlements in higher-cost rural areas, but the overall level of affordable housing provision is declining and falls far short of estimates of need, especially in the smaller settlements. The approach of allocating land specifically for affordable housing in LDFs appears to be successful in bringing forward more sites for development and in speeding up the lengthy process, so achieving the step change necessary to meet rural needs, but it may be a more expensive approach and again there is a question as to how far it should be targeted on the larger settlements. It will be important to monitor the progress of this pilot.

In addition to addressing the general issue of housing availability and affordability, the concentration of new development, and especially social housing provision, in larger settlements such as the market towns means that provision for 'special needs' groups in rural areas will be concentrated there. One important element is housing for the elderly, which forms a significant part of the output of many housing associations. To an extent this also reflects patterns of locational preference. The State of the Countryside report (CRC

2006b), for example, reveals that while younger people (those in the age range 25 to 34) have a greater-than-average preference for a move to a city or large town, and those in the age group 35 to 54 have a greater-than-average preference for life in a country village, the older groups (65 to 74 years) have 'a greater-than-average preference for a move to a slightly larger settlement, such as a market or small town' (p28). This does, of course, reinforce the trend towards the 'greying' of market towns.

Market towns, housing and social inclusion

The notion of the 'intermediate' status of the market town, somewhere between the truly rural and the truly urban, is seen in sharp focus when social inclusion and regeneration issues and policies are considered.

It has long been recognised (Walker 1978; Lowe *et al.* 1986; Chapman 1998) that beneath the rural idyll lay substantial issues of rural poverty and deprivation, but this has typically been viewed as distinctly different in character from urban deprivation. Rural poverty is usually viewed as involving a combination of low rural incomes, problems of access to affordable housing and mobility deprivation limiting access to services and opportunities. In general, problems such as these are likely to be ameliorated in market towns with their better access to services, housing and employment. On the other hand, market towns are more likely to experience what might be thought of as aspects of urban deprivation, including the decline of their traditional economic base and the existence of pockets of poverty and social exclusion in particular housing neighbourhoods. The issue facing market towns is they may face 'urban' problems of disadvantaged households and communities and economic decline without access to the regeneration funding regimes that are available only to larger towns and cities.

As will be discussed below, under the Labour government of Tony Blair there has been some intensification of this urban focus to social inclusion and regeneration funding. At the same time, New Labour's Sustainable Communities agenda, mentioned above, has also raised questions about the opportunities for market towns facing problems of decline to take advantage of what might be called 'housing-led regeneration'.

Funding for social inclusion and regeneration

The urban focus of funding often presents a particular problem in meeting the regeneration needs of market towns. These needs are perhaps at their most acute for towns embedded in former coalfield areas, but can be found in other markets towns, especially away from the more prosperous and pressured rural regions (which of course do have their own issues of housing availability and affordability).

The North East of England provides a particularly good example of this need for support for social inclusion and regeneration beyond the major cities. In part it is a product of the region's industrial history and its legacy of small industrial towns and, in particular, of former coalfield communities that in terms of economic, social and environmental problems have much in common with urban areas but are characterised by small, dispersed settlements. In addition, what might be called the 'truly rural' areas of the region, amongst the most remote in England, also have their share of problems, with issues of transport and physical exclusion, low income, and low aspirations and skills.

From the inception of explicit urban regeneration policies and programmes in the late 1960s, they have mostly been exclusively targeted on major urban centres. During the 1990s, though, some funding streams did provide more opportunities outside of the major cities. The Estate Action programme of the Department of the Environment, providing funding for the regeneration of run-down council estates, was not explicitly spatially targeted. More importantly, from the mid-1990s the Single Regeneration Budget (SRB) Challenge Fund (which incorporated Estate Action) provided resources for a wide range of initiatives, awarded through competitive bidding but not geographically limited. Although, naturally, the bulk of spending was in the cities, SRB did fund programmes in smaller towns and other localities that previously had almost no access to that kind of support.

The potential flexibility of this funding regime is indicated in the North East by the example of Alnwick. The most northerly market town in England, situated in one of its most rural areas, it epitomises the image that is conjured by the term 'market town': very attractive, set in beautiful countryside and gaining top marks on assessments of 'quality of life'. Nevertheless, even here problems of 'urban deprivation' were to be found, especially in a council housing neighbourhood that exhibited all the social and economic problems of an inner-urban 'sink' estate. Under the Estate Action/SRB regime the local authority was able to obtain funding for an integrated regeneration programme for the area.

However, the major New Labour programme for addressing issues of social deprivation and exclusion, the Neighbourhood Renewal Strategy (Social Exclusion Unit 1998; 2001) re-imposed a sharp urban focus. Using again the example of the North East, the targeting of the Neighbourhood Renewal Strategy programme has been a key and controversial issue. Nationally, this targeting involved the designation of eighty-eight local authorities within England, on the basis of the scoring of wards on the Index of Multiple Deprivation, as eligible for Neighbourhood Renewal Fund (NRF) and related programmes. In all, fourteen of the twenty-two districts in the North East region are eligible for NRF, but there are in the region a number of districts with extensive areas that share the problems of the NRF districts, but which just miss out on designation. It is particularly in the former coalfield areas where this issue impinges, where the chance of which district a settlement lies in determines its access to resources to address the often appalling social, economic, environmental and health legacies of the mining industry and its decline, though the problem of access to funding for social regeneration also affects the more remote rural areas.

One important New Labour innovation, the RDAs and the Sub-Regional Partnerships (SRPs) that deliver some aspects of RDA programmes, do provide a potential source of support for market towns and rural areas. The Northumberland Strategic Partnership provides an example of how this compensatory role can operate, explicitly seeking to address the 'rural deficit' in funding. The RDA's Single Programme is allocated on an approximate 50/50 split between urban and rural districts in Northumberland, with the most rural districts, Alnwick and Berwick, getting an equal share of funding despite their smaller population size. However, the wider geographical scope of the Single Programme funding through the RDA/SRP nexus is balanced by its narrow economic focus, stemming from the essentially economic remit of the RDAs. This means that funding for more socially oriented programmes is more limited. The MTI, Rural Development Programme and SRBs, which all had an important social dimension, were transferred to the RDAs and have been phased out and incorporated into the RDA Single Programme, with its mainly economic development priorities.

Market towns and their rural hinterlands do have some advantages, in particular their strong grass-roots potential for voluntary and community action and initiative, but they tend to lack the integrated support and funding to make best use of this potential.

The Haskins (2003) Rural Delivery Review for DEFRA made many of these points, for example the problems caused by the run-down of the Rural Development Programme and the complexity of agencies and schemes. Its recommendation included the proposal that RDAs need to have more of a regional coordinating role to play on funding administered by DEFRA, and that this funding should be more locally determined, and some progress is now being made towards these objectives (DEFRA 2006b).

At the same time, in northern England, the RDAs are now working within a framework of a cross-regional development strategy known as the Northern Way, which is placing increasing emphasis on city regions (DCLG 2006b), and their core cities as the key regional growth and development dynamic. The Northern Way (ODPM 2004c) was developed as part of the Sustainable Communities programme, which is the most recent major New Labour regeneration initiative. The place of market towns within Sustainable Communities, and the impact on them of the urban development dynamic, is discussed below.

Sustainable Communities and planned housing allocations in market towns

The Sustainable Communities agenda presses for urban containment primarily on the grounds of environmental sustainability, arguing in particular that it prevents long-distance, car-based commuting and the emissions that this produces. Within this perspective, market towns might be either part of the solution or part of the problem. They may be seen as sustainable communities, providing a focus for balanced employment and housing that limits commuting, or they may be seen as attractive destinations for affluent commuters moving from cities.

As noted above, the politics of planned housing development has often created an 'unholy alliance' between planning objectives and local elites to constrain rural housing development, especially in the pressured rural areas of Southern England. (Murdoch and Abram 2002). However, as Smullian (2006: 14) asks in discussing a controversy over house building in Dorset, 'what happens when a council's allocation of new homes is too low, rather than the more familiar complaint of being too high?' In this case, protests centred on containment policies that provide insufficient housing to meet needs in rural area in order to focus new development in the urban areas of the county. Thus, in the tradition of key settlement policy, it involved policies to direct housing development to market towns. However, in Northern England this reversal of the assumption of opposition to rural housing development is of a different kind and scale and affects market towns in a different way.

Here a more widespread assertion of the need for more, not fewer, housing allocations in rural areas is based not so much on the level of local housing need (though this may be a factor) but on the opportunities for what can be termed 'housing-led regeneration' – the notion that new housing development can provide an engine of economic growth and regeneration in a locality. In the North East, for example, in interviews with regeneration practitioners throughout the region it was suggested that, especially in former coalfield areas, housing-led regeneration involving new private development and through it the attraction of more affluent newcomers, could have a positive effect on deprived and declining communities. It was argued, for example, that housing-led regeneration had been successful in small towns and villages in the former coalfield areas of South Northumberland and Durham. In rural areas, too, there was a contention that – in addition to meeting housing needs – new housing development could boost economic regeneration and attract a skilled workforce.

However, this demand for housing-led regeneration in smaller towns and more sparsely populated areas in the North may be undermined by policies that emphasise the renaissance of major cities as the renewal of their housing markets, and which as a result suck housing allocations into the main urban areas and limit development elsewhere.

Ironically, it was concern over low housing demand and surplus housing stock in some neighbourhoods in large northern cities such as Manchester and Newcastle that was the original *raison d'etre* of the programme of Housing Market Renewal Pathfinders introduced within the Sustainable Communities plan (ODPM 2003a). However, as these and related proposals have developed, it has become clear that while they propose the clearance of some existing housing, they often propose the construction of even more new housing. Clearance and redevelopment within northern cities is increasingly seen as a means to modernise their housing stock and the environment in order to facilitate economic regeneration, rather than simply to address problems of vacancy and low demand (Cameron 2006). The Northern Way strategy of city regions, with cities as the main drivers of regional economic development, reinforces this concentration on new development within major urban areas.

At the same time, though, the system of planning that aggregates new housing alloca-tions for regions, initially under Regional Planning Guidance and now within the RSSs, has taken the fact that in the northern regions projections of population and household change typically suggest limited growth, or continuing decline, to imply a limited requirement for new housing development. As a result, in regions such as the North West and North East, controversy has arisen over the limited scale of new housing allocations made to the region by central government.

In a sense this debate about housing numbers presents a mirror image of the critique of a 'predict and provide' approach to planning for housing mentioned above. While, especially in the South East, it was argued that 'predict and provide' over-estimated housing need and imposed unacceptably high targets for housing and housing land (Bramley 1995), the argument over housing numbers in the North involves the assertion that a 'predict and provide' approach delivers targets for new housing numbers that are far too small. In the words of an official in the North East: 'Regional housing allocations are a blunt instrument and may be a barrier to regeneration aspirations. In economic terms there is a need for housing to subsidise other development' (see Chapter 8 for a detail discussion of these issues).

It is, though, localities outside of the major urban areas, including the market towns, that tend to feel the squeeze of limited regional allocations of housing on the one hand, and the concentration on regeneration and development within the main urban areas on the other. Within the northern regions, additional housing allocations are seen as a resource for regeneration but are a resource that is scarce and contested, and in the competition rural areas, and the market towns within them, tend to lose out.

At the regional level, economic, spatial planning and housing strategies all come together to reinforce this 'city' focus. This applies not only to housing development as a whole, but also to funding for social housing, with for example the Housing Corporation's funding for housing associations in northern regions focused mainly on supporting regeneration in urban areas, with little left over for market towns and the more rural parts of the regions. Thus the pressure on affordable housing provision in market towns is a national phenomenon, and not just limited to the pressured areas of the South.

Conclusions

Market towns occupy a crucial position in terms of rural housing needs and provision. They have the only relatively affordable owner-occupied housing and some remnants of former council housing, and now they are the primary location in which it is possible to build new social housing, both on planning grounds and in terms of the possibilities of obtaining cross-subsidy from open market developments. They may be the only 'mixed communities' left in rural areas, with an important wider role in relation to the economic and social needs of the smaller surrounding communities.

The ability of market towns to fulfil this role is, though, coming under pressure in different ways from different ends of the spectrum of the 'regionalised countryside'. In the most pressured areas the key problem is maintaining their function of affordable housing provision in the face of escalating housing markets and housing land costs. In depressed and declining rural areas, the challenge is accessing financial resources for regeneration and the 'resource' of planned housing allocations to support housing-led regeneration in the face of policies pulling funding and development into major urban areas.

Chapter 8

Capacity vs. need

Exploring regional differences in housing
provision in market towns

Susannah Gunn and Neil Powe

Introduction

The primary emphasis of rural planning policies is on the concentration of new development in 'local service centres' (DETR 2001; ODPM 2004a), and it is argued that this offers a more sustainable pattern of development. Such places are more likely to achieve the co-location of employment, housing (including affordable housing), services and other facilities, and it is thought that such a pattern of development will help generate more sustainable patterns of behaviour. This has led market towns to become one of the main focuses for development, and specially housing development, in rural localities (ODPM 2004a). Indeed, it was suggested in Chapter 7 that, by and large, market towns are virtually the only rural locations identified in local plans (local development frameworks) where new housing will be permitted. Market towns are being asked to accommodate housing development that contributes to meeting both rural housing needs and helping satisfy more general housing requirements identified in regional strategies.

But levels of pressure for development can be seen to vary between regions, and this is likely to give rise to different policy debates and contexts for market towns in different regions. Different levels of economic performance play a large part in driving demand for housing development. While the north/south divide is not such a prominent feature of national debate as in the 1980s, significant levels of inter-regional difference continue to exist. So, in the case of the North East, key priorities are seen as being 'employment creation and area regeneration' (Richardson *et al.* 1999: 145), while the East of England has been characterised by 'high levels of economic prosperity . . . both driven by and followed by relatively rapid rates of increase in population' (Townroe and Moore 1999: 55). Such differences are evident in past aspects of development, where the North East saw a 19 per cent increase in the number of households between 1971 and 2001, while in the East of England a 49 per cent increase occurred (Holmans *et al.* 2007).

Kate Barker (2003) has raised the issue of whether the planning land allocation system is sufficiently responsive to changing levels of demand pressure. Trends in house prices and affordability (Bramley 2007) and price elasticities (Barker 2003:44) suggest that in southern regions in particular insufficient housing sites are being brought forward to satisfy the strong demand pressures evident there. Interestingly, Haughton and Counsell (2004), in a study of regional planning, found a tendency for planners in economically more buoyant regions to attempt to constrain housing growth while those in areas of industrial decline such as the North East sought a more relaxed approach.

This chapter investigates how these pressures and tensions play out in two contrasting regions – the North East and the East of England – by considering evidence for two market towns in each of those regions (Alnwick and Morpeth; Downham Market and Wymondham). Data from resident surveys then provides a further understanding of the implications of housing development for these towns. These case studies give a flavour of the discussion currently occurring across the country, and draw out the particular issues being felt in two very different regions and in four very different market towns. The chapter begins with a brief consideration of the derivation of the population and household figures that currently shape regional strategies.

Population dynamics, household projection and housing allocations

Haughton and Counsell (2004: 138) note 'the lack of a national spatial strategy' but the presence of a 'considerable body of government guidance'. In addition to policy guidance, population and household forecasts are produced nationally that provide a framework for the development of regional and more local figures and thus provide an element of a de facto national planning framework and strategy. National population projections are produced by the Government Actuary and consistent sub-national projections are produced by the Office of National Statistics.

In determining future population levels, at national and regional levels, changes in migration are both more important and more difficult to predict than changes in births and deaths, where trends are fairly stable. Population forecasts are translated into projections of numbers of households, using household headship rates and other data (Gallent 2005). Some suggest that the use of other data creates further unreliability (Adams and Watkins 2002; Gallent 2005) whilst others have indicated the need to focus on other contextual influences that may affect the formation and migration of households (Wong and Madden 2000). One such factor is likely to be regional and local economic conditions, with a more buoyant economy encouraging household formation and in-migration, particularly of those in higher skills brackets (DETR 1999; Wong and Madden 2000; Holmans 2001; Dixon 2003; Llewelyn Davies Yeang 2006; Ove Arup & Partners Ltd 2006). In the development of RSSs, greater account is being taken of these economic factors than was the case with earlier regional plans, but the magnitude of the effect that greater economic buoyancy can have on household formation rates and migration remains contentious and has added to the level of debate on housing numbers at enquiries into RSSs.

Once the estimated number of households has been established, the Regional Planning Body allocates the required number of houses to the various sub-regions partly based on local household estimates. These are also based on other housing information (sub-regional housing market and needs assessments; local housing land availability studies; urban capacity studies) and wider policy objectives, such as meeting the requirements of national planning policy and other regional priorities. Figures are given for the average number of dwellings to be built each year (dw/yr) and the number of dwellings to be built over the plan period, which is usually 15 years.

The regional and local household projections, the level of housing provision and its distribution are rigorously debated in all regions. This is partly because of the way that these allocations are determined but it is also because of the implications they have for the future development prospects of the affected settlements. Based on regional and sub-regional fortunes, as well as local circumstances, some communities perceive new housing as an opportunity to be grasped whilst other communities find the prospect more threatening. This is as true for market towns as it is for other settlements.

New housing in market towns: an opportunity or a threat?

The impact of new housing development on a town will depend on a wide range of variables related to the circumstances of the town, the scale and nature of the new development, and the characteristics and lifestyles of those occupying the new housing.

Williams (2000: 156) has noted that 'New house-building . . . could provide the right stimulus for increasing the number and quality of local services', and that loss of 'existing services could also be prevented by the use of housing development to increase the resident population size in settlements in which local provision is becoming economically unviable.' However, realising such benefits may be hampered by limited capacity within the town to absorb new development to accommodate services or the roads and car parking to give access to them. Accommodating new service development may also pose a threat to the character of historic town centres – a key asset for many market towns – or if new large housing developments take place on greenfield sites, usually on the outskirts of the towns, this may also threaten their distinctiveness and 'countryside' feel.

The extent to which such opportunities or threats become reality depends on the nature of the relationship of new residents to the town and its services. Research on existing patterns of behaviour (SERRL 2004) found that a significant proportion of town and hinterland residents travelled far and wide for services and employment rather than focus their activities on the 'local service centre'. The building of new houses in market towns may accentuate such trends, with urban-to-rural migrants hanging on to their urban links and being perhaps more likely to work and shop outside the town. However, Renkow and Hoover (2000) suggest that residents' engagement with their local town may improve over time, and while leakages of spending may be significant, studies have found that new housing undoubtedly increased the trade within market towns (Civic Trust 2000; Richardson and Powe 2004). In addition it has been shown that in-migrants can also create employment locally (Findlay *et al.* 2000).

However, realising this potential does not happen automatically, and the success of market town centres will depend very much upon their ability to provide the quality and range of services sought by new residents. Success may also be influenced by the type and location of housing. For example, the Civic Trust (2000) found that residents of new housing living close to centres were more likely to give patronage to town centre shops and services. As has been shown in Chapter 6, the age profile of town residents can affect their behaviour and the fact that in-migration is tending to raise the age profile of market towns needs to be taken into account.

The extent to which in-migrants contribute to the social capital of the towns, particularly through participation in voluntary and community activities, is also important. For example, Smith and Phillips (2001) found in-migrants brought new ideas to their towns and contributed significantly to local politics, while Liu and Besser (2003) demonstrate the potential for elderly residents to be involved. This too suggests that additional housing development can increase the vitality of the towns, as they allow for in-migrants to become part of a growing community, and provides more opportunities for locals to remain local in the focus of their activities. However, concerns have also been raised that such involvement in voluntary organisations may lead to them becoming dominated by new, mainly middle class, arrivals, possibly leading to the exclusion of others (Murdoch and Day 1998) and changing the character of towns from that to which established residents feel an attachment.

Finally, the extent to which any uplift in land value consequent on the pressure for development can be captured for the benefit of the local community also affects the balance struck between opportunity and threat. As an opportunity it provides the potential for local planners to negotiate planning gain to help meet a range of local needs, such as schools, recreation and community facilities, and new infrastructure. As a threat, the growing demand for more housing can itself exacerbate existing challenges, such as those concerned with affordable housing, and this in itself can become an issue for negotiation (see Chapter 7).

How the balance is struck depends on a number of factors, including the skills and capability of the local authority in negotiating planning gain (Campbell *et al.* 2001). It will also be affected by the nature of the local land and property market. Significant factors in play include the typically smaller sizes of sites available in many market towns, and the historic nature of most market towns, making sites more complicated to develop, more costly and potentially risky. A further important factor is the extent of the pressure for development, with localities with higher pressures for development enjoying greater scope to generate and capture planning gain.

Regional context of the case study towns

Both the North East and East of England regions are highly rural, with the ODPM indicating that 'the majority of the [North East] region is very rural' (ODPM 2003b: 4) and the East of England Development Agency (EEDA) suggesting that the East of England region is atypical in not having any 'traditionally large city or an obvious regional capital' (EEDA 2004: 11). Instead it consists of a rural hinterland supported by 'medium sized cities, new towns, urban areas and the largest number of market towns in England' (EEDA 2004: 11). In both instances the case study counties, Northumberland and Norfolk, are the most rural and most peripheral counties in their respective regions.

The North East has a population of 2.5 million (ODPM 2003b), two-thirds of whom live in major conurbations. The remaining residents live in very sparsely-populated rural areas, mainly in market towns and villages. Although the most recent figures show a net in-migration for 2002–2003, the North East as a region was losing population throughout the 1990s (NERA 2005). In terms of the thirteen North East MTI towns between 1991 and 2001 there was actually a small decline in population (-2 per cent), the only average decline within the sample (see Table 2.5). In stark contrast to other regions, the North East has also been experiencing, in aggregate terms, a housing surplus rather than a shortfall. The East of England has a population of almost 5.5 million (EERA 2005) and has been one of the English regions that has consistently grown in population. The East of England Regional Assembly (EERA 2005) suggests that this trend is set to continue, with a 12.2 per cent projected population increase for the period 1996–2021, accompanied by an increase in households of 24.7 per cent. In terms of the twenty-eight East of England MTI towns they experienced the largest average regional population increase between 1991 and 2001 (19 per cent) (see Table 2.6).

In the North East, a mismatch has developed between the housing stock that is available and the property aspirations of the region's population. This has been exacerbated by the region's loss of population, and has been reflected in the abandonment of some areas of the conurbations. To promote sustainability and to meet housing market renewal objectives, national and regional policies in the North East have focused on the local conurbations, through the Housing Market Renewal Pathfinder (HMRP) initiatives and the Northern Way's development of strategies based on the city region (ODPM 2003a; Northern Way Steering Group 2004). As Cameron and Shucksmith noted in Chapter 7, this has had the effect of giving relatively high housing allocations to the urban areas of Tyne and Wear, but has left market towns with much lower allocations to achieve the housing stock restructuring that might be thought necessary to achieve rural regeneration.

Both central government and the EERA identify the high and rapidly rising housing prices in the East of England as a major concern, with the impact this is having on recruiting and retaining staff an additional concern (ODPM 2003c; EERA 2004). Current debate (Barker 2004) suggests that, to rectify these failings, planning for housing provision needs to be more closely linked to housing market performance and the delivery of housing. However, the Regional Assembly also suggests that housing demand is outstripping the ability of house builders to provide additional housing (EERA 2004: 127), which is further exacerbating the problems of house price inflation and affordability (EERA 2005). This was felt to be particularly serious in the Cambridge sub-region, but in Norfolk the combination of relatively low rural incomes, demand from people moving into the area to retire or commute, and the buying of properties for second homes and tourism has also generated an affordability gap and a gap in provision for local people wanting to stay to live and work in the area (North Norfolk District Council 2004: 56). So, the East of England's RSS (EERA 2004) gives more space to the role and the requirements of market towns than the North East's RSS. However, the East of England RSS is also necessarily concerned with the demands that growth will make on the Cambridge sub-region, Milton Keynes growth area and the northern arm of the Thames Gateway, which are all ear-marked for significant increases in housing by the Sustainable Communities agenda.

Economically, the North East region continues to be one of the poorer regions in the UK, and the East of England one of the more prosperous. However, considerable economic variation occurs across all regions and Norfolk represents one of the poorer areas of the East of England region (EEDA 2004), whilst Northumberland is relatively wealthy compared to other parts of the North East (One NE 2006). Nevertheless, in both regions there is at least a tacit understanding that market towns will be instrumental in the regeneration of their local rural economies, and will provide accessible employment, housing and services to a wider rural hinterland.

In the North East this is expressed in both the Regional Economic Strategy (RES) and the RSS, but is expressed more strongly in the RES (One NE 2006), which tempers the RSS's emphasis on the core cities of the region perhaps at the expense of more rural localities (NERA 2005). The RES highlights the importance of the region's market towns in providing a complementary economic approach to the city regions, whereby strong market towns can be used to revitalise the more rural areas, providing economic, social and service infrastructure for their wider hinterlands (One NE 2006).

The East of England RSS (EERA 2004) argues for a familiar rural housing policy of developing more contained key settlements and market towns to prevent a less sustainable, more dispersed development pattern emerging. The East of England RSS celebrates the vibrancy and self-sufficiency of its many market towns, but notes that within the Norwich area (the only city in Norfolk) many of these towns also have cultural and economic links with Norwich itself. The other main issue identified is the need to improve transport and water infrastructure as well as the capacity of social facilities such as health and education (EERA 2004: 127). This is linked to an aspiration of ensuring that the benefits of economic growth are directed towards those areas experiencing peripherality – such as the market towns in Norfolk and their rural hinterlands.

Case study towns

Introducing the towns

A short profile of the case study towns is provided in Table 8.1; they are also discussed in Chapter 3. One of the two towns from each region was chosen for its remoteness from a large urban area: Alnwick in the North East (population *c.* 8,000), and Downham Market in the East of England (population *c.* 7,000). Alnwick is located 35 miles from the city of Newcastle upon Tyne, whereas Downham Market is fairly remote from the urban centres of Norwich (44 miles away), Peterborough (33 miles away) and Cambridge (33 miles away), but is located only 13 miles from the larger town of King's Lynn (population *c.* 19,000). The other two towns were chosen because they were more accessible: from the North East the town of Morpeth (population *c.* 13,500) and from the East of England, Wymondham (population *c.* 11,500). Both these towns act as commuter towns for their local cities, and attract some commuting in-migration as a matter of course.

Table 8.1 Description of the case study 'market towns'

Morpeth	Morpeth is the centre for administration in the county, with consequent impacts on employment identified in Chapter 2. Tourism is important to the town with the thirteenth-century chantry that houses a bagpipe museum being a key attraction. The town has a railway station on the North East main line, with direct links to Newcastle, Edinburgh and London. The town is facing house prices above and rising above the county average. In-migration, however, remains below the county average.
Alnwick	Tourism is important, with the castle being a key visitor magnet (now of Harry Potter fame) and the water gardens providing a more recent attraction. The results in Chapter 2 identified the importance of employment in public administration, where a sub-regional centre for local government is located close to a Royal Air Force base (currently being significantly downsized). The town is facing house prices similar to the county average but they have recently been rising above the county average. This has been partly fuelled by in-migration at levels above the county average.
Wymondham	The town is steeped in history, with an attractive market cross and abbey near its centre, as well as an award-winning railway station. The results in Chapter 2 do not identify any particular characteristics of the town. The town is facing house prices similar to the county average but rising at a rate above the county average, with in-migration below the county average. In-migration is likely to increase with major housing building planned.
Downham Market	The town has a railway station with a direct line to London, and it is just within commutable distance (1 hour 30 minutes from King's Cross). An attractive feature of the town is its Victorian clock tower. A notable characteristic of the town, identified in Chapter 2, is the high proportion of population who are retired. The town is facing house prices similar to the county average, but they are now rising above the county average and in-migration is above the county average.

All four towns are located in close proximity to attractive rural areas and have histories dating back to medieval times, which are still visible in their layout and architecture. All the towns can be considered as attractive places to live. Although all have a medium–sized supermarket somewhere within the town, the level of retail provision varies, with Morpeth perhaps being the best served in terms of comparison shopping and leisure facilities and Downham Market the least well served. All four towns have experienced relatively recent new housing development and in-migration (see Plate 8) but these developments have varied considerably in scale. These towns have also been subject to much discussion regarding further retail investment, with Alnwick and Morpeth recently gaining permission for such developments (see Chapters 10 and 11). In the case of Downham Market, the town centre has been subject to recent improvement (see Chapter 11).

Housing allocations for the case study market towns

In both the East of England case study towns the actual housing allocations remain undecided at the time of writing, as the relevant LDFs have yet to emerge. Wymondham is part of the Norwich sub-region and South Norfolk District Council. This sub-region is less pressured than other parts of the region but it is still expected to deliver 45,500 dwellings by 2021 (EEDA 2004: 67). South Norfolk has been allocated 11,200 dwellings by 2021 (560 dw/yr) (EEDA 2004: 67). Many of these additional dwellings have been allocated to the Norwich

Plate 1
Market cross in
Alnwick, which
dominates the recently
redeveloped market
place

Plate 2
Market cross in
Wymondham, being
renovated for their
900th birthday in 2007.
The market cross is
thought to date back to
the early seventeenth
century, but now
appropriately functions
as a tourist information
centre

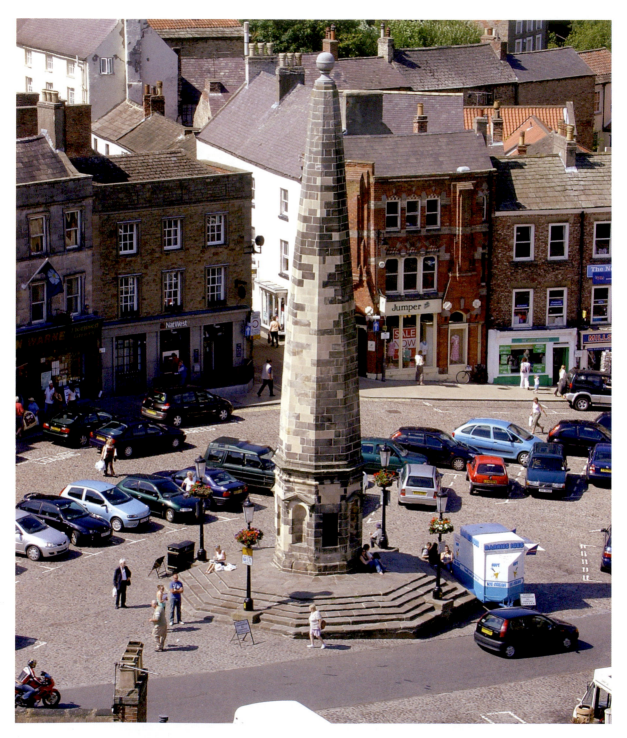

Plate 3
Obelisk, which replaced the market cross within Richmond's
(North Yorkshire) large market place in Georgian times

Plate 4
Keswick's mountainous backdrop

Plate 5
Keswick's pedestrianised town centre with the attractive Moot Hall, which houses the tourist information centre

*Plate 6
Wymondham town
plaque and the
town's oldest inn –
the 'Green Dragon'*

*Plate 7
Housing estate on the
outskirts of
Wymondham,
separated from the
town by a main road
and located near to the
A11, convenient for
'out-shopping' and
'out-working'*

Plate 10
One of three sculptured seats in Alnwick's medieval market square

Plate 11
Independent
department store in
Morpeth, found to be a
key 'anchor' for the
town

Plate 12
Independent furniture
store in Downham
Market, described as an
important 'anchor' for
the town

Plate 13
Traditional shop frontage in Richmond

Plate 14
Marketplace in Downham Market and Victorian clock tower, recently redeveloped. The market has been relocated to its original location and the clock renovated

Plate 15
The Playhouse in
Alnwick, a very popular
cinema/theatre among
town and hinterland
residents

Plate 16
The Theatre by the Lake
in Keswick is located
close to the shore of
the picturesque
Derwent Water, and
successfully attracts
people from all over the
county for
performances

Plate 17
Inside Todmorden
market

Plate 18
Redeveloped
marketplace in
Morpeth, showing the
new Marks & Spencer
store that has been
attracted to this prime
location

Policy Area (8,400) which leaves 2,600 dwellings to be located elsewhere. Wymondham has been identified as a place for future employment growth and housing development (EEDA 2004), because of its strategic transport links and extensive services. Downham Market, situated in the Borough Council of King's Lynn and West Norfolk, is part of the King's Lynn sub-region's urban area (EEDA 2004), which has been allocated 11,000 dwellings. Currently, the possibilities for growth and regeneration of King's Lynn are being explored, and it is suggested that about 7,000 dwellings will be located to King's Lynn (King's Lynn & West Norfolk Borough Council and Partners 2005a). As it stands there is currently a shortfall of 4,000 dwellings (267 dw/yr) that will need to be located somewhere in the sub-region, and Downham Market would appear to be one of the likely recipients.

With the North East's very different regional context, Alnwick District and Morpeth Borough Councils have both been awarded lower housing allocations than their East of England counterparts: Alnwick 79 dw/yr and Morpeth 125 dw/yr (NERA 2005). These allocations are for the whole district, although the expectation is that Alnwick and Morpeth will be the recipients of most of the allocation.

Northumberland

Both Castle Morpeth and Alnwick District Councils have suggested that their allocations are too low (Alnwick District Council 2005a; Castle Morpeth Area Committee 2005). In both cases they are able to identify sufficient housing land on previously developed land within their urban capacity studies (Castle Morpeth Borough Council 2002a; Alnwick District Council 2003; 2004) and highlight their ability to accommodate additional allocations in line with those found in the old Regional Planning Guidance. Consequently they have already given permissions beyond the new RSS housing allocations (Alnwick District Council 2003). The councils argue that there is a need to maintain these pre-existing allocations, particularly in relation to their ability to manage their housing stock, to achieve affordable housing and to realise the sustainable rural regeneration that the RSS seeks to accomplish (Alnwick District Council 2003; 2005b; Castle Morpeth Area Committee 2005). These feelings are illustrated by the following quote:

> It is considered that adopting this figure [RSS's proposed housing allocations figure for Alnwick district] takes no account, however, of other objectives in the RPG [Regional Planning Guidance] and indeed the Rural White Paper which seek to enhance the role of market towns and achieve rural regeneration in order to combat social exclusion, improve access to services and sustain viable local communities. It is considered that this significant reduction in house building would undermine the district's ability to achieve the rural regeneration aims set out in the Economic Regeneration and Tourism Strategy and in particular could undermine the ability to improve the vitality and viability of market towns.
>
> (Alnwick District Council 2003: 9)

Indeed, Alnwick's and Morpeth's allocations contrast with the North East RSS (NERA 2005) reflections on the contribution market towns make to rural areas. This identifies the need to strengthen the role of Alnwick and Morpeth as 'main rural service centres' (56), and to develop at a scale that 'sustains a . . . vibrant rural economy' (57), and to address affordable housing problems. Northumberland County Council and Northumberland National Park also indicate the importance of market towns in ensuring a wider rural regeneration, although they also indicate that Castle Morpeth's green belt may constrain its contribution (Northumberland County and Northumberland National Park 2003).

Norfolk

In contrast, in the towns of Wymondham and Downham Market there is a concern that their allocations of new housing are too high. The preferred policy option, voiced by both Wymondham's and Downham's councils, is to locate considerable amounts of housing in the neighbouring principle settlements of Norwich and King's Lynn, thus reducing the amount they have to accommodate. Wymondham has suggested that 'South Norfolk Council (should) not put all its eggs in one basket by allocating most of the new housing to Wymondham' but instead 'all market towns must be asked to share the load of the district's future housing needs' (Wymondham Town Council undated: 1). Wymondham sees the volume of new housing to be accommodated as something of a burden.

A key challenge is seen as maintaining the original character of the towns, with Wymondham emphasising the need to give priority to protecting the town's environment and heritage when deciding where housing should be located (Wymondham Town Council undated). Issues relating to services and infrastructure are also important, with the town council expressing concern that 'all aspects of Wymondham life, such as the provision of retail space, access, leisure, housing, transport, biodiversity use of existing sites, cycle routes, open spaces, general infrastructure items, sports facilities and cultural needs should be considered' (Wymondham Town Council undated: 1) to ensure the town's growth is adequately provided for, and the quality of life is not adversely affected. In response to infrastructure issues relating to Downham Market, King's Lynn and West Norfolk Borough Council recognise that new housing has already placed great demands on existing infrastructure, so the current policy proposal seeks to improve leisure facilities, as well as retail and employment opportunities (King's Lynn and West Norfolk Borough Council and Partners 2005).

While Norfolk appears to be experiencing less of the housing pressure generated by Cambridge and London commuting patterns, and its house prices are relatively affordable compared to other parts of the region, they are still high compared with the relatively low incomes of many of the locals. In this respect it is similar to the North East. However, unlike the North East, the whole region is experiencing very high prices so the local population have even less opportunity to find alternative affordable housing elsewhere if they cannot afford what is available in their local housing market. In response to this, Norfolk County Council has recently decided to allocate additional finances to affordable housing projects (Norfolk County Strategic Partnership 2005), using money that has been generated from the second homes tax regime. The relevant local plans for Wymondham and Downham Market include a requirement for affordable housing to be considered on particular housing sites (King's Lynn and West Norfolk Borough Council 1998; South Norfolk Council 2003). King's Lynn and West Norfolk also intend to produce guidance on affordable housing as their first supplementary planning document after completing their initial LDF planning documents (King's Lynn and West Norfolk Borough Council 2006).

Impacts of housing expansion

Through surveys of residents in the four towns it has been possible to investigate the behaviour of new residents and resident attitudes towards housing development – or lack of housing development. This section considers the results of resident surveys undertaken within the case study towns. These results throw some light on how far the potential threats and opportunities identified above play out in the four towns.

Resident engagement with the town

Our interviews with key actors in market towns (see Chapter 11) revealed something of a consensus that those migrating into the towns contribute relatively little to the economy and community. However, Table 8.2 provides summary statistics from the resident surveys that question this view. These results suggest that although engagement within the town is not high, on the whole in-migrants do not behave very differently from existing longer-term residents. Residents' engagement with their towns is considered in relation to a number of activities: working in the town, shopping (food and non-food), evenings out and their contribution to local community activities. These are reported in the left-hand column of Table 8.2.

A sizeable proportion of those living in Alnwick and of working age worked in the town, but this was not the case with the other towns. This was the expected picture for Morpeth and Wymondham, because of their proximity to larger settlements, and they show 44 per cent and 48 per cent respectively working in larger urban areas, but it was less expected of Downham Market. Although Downham Market is remote, it was seen as a convenient location for rural employment, within the nearby larger market town of King's Lynn but also the wider rural area, including nearby air force bases. Downham Market also has a direct rail link to Cambridge and London, but commuting to such large urban areas (by whatever mode of transport) was only undertaken by 18 per cent of the respondents (compared to 13 per cent for Alnwick). When compared with longer-term residents, in-migrants were consistently found to be more likely to work elsewhere. Whether these relatively new residents will tire of travelling and look for or create more local employment opportunities in the longer term remains a matter for speculation. Examining the percentages working outside the towns, in-migrants did not behave uniformly between towns. Indeed, approximately half of in-migrants in Alnwick actually worked in the town. Although lower than the Alnwick average, it is considerably higher than the average for the other towns. This suggests that when deciding where to build new housing, perhaps choosing the 'right' town is more important than its type and location.

Residents' engagement with retail (considered in more detail within the next chapter) is higher for food than non-food (mostly comparison) purchases, and few respondents did their main non-food shopping in the towns. So, although the town residents provide significant custom for local shops, 'out-shopping' remains common. Table 8.2 considers the evening economy by looking at numbers visiting a public house or a restaurant in the last month.

Table 8.2 In-migrators' engagement with activities within the town

	Alnwick		Morpeth		Wymondham		Downham Market	
	Total population	In-migrants	Total population	In-migrants	Total population	In-migrants	Total population	In-migrants
Work in town (% of those working)	61	49*(–)	38	24*(–)	26	22*(–)	21	14*(–)
Main food shopping in town (%)	61	62	64	62	42	44	74	71
Regular non-food shopping in town (%)	44	48	51	58	52	51	40	42
Evening out in town (pub or restaurant last month) (%)	47	47	46	59*(+)	33	35	31	31
Local community activity (%)	38	47*(+)	No data	No data	42	41	37	33

Notes: * Significantly different from longer-term residents at the 5% level.
      Due to different objectives of the Morpeth survey, no data was collected on community activities.

In-migrants' behaviour is very similar to that of the longer-term residents, but those in Morpeth were found to be actually more likely to go out in the evening to the town.

A large minority of both in-migrants and longer-term residents took part in community activities. Though the majority were merely members of clubs, the results also suggested that a minority were making an important contribution to their towns through voluntary work – for example, through helping in schools, clubs and local heritage groups. In Alnwick, in-migrants were more likely to be involved in community activities but the survey uncovered no evidence that longer-term residents saw this as a 'takeover'.

Changes in the towns

Residents were asked whether they thought the character of their town was changing and were asked to discuss whether they thought these changes were good or bad for the town; a summary of responses is shown in Table 8.3. Listed in order of their average importance, the population growth issue dominated in Wymondham and Downham Market (81 per cent and 51 per cent respectively), and generated a number of detailed comments regarding the effects of new housing. In Alnwick the publicity that followed the opening of the water gardens and filming of Harry Potter has led to an increase in the perceived impact of tourism within the town (52 per cent).

While some responses saw housing growth as good for the towns, bringing more amenities, housing and families, the majority felt it generated problems; this was particularly the case in the East of England towns. The key issues raised were that new housing had stretched existing services (for example, schools and medical services) and infrastructure (roads) (29 per cent Wymondham; 22 per cent Downham Market), and would lead to a change in the character of the towns (21 per cent Wymondham and 7 per cent Downham Market).

The strength of feeling regarding population growth was strongest in Wymondham, where comments suggested that the town has become more impersonal and a dormitory town with little engagement from new residents. The new estates were criticised for lacking character and for being in some way disconnected from the town. Others focused on the loss of the town's rural character, suggesting it was no longer a small or country town, becoming instead a suburb of the nearby city of Norwich. These views were as likely to be held by in-migrants as longer-term residents. Although mentioned less frequently, the

Table 8.3 Respondents' perception of town's changes (%)

Topic	Alnwick	Wymondham	Downham Market	Average
Population expansion	9	81	58	49
Stretched services/infrastructure	1	29	22	17
Becoming more touristy	52	0	0	17
Changing character	6	21	7	11
In-migration	5	8	20	11
Crime/anti-social behaviour	8	9	7	8
Being regenerated	1	0	19	7
Change in shopping	7	2	9	6
Lack of change	7	1	0	3
Becoming run down	6	0	0	2
Increasing house prices	3	0	1	1
Sample (those responding)	120 (56% of sample)	161 (62% of sample)	145 (62% of sample)	426 (60% of sample)

Note: Due to different objectives of the Morpeth survey no data was collected on this issue.

Downham Market data showed those concerned with change in the character of the town were more likely to be longer-term residents. Downham Market residents noted similar issues relating to the community and town character, and questioned the engagement of new residents. For example, one participant stated 'I used to know nearly everyone, now it's [Downham Market] full of strangers' and another suggesting the town is becoming more of a 'new town' in character.

Housing issues

In addition to concern about pressures on services and impacts on town character – especially in the Norfolk towns (see Table 8.4) – affordability is a key issue particularly for young residents, with high house prices resulting from external demand being mentioned. Consistent with the discussion above, the issue of affordability was particularly noted by Alnwick respondents; indeed, a number noted personal difficulties relating to housing. In Alnwick, a lack of rental/council houses was cited as a particular problem, whereas comments from Wymondham and Downham Market related almost exclusively to market housing. With most 'affordable' housing provision coming from quotas (see Chapter 7), the housing allocations in Alnwick are unlikely to lead to the construction of many new rented houses.

Conclusion

For all these towns the scale of the future allocation of housing is seen as an important issue that will ultimately affect the towns' sustainability, vitality, and distinctiveness. Current population and migration patterns generate very different housing requirements in the North East and East of England, and these are then reflected in very different housing allocations. In the North East, levels of population growth are comparatively low and, in aggregate, there is no shortage of houses, while the East of England continues to experience high levels of population and household growth, and aggregate shortages of housing are in evidence. On the one hand, councils in the North East are asking for higher allocations to ensure the viability of services in their market towns (need), whilst in the East of England they are seeking to reduce their allocations to protect their towns' character and because they feel they have insufficient infrastructure and service capacity to meet the needs of an expanded population (capacity); this very much reflects the views of local residents. However, all four towns studied questioned their physical and socio-economic ability to remain

Table 8.4 Respondents' perception of housing issues (%)

Topic	Alnwick	Wymondham	Downham Market	Average
Affordability	80	24	23	42
Too many new houses	5	49	43	32
Imbalance of population and service/infrastructure	3	40	40	28
Inappropriate development	12	12	18	14
Loss of character	1	9	8	6
Too few rental/council houses	16	2	4	7
Poor-quality housing	5	0	0	2
No problem	3	2	3	3
Sample (those responding)		202	171	
	(% of sample)	(78% of sample)	(73% of sample)	(% of sample)

sustainable and distinctive in the face of the changes they have been asked to make by new housing allocations.

Alnwick and Morpeth are both struggling with the impact of policy, which minimises their allocations whilst requiring them to continue to find affordable housing and to maintain services. In Alnwick, in particular, there is a need to change the profile of the housing stock to help accommodate those employed locally on relatively low salaries compared with many of the in-migrants retiring into or commuting from Alnwick. The current regional policy focus of locating housing in the conurbations seeks to reduce out-migration from main urban centres and fits with central government's urban renaissance agenda. However, there is a general recognition that city-centre living is attractive to younger adults, whilst older people are inclined to seek housing in more rural locations, but there is a question as to the extent to which current policy in the North East recognises this. Ignoring the important impact of younger people leaving towns like Alnwick (and to a lesser extent Morpeth) and older people moving into these towns leads to problems with housing provision, services and retail provision, and employment opportunity.

In common with the rest of the south, in the East of England there is a continuing need to provide sufficient housing to meet the market demand. The scale of the need is seen as being substantial, and rural settlements such as market towns are popular places to live. The cumulative effect of recent allocations and past policies and levels of development underline residents' and councils' concerns about the balance between development and the ability to absorb it. An additional concern, particularly in Wymondham, is that the towns are losing their characteristic small-town feel, and their sense of a close-knit community. This provides something of a challenge particularly for councils but also for house builders, housing associations and other service providers. There is a need to find creative ways of planning and of providing enough well-designed housing, including affordable housing, and sufficient infrastructure to meet the needs of both the existing and future residents of these market towns without losing their particular distinctiveness.

There is undoubtedly an important role that housing development can play in maintaining the sustainability of market towns in general and these towns in particular, through providing (potential) additional custom for shops and to supplement local social capital. As has been pointed out elsewhere in this book, new development can also contribute to the generation of employment and housing-led regeneration. So housing development can provide opportunities for market towns but it also brings tensions, and providing housing alone is not enough. The appropriate facilities and infrastructure also need to come along at the right time to service new demands, and these need to be appropriate for the new population profiles and characteristics of market towns. The possibility of harnessing planning gain needs to be maximised to contribute to the achievement of this balance between development and services.

Nevertheless, to help ensure the viability of market towns in the face of population changes and rising house prices, market towns will need to expand. If they attempt to stand still they could stagnate, and some concern has already been shown that in the North East this could be a problem. If they expand, particularly at the rate likely in the East of England, then the existing character of these towns will be altered to provide a different rendition of the role and identity of the market town for its residents, its working community, its visitors, and its wider hinterland. Finding the balance between over- and under-expansion to achieve the vitality and vibrancy that everybody wants for these towns will continue to be the challenge for many years.

Chapter 9

Market towns and rural employment

Trevor Hart and Neil Powe

Introduction

Chapter 3 identified 'specialised employment' as a functional role for a number of market towns, where there is one dominant employer or sector of employment, such as defence or manufacturing. Market towns performing such a role were identified as accounting for just less than 20 per cent of towns studied. However, the development of a wider role for market towns to act as centres for employment has been a basic tenet of policy for some years, but the extent to which they perform this role has been questioned by recent research (SERRL 2004). Nonetheless, acting as a source of local employment – and consequently, a contributor to local prosperity – remains a role and an aspiration for most towns. This chapter explores the scope for market towns to act as centres for employment, and considers the contribution of employment development to the fortunes and futures of the towns in a number of related dimensions. It begins by considering the context in which they operate, by reviewing employment trends in rural areas, before reviewing evidence on employment in market towns, from literature and from the work with the 11 case study towns.

Employment trends in rural areas

The economies of market towns, and the employment that is an expression of that economy, do not operate in a vacuum. They are subject to the same forces that affect other parts of the economy, but it may be the case that some of the attributes of market towns act to shape those forces and outcomes in a particular way; for example, Hepworth *et al.* (2004) point to regional differences in the emergence of the rural knowledge economy.[1] Alternatively, market towns might be well placed in capturing a share of employment in growing sectors such as tourism. Similarly, market towns are still, to a large extent, firmly tied into the fortunes of their wider localities. For example, towns in prosperous regions stand a better chance of being prosperous than those in deprived regions. However, specific trends and forces affecting the economies and employment in rural areas have been highlighted by a number of studies, and it is important to try to understand the nature of the influences that might be exerted on market towns by their 'rurality'.

Compared with urban areas, employment trends in rural areas have been broadly positive: rural areas have gained employment while urban areas have lost jobs, and generally unemployment levels have been lower in rural areas than in urban. However, a less positive picture is evident in some rural localities, with higher and more persistent levels of unemployment in some coastal towns and former coalfield areas, and continuing job losses in primary industries (Tarling *et al.* 1993; Gudgin 1990; CRC 2006b).

Growth in jobs in rural areas has been ascribed in the past to the movement of industry from urban areas, to avoid the diseconomies of operating on restricted urban sites where businesses might be subject to high levels of labour turnover, to more economical and efficient rural locations – the so-called urban-rural shift (Fothergill and Gudgin 1982). Increases in employment have also come, as has been the case elsewhere, through the growth of the service sector. Gillespie (1999) suggests that, in areas away from the major settlements, this could be linked to a number of factors including: the growth in service employment mirroring or following the growth of population in rural areas; the greater facility offered by ICT in decentralising activities; the development of flexible working practices, which, along with the diffusion of ICT, have made 'mobile working' possible; the readier availability of premises in a range of decentralised locations and the impact of workers exercising their residential preferences, particularly in the case of the self-employed and those starting new businesses. In relation to the latter, Gillespie points out that, apart from three central London boroughs, all of the top thirty places for non-manual home-based work are rural areas.

Butt (1999) reported that there had been 'a growing convergence of the industrial structures of urban and rural areas' (36). Indeed, Chapter 2 identified that the structure of the economy in market towns is similar to that of the nation as a whole. However, subtle differences were observed, with a higher proportion of 'manufacturing', less 'real estate renting and business activities' and 'financial intermediation'. These results are consistent with those of SERRL (2004), whose regional analysis suggests that there is a strong focus in market towns on financial and business services – typically weaker in rural areas – in the South East; a strong focus on public administration in the North East (due in part to the location of Ministry of Defence establishments) and tourism in the South West. Knowledge-intensive sectors remain under-represented in rural areas vis-à-vis the national average (Green and Hardill 2003).

More recent work by the CRC (2006b) identifies a number of other, mainly positive, ways in which rural employment differs from urban employment, namely: a lower proportion of the overall population of working age; a higher rate of employment; a higher rate of self-employment; a lower rate of unemployment and a lower level of economic inactivity. Alongside these positive factors a number of less positive and largely less visible features need to be noted.

First, the favourable employment picture continues to be balanced by a poorer choice of job opportunities, both qualitatively and quantitatively. Indeed, reporting findings for the rural East Midlands, Green (1999) suggests: young people (particularly those with "aspirations"), women seeking full-time employment in high level non-manual occupations, and men in specialist occupations (particularly if they lost their jobs) were amongst the most likely to find their employment opportunities constrained by such location' (42). This lack of choice of employment is, in some significant part, related to the extent to which transport and accessibility issues act as a barrier to employability.

Matching jobs and workers can be problematic in rural areas. In addition to problems posed by lack of transport and childcare, mismatches between skills have been found to be prevalent (Monk *et al*. 1999), both in the sense of workers lacking the skills demanded by employers and in workers possessing skills above the levels in demand locally. It can be difficult for workers to remedy skills gaps, both because it is hard to know what skills to acquire for a small area of job search and because of the difficulties of accessing training. Mechanisms for matching jobs and workers can also be problematic. There is a tendency for small firms to rely on informal networks to recruit staff, and this is particularly common in rural areas: workers who are not part of such networks are disadvantaged in finding work, and public sector services such as Jobcentre Plus are sometimes not locally available or can be seen as not fully recognising the nature of workers' needs (Marsden *et al*. 2005).

This relative shortage of choices is likely to encourage – or perhaps reflect – rural-urban commuting and, indeed, between 6.3 per cent (in the North West of England) and 26.8 per cent (East Midlands) of rural residents travel to urban areas to work. Lowe (1999) identifies a difference between residents of remote rural areas, where between 80 and 90 per cent found work in rural areas, and more accessible rural areas, where between 40 and 60 per cent of residents were commuting to urban areas for work. Interestingly, Green and Hardill (2003) note that the increasing penetration of ICT and flexible working practices into more areas of working life opens up new opportunities for the geographical expression of labour market careers.

Second, even if unemployment rates are generally lower, there is a significant level of under-employment in rural areas, which encapsulates both people working below their capacity and capability – taking part-time or seasonal and casual work when they would really like full-time work – and people working in jobs below their skill levels (although this can be part of a 'lifestyle choice'). An alternative perspective on this is illustrated by the tendency of graduates to 'educate out' of rural areas (Green and Hardill 2003).

Third, businesses in rural areas are predominantly small in size and as such will exhibit many of the postulated advantages and disadvantages associated with small and medium-sized enterprises (SMEs). Disadvantages identified tend to focus on the capacity of smaller firms to develop and exploit market opportunities, and there are a number of features of rural areas that can exacerbate these difficulties. The pattern of growth in employment in rural areas was paralleled by the attribution of some advantages to rural SMEs, but differences between urban and rural SMEs are perhaps less evident than has been thought to be the case. Although rural firms are more likely to be micro-businesses, previously observed advantages over their urban equivalents in areas such as innovation, application of ICT and growth orientation seem to have evaporated (Smallbone *et al.* 2002).

Small rural firms face a number of competitive disadvantages compared with their urban counterparts. The fact that rural SMEs are distant from major national and international markets leads to a greater reliance on smaller local markets or niche markets. High levels of local interaction and exchange can be beneficial to local economies, in that it minimises economic 'leakages'; however, evidence on how far this happens is limited and equivocal (Courtney and Errington 2000; Blackburn and Curran 1993; SERRL 2004). It is also the case that the small size and occupational composition of local labour markets can impose constraints on growing firms, or firms seeking to innovate. This problem is exacerbated by the cost and difficulty of accessing training and business support services (SQW 2006).

The risk facing small businesses in rural areas lies in becoming trapped in limited, low-value-added markets, which poses a risk for rural communities of becoming low-skill and low-wage economies. Alternatively, potential exists for capitalising on positive environmental factors (attractive to certain skilled and well-resourced entrepreneurs), effective links and synergies with urban economies and some of the cost advantages identified by studies on urban–rural shift, to build strong and growing economies. The diversity of rural areas results in variations within rural areas tending to be greater than those between rural and urban areas. The fortunes of rural areas and the small firms that inhabit them – and of market towns – will vary between localities.

Fourth, skills and training have been seen as important to rural areas, as a means of helping in the process of adaptation to economic change, and for individuals, as a means of developing employment and career opportunities (Errington *et al.* 1989). They observed that: 'rural businesses, rural employers, rural employees and the rural workforce as a whole are at a significant disadvantage compared to their urban counterparts. This disadvantage stems largely from the small size of rural firms and their distance from existing training providers' (54). To a large extent this problem can be seen as one of cost, and in particular the higher fixed administrative and travel costs associated with service delivery in areas of dispersed population. This is exacerbated by the difficulties for smaller firms in releasing employees from day-to-day activities to undertake training, and for those seeking training readily accessing what they need (Green and Hardill 2003). The issues with training can be seen to be replicated in the case of business support services, where problems of cost, choice and sometimes quality are also apparent (Smallbone *et al.* 2002). Policy responses have been criticised as lacking a proper awareness of the needs of rural business for advice and support (Smallbone *et al.* 2002). In part, this may be a result of funding mechanisms failing to fully reflect the costs of catering for a dispersed population of clients (Hart 1996).

Fifth, low levels of pay contribute to high levels of poverty in rural areas. Studies by McLaughlin (1986) and Cloke *et al.* (1994) identified between a quarter and a fifth of all rural households being in poverty. To some extent this is a reflection of the employment and occupational structure of rural areas, where high-wage industries and occupations[2] are under-represented (Green and Hardill 2003), but it may also reflect competitive conditions in rural labour markets.[3] While the Commission for Rural Communities (2006a) reported an average £130 per week urban to rural differential (approximately €185), the picture will vary between rural localities. Wages are consistently lower in more sparsely populated locations,[4] again possibly reflecting lower levels of labour market competition. Although not explicitly explored, it is expected that wage rates in market towns are likely to reflect the wider trends within their hinterlands.

Employment in market towns

There are few, if any, studies that address a full range of employment issues in relation to market towns. Recent evidence, however, suggests their performance to be lagging behind their surrounding rural areas, where for the period 1995–2000 in England and Wales, Farthing *et al.* (2005) found employment in rural areas (24 per cent) was growing more rapidly than in small towns (12 per cent). Explanations for this difference were left to future research. In principle, market towns could be seen as possessing most of the advantages outlined earlier for rural economies and to be better placed to overcome the disadvantages. Their size and role, as local service hubs, increases their potential to offer the range of business and training services the predominantly small local businesses need; these attributes can act as advantages to both employers and workforce. To the extent that market towns continue to act as a focus for trade they can provide a 'market' within which a business can trade and develop supply chain linkages. As often the more accessible locations within rural areas, market towns may offer easier labour access for employers and a better choice of work for employees. As such the findings of Farthing *et al.* (2005) are inconsistent with expectations, and need to be the subject of future research.

Considering the situation in small towns, SERRL (2004) revealed that, while they do act as employment centres for their surrounding rural area and for local residents, the extent of this role is less than has been assumed in policy. Two reasons are identified for this: the 'cheap mobility' on offer as a result of falling private transport costs; and that the choice of place of residence is not strongly connected with choice of work location. Generally, the role of employment centre is more significant to town residents than inhabitants of the town hinterland.

A study of six towns in Somerset[5] (Cousins *et al.* 2004) reviewed a wider range of labour market factors. It found that the towns were all affected by a tight labour market, experienced low levels of unemployment and employers were experiencing difficulties recruiting to lower-paid 'less attractive' jobs. However, the labour force was seen as having poor endowments of basic skills and higher-level qualifications, and the towns were characterised by a prevalence of low-paid occupations, reflected in average wage levels being in some cases no higher than 70 per cent of national figures. The economies of the towns were regarded as 'vulnerable', because their employment was skewed towards declining sectors and away from growth and knowledge-based sectors. Therefore, diversifying employment was seen as a priority. Scope for development was limited by a number of factors including: the size and quality of the local labour supply; the patchy availability of training and business support services; difficulties in attracting higher-skilled professionals into the towns in spite of the perceived 'lifestyle advantages' of the county; and the need for employees to 'move on' to achieve career progression. Also absent was 'an explicit vision for the future', based on a clear understanding of their strengths and weaknesses, and around which marketing and development efforts could be focused.

A number of studies have pointed to potential positive impacts of in-migration, but for the most part these studies have focused on rural areas generally rather than specifically on market towns. Although increased in-migration is likely to lead to more commuting, the long-term effect may be more positive. Renkow and Hoover (2000) suggest it is unlikely that in-migrants will both move into rural areas and simultaneously change employment. They suggest instead that this may come later. In an English context, Keeble and Tyler (1995) find evidence to support this two-stage process, with 36 per cent of remote rural and 53 per cent of accessible rural businesses surveyed suggesting that the entrepreneur moved to the area prior to setting up the business. Considering the benefits of in-migration more generally by using surveys of in-migrants in Scotland, Findlay *et al.* (2000) found 22 per cent of the sample to be self-employed, nearly all of whom (85 per cent) had based their business locally (less than 20 km of home). Bosworth (2006) has provided further support for these findings by considering micro-businesses in the rural areas of Northumberland. He found that 40 per cent of micro-businesses were run by in-migrants and that these businesses also employed an average of approximately two employees per firm. Micro-businesses run by those migrating into the area were also found to be more growth-oriented, suggesting these businesses were more likely to provide future job creation than micro-businesses run by established residents.

In Chapters 2 and 3, the local distinctiveness of market towns (history, tradition, architecture) was identified as a key motivation for moving to the towns, for purposes of commuting or living and working in the town. With market towns also likely to have lower average house prices than their hinterlands (see Chapter 7), there may also be an element of achieving 'second best' providing the closest achievable approximation to the rural idyll. For those residents working within rural areas outside the market towns, they may provide the only feasible option for housing. Indeed, the data presented in Chapter 7 shows how market towns are often likely to provide the only realistic option in terms of the availability of social rented housing. Furthermore, in remoter areas market towns may provide convenient locations for dual-income households to find a compromise between locations of employment. This role of housing rural employees is likely to be important for the vitality of the rural economy and, more particularly, in addressing some of the issues of labour shortage identified in studies cited above.

In addition to impacts such as adding to local prosperity, developing employment in market towns can have wider benefits. It is possible that having local employment will increase 'engagement' within the towns, by both businesses and employees. For example, local firms are likely to be more favourable to the idea of providing sponsorship for activities within the towns. It may also be true that residents working in the town may be more engaged with the town in other aspects of their lives. For example, previous research has suggested that those working in the towns may be more likely to shop in the town, though the findings vary between good purchased (Pinkerton *et al.* 1995; Civic Trust 2000; Findlay *et al.* 2001; Courtney *et al.* 2006). This may have implications both in terms of the contribution of out-commuters to the local economy and also car usage.

Rural job opportunities may contribute to maintaining a younger population, with aggregated data suggesting that towns with better-paid employment options[6] tend to have younger populations and have more contained work patterns, such that average distance travelled to work is less than in other towns (see Chapter 2). Ideally, jobs would be filled mainly by those living within the towns and their immediate hinterland, or by those moving to the area with the intent of settling and engaging with other activities in the towns.

Findings from the case study towns

The case study towns expose a number of key issues affecting employment in market towns. First, many of the towns face constraints on development, frequently of what might loosely be termed 'environmental' in nature. These include the towns being sited in sensitive environments – for example, green belt and AONB in the case of Haslemere – or topography – for example, Minehead's coastal location on the edge of moorland means that flood risk and steep gradients severely limit scope for development. In addition, the 'heritage' element in many of the settlements means that there can be local resistance to development that is not seen as complementing the character of the town. If such environmental barriers can be overcome, there is still a need for some form of coordinated initiative to achieve development. Getting key agencies – local interests, county and district councils and regional development agencies – to work together was not always easy, and failure to do so was seen to be slowing development in Minehead and Todmorden.

Development problems can be exacerbated by the unsatisfactory quality of road linkages. A number of our case study towns faced somewhat tortuous road journeys to the nearest large town or motorway link while others face congested roads, slowing business journeys at peak travel times.

Second, employment can be concentrated in a single sector or in a limited number of businesses, adding a certain vulnerability to the local economy. In an historical dimension, Todmorden, which has lost all its employment in the cotton industry, provides one example; another more recent example is provided by Crediton, where the closure of a large local food producer is evident from its still-derelict site adjoining the railway station. In other cases, dominance provides a potential risk. So, in the case of Richmond, the current planned expansion of the nearby garrison promises to be a significant addition to the local economy, but the political decisions that brought the expansion could be reversed at a later stage. In Minehead, the dependence on the tourism sector and particularly one employer – Butlins – means that changes in taste may have significant direct and induced impacts on employment. In the case of Keswick, the planned relocation of the historic pencil factory to Workington will have an impact on the town, but this might be less than it first appears as so many of the employees of the factory commute to work, many from the Workington area.

Third, local employment often offered only low levels of wages. Low wages were particularly evident in areas where linkages to rural industries were still strong, where there was a strong dominance of low-paying industries and where there was a history of industrial decline. In such locations, many of the jobs on offer paid at or near the national minimum wage. Combined with other factors this was seen as a contributor to social exclusion. In other locations – particularly commuter or retirement towns – a combination of low pay in local jobs and high house prices added up to a significant social issue for the town. The starkest example of this was in Haslemere, where low rates of pay in service employment in the town contrasted sharply with house prices in many cases starting at around £500,000.

Fourth, business services and labour market institutions are not always well located in relation to the needs of the users. While 9 of the 11 case study towns have a Jobcentre Plus office (only Crediton and Haslemere lack an office), few of the towns have offices of private sector employment agencies, recruitment mechanisms commonly used by small businesses. Training provision was hard to analyse for the towns, as the key issue for business is finding the *appropriate* provision, both in the sense of the skills set and the location, but none of the towns are close to a Business Link office. This is perhaps significant, as Business Link is the public policy mechanism designed to support the small businesses that dominate the economy of the market towns. So, for example, in Oswestry Business Link worked closely with the MTI group in helping them to identify problems and address potential solutions as too did Advantage West Midlands (RDA). Unfortunately, the Business Link in the area was consolidated to a distant large urban area. Most towns had some form of gateway to business advice in the form of accountants and bank branches, but none of the towns appeared to offer a range of services; those seeking any degree of choice would have to search outside the town.

So, while policy might place an emphasis on such towns as places where growth could happen in the future, their capacity and capability to accommodate growth will vary. Most will face some form of constraint to be overcome if they are to make the most of the potential they possess, and it is by no means clear that, with or without participation in an MTI or its successor, they will have ready access to the resources necessary to assist them in action to address the constraints.

As outlined in Chapter 8, further interviews and surveys were undertaken in four towns – Alnwick and Morpeth in Northumberland, and Wymondham and Downham Market in Norfolk. These made possible an exploration of some of the detail of work and social lives of residents of the towns and thus consider some of the relationships between the town as an entity and its employment patterns.

Some results of this work were considered in Chapter 8, where Table 8.2 suggests that Alnwick performs the role of a key rural employment centre (61 per cent of residents working, work in the town – see Box 9.1), whereas Wymondham and Downham Market would appear to be commuter towns (only 26 per cent and 21 per cent of residents working, work in the town). Despite its location close to Newcastle, Morpeth would appear to fall somewhere between rural employment centre and commuter town (38 per cent of residents working, work in the town). Interestingly, when considering those working in larger urban areas or further afield, statistically the two more remote towns of Alnwick and Downham Market are indistinguishable (5 per cent level of significance – 13 per cent and 18 per cent respectively).[7] Instead, the difference between Alnwick and Downham Market is revealed in other terms, with Alnwick being highlighted as a rural service centre and Downham Market as a location for housing for rural employment (see Box 9.2).

In Chapter 8 it was shown that those migrating to the towns within the last 15 years were consistently more likely to work outside the towns. However this pattern did vary between towns. Examining the percentages out-working, in-migrants did not behave uniformly between towns. Indeed, approximately half of in-migrants in Alnwick actually worked in the town. For those commuting out to work, the use of the car dominated.

Box 9.1 Alnwick: rural employment centre

Alnwick clearly acts as an important rural employment centre. In addition to the 61 per cent of working residents actually working in the town, 23 per cent of working hinterland residents also work in the town (Powe and Shaw 2004). Although noted for its tourism, discussed in the next chapter, some major employers in the town also include: House of Hardy and Greys of Alnwick, world-renowned makers of fly-fishing tackle; Northumberland Estates, which manages the Duke of Northumberland's agricultural, forestry and property interests; Sanofi Alnwick Research Centre, a very large pharmaceutical research and testing centre; Alnwick District Council; Tagish Ltd, an independent company specialising in the delivery of ICT solutions and consultancy; and the translating company Eclipse Translations Ltd. Whereas the rural location fits with the specialism in fishing tackle, other businesses can be considered to be more 'footloose' in terms of their requirements.

Alnwick as a district has also been characterised as enterprising, with Stockdale (2005) reporting that of the five areas considered within her English study (Alnwick, Ashford (Kent), East Devon, South Warwickshire and Wear Valley), the highest level of self-employed in-migrants was in the District of Alnwick (25 per cent). However, this is something of a contrast to the findings of Courtney *et al.* (2004) who rated the district as performing poorly, largely as a result of 'the relatively poor quality of its human capital' and a 'sense of comfortable inertia' (x). Compared with its neighbouring district of Tynedale, it was felt to lack the accessibility and culture to attract and retain enterprise.

Box 9.2 Downham Market: housing rural employees

Downham Market is fairly remote from the urban centres of Norwich (44 miles away), Peterborough (33 miles away) and Cambridge (33 miles away), but is located only 13 miles from the larger town of King's Lynn (population of approximately 19,000). There is a plentiful supply of new housing that is priced similarly to the Norfolk average, but below the nearby Cambridgeshire average. Considering the list of places where Downham Market residents work provides a speckled pattern of rural areas within Cambridgeshire, Lincolnshire and Norfolk, with the only clusters being 10 per cent of Downham Market working residents located at a nearby Royal Air Force base and a further 10 per cent at the nearby larger town of King's Lynn. Although in Downham Market in-migrants were more likely to work in larger urban areas the role of the town as housing rural employees is likely to continue.

Despite the central location of train stations within three of the towns, only a small proportion used these facilities to travel to work beyond the town (Morpeth, 6 per cent; Wymondham, 6 per cent; Downham, 10 per cent). Use of the bus service was also minimal, but was more important in the less remote towns (Alnwick, 0 per cent; Morpeth, 6 per cent; Wymondham, 8 per cent; Downham, 0 per cent). On the other hand, approximately half the respondents living in the town did not use the car to get to work (Morpeth, 50 per cent; Alnwick, 52 per cent; Wymondham, 54 per cent; Downham, 53 per cent).

Table 9.1 considers the extent to which those working engage with the towns. With the exception of Morpeth, where those working in the town were also more likely to do their main food shopping in the town, the main differences were observed between those working and not working. Indeed, in general whether respondents worked in the town or elsewhere would appear to make little difference to other forms of engagement with the towns. Although working in the town leads to a more contained lifestyle, those working in the town are not otherwise more likely to engage with the towns.

Reaping the benefits of attractive towns

To realise the potential benefits of their location and lifestyle attributes, market towns will need to address some of the shortcomings identified above. They will need to try to address education and skills gaps, and to maximise the advantage offered by environmental quality through careful planning and marketing. However, as a number of lifestyle surveys have emphasised, market towns are considered some of the most attractive places to live, and a number of studies have addressed the question of how far the forces of counter-urbanisation are linked to enterprise development. Although often distant from larger urban areas and their markets, with improvements in communication technologies, the presence of a wider range of services than found in more remote locations, and often good infrastructure links to elsewhere, both businesses and labour may be attracted and develop.

These issues have been considered by Keeble and Tyler (1995), where using a 'matched pairs' approach, they surveyed business within remote rural, accessible rural and urban areas. This revealed that residential and environmental attractiveness were key stimuli for the location of business, with nearness to the founder's home being the most important reason for its location. As such, rural areas have been able to attract actual and potential entrepreneurs through their desirable residential characteristics and this has contributed to rural employment growth. Comparing rural to urban locations, Keeble and Tyler (1995) suggest that as well as attractive residential locations, rural areas may also offer 'production

Table 9.1 Engagement of working residents (%)

	Main food shopping in the town	Regular non-food shopping in the town	Evening out in town (pub or restaurant in last month)	Local community activity
Morpeth				
Sample	69	48	20	N/A
Sample working	59	53	67	N/A
Working in town	73*(+)	54	66	N/A
Working in large urban area	44*(−)	57	65	N/A
Alnwick				
Sample	67	45	33	54
Sample working	58	43	55*(+)	29*(−)
Working in town	61	40	52	31
Working in large urban area	61	61	72	22
Wymondham				
Sample	47	67	19	47
Sample working	38	43*(−)	41*(+)	40
Working in town	42	42	35	44
Working in large urban area	38	44	40	39
Downham				
Sample	80	43	18	47
Sample working	70	39	39*(+)	31*(−)
Working in town	77	40	47	32
Working in large urban area	69	39	23	23

Notes:
1 * 5% level.
2 Sample working is compared to not working; those working in the town compared to those working elsewhere; and those working in large urban area compared to those not.

cost' benefits in terms of lower rural labour costs and the availability and cost of rural premises. Against this, urban areas provide better access to clients, staff and suppliers. Hence, the choice of location will depend upon the importance of these factors, and this will depend on the characteristics of the businesses. Keeble and Tyler (1995) suggest 'changes in the nature of the production process which allow manufacturing and service activity to be more footloose have also reduced the need for traditional urban locations' (995). However, a more recent study by Courtney *et al.* (2004), taking matched pairs of successful and less successful rural districts, pinpointed the importance of accessibility and proximity to large urban centres – particularly London and other major cities – in determining levels of economic performance. This finding was extended to localities within the districts, with those enjoying better intra-regional accessibility exhibiting better economic performance.

The relevance of Keeble and Tyler's findings depends on the extent to which residential location attracts people for employment as well as a home, or whether the willingness and ability to commute dominates. In her survey of practitioners from the North West and Eastern regions of the UK, Wong (1998) found that there was a general opinion that quality of life was not a primary consideration as there are usually attractive areas within commutable distance from the businesses office or factory. For example:

> High quality of living in terms of attractive surroundings and a good quality market are factors that attract people to move to the area, but these are commuters not

businesses. High quality of living does not override the land, skills, infrastructural constraints which new businesses face when considering the move to an area (local authority in Essex)

(Wong 2001: 27).

This was further demonstrated by Wong (2001) using house price and commuting distances in the North West of England, where those living in more prosperous counties had the highest house prices and were found to be commuting the furthest. Areas with more industrial and mining employment were found to have more in-commuting than out-commuting. More generally, in her study of practitioners, the consideration of traditional economic factors (land, skills and infrastructure) was seen to be the first of a 'two-tier sieving' process in which 'only after these basic factors are satisfied, one may turn to the softer, more intangible factors such as business culture, image and quality of life' (Wong 1998: 718).

These findings are reinforced by the work of Courtney *et al.* (2004). While they emphasised that 'a high quality natural and built environment stimulates the local economy through in-migration, business start-ups and tourism' and that 'business start-ups are a significant driver of the employment rate' (xii), 'hard' factors remain of fundamental importance. Central among such factors are ready access to main urban centres for a variety of supply chain linkages, and local institutional effectiveness, both in the sense of the availability and delivery of high-quality public services and the existence of strong local networks able to contribute to local capacity.

Despite these general findings, there are likely to be exceptions, which may depend on the nature of the businesses considered; indeed, Courtney *et al.* (2004) warn against overstating differences based on locality research. For example, it was reported in Richmond that a software firm has set up in the area primarily because of the quality of life that the town provides. Wong (2001), echoing earlier work, found quality of life to be more important within the East of England region, which is built on the growth of high-technology industries and services. Clearly, areas that provide both the traditional economic factors and quality of life will be most successful in attracting and developing businesses. In his review of literature in both personal and business migration, Rogerson (1999) found quality of life to be one of a number of factors that will be considered in making personal and business decisions.

Whether attractive locations also attract quality staff has not been the subject of much research. However, Keeble and Tyler (1995) found shortages of skilled staff to be greatest in more remote rural locations. Given the 'intermediary' role of market towns between urban and rural, perhaps they provide a compromise between the urban and rural advantages.

As perception can play a large part in determining the attraction of a locality, the way in which towns and regions are marketed can become important. Courtney *et al.* (2004) identify a strong and visible local identity as an aid to 'branding' and a key element in development. Recent literature has considered the extent to which the countryside – as opposed to market towns specifically – can be 'commodified' (Cloke 2006; Fløysand and Jakobsen 2007), through marketing of a rural idyll. This has brought benefits in terms of tourism and product promotion such as foods and craft products. It may be possible to promote market towns – and some of their businesses – in a similar way, as coming from somewhere steeped in history and having a character that is 'different from urban'.

There has been little if any research on how decisions are influenced by these types of marketing initiatives, and even deciding on would-be material is problematic. The identity of 'market towns' as a genus is established through many indirect processes, and the picture held by any one individual is likely to be the product of an accretion of images accumulated through both random and systematic processes. So, attempting to judge the effectiveness of market town branding through considering just one source of material is fraught with difficulty. Websites are becoming a main route to finding information about places and services, but a review of websites for the 11 case study towns reveals a highly variable approach to marketing through this medium. In many cases there is no one obvious gateway to choose to gain an understanding of the character of the town and few offer information directly relevant to business decisions. Most tend to emphasise the heritage and environmental attractions of the town and link this to local products in a way that helps reinforce the positive images on which the towns may need to build. However, few provide links between these advantages and the 'hard' elements influential in business decisions. One example is provided by 'Richmond Online', which highlights examples of businesses that have located in the area and what has helped them succeed. Using the example of the software firm quoted above, it notes the availability and importance of local transport and high-speed data links in the success of the business.

Policy responses

Throughout this chapter it has been emphasised that market towns possess a variety of factors that can both advantage and disadvantage them when they are seeking to develop and improve the local economy. Courtney *et al.* (2004) identified eight factors that influenced local levels of economic performance in rural areas, some of which have been fully discussed above:

- skills and education;
- accessibility and transport;
- an 'open' economy and society, focusing on the ability to attract in-migrants and use their skills to develop products, services and markets;
- environmental qualities and planning;
- entrepreneurship and enterprise, pointing to the need for such qualities to be complemented by an environment conducive to their development; this is shaped by local agencies;
- cultural capacity, emphasising the value of a forward looking attitude embedded in a cohesive community;
- marketing and identity;
- institutional effectiveness.

This wide range of factors can be related to what has been an important paradigm in rural economic development, the pursuit of 'integrated rural development' that sees economic development as part of a suit of complementary activities that are necessarily interdependent. Such an approach was exemplified in the 1960s and 70s by the work of the Highlands and Islands Development Board and the Development Board for Rural Wales, to an extent in the Rural Development Programmes of the Rural Development Commission, and possibly in the approach adopted in some of the MTI Action Plans. This approach emphasised the need for both analysis and policy to be coordinated – a feature of the Rural White Papers and the development of rural proofing – but also pointed to the need for prolonged engagement, yielding more sustainable solutions to problems.

Perhaps the current arena for developing integrated approaches is the LSP, which brings together the key local actors to develop an approach to addressing local economic, social and environmental issues. These in turn, through the emerging LAAs, will allow the pooling of existing funding streams to enable the delivery of locally identified priorities; one of the four key themes of all LAAs has to be 'economy and enterprise'. However, there is some doubt as to where and how market town partnerships – and their identified priorities – feature in this process. While the LSP is bound to take on board and reflect community wishes, it is by no means set down who should champion the needs of market towns and how. So, in the case of Crediton, there was felt to be a need for someone to act as 'champion' for the town in the LSP deliberations but who this would be and how they might relate to existing organisations in the town was by no means clear. The complexity of tiers and layers of policy and process involved in shaping and developing policies and programmes makes significant demands on the time and resourcefulness of local actors, and it was noted in Chapter 4 that such assets are not always available to market towns. The identified importance of a dedicated market towns officer to drive programmes forward, and the lack of progress that is apparent when such an officer is not available, serve to emphasise the importance of capacity in effectively engaging with such processes.

Since the reorganisation of rural services and the changed role given to the Countryside Agency, the prime responsibility for the market towns programme rests with the RDAs, established in 1999. The White Paper *Building partnerships for prosperity* (DETR 1998a) suggested that the RDAs will design rural development programmes targeted at their most deprived rural areas; this was subsequently amplified (DETR 1998b) by guidance on their rural priorities and who their 'key rural partners' should be. The emergence of a greater priority for rural matters and impetus behind market towns programmes coincided with the outbreak of foot and mouth disease in 2001.

But a number of questions have been raised about the nature of RDAs' involvement in rural economic development, some of which relate to the emergence on the national agenda of the urban renaissance and the city region as a focus of activity. More particularly, Ward (2006) contends that 'nationally prescribed performance targets strongly influence RDAs' investment priorities and militate against large numbers of small investments for relatively modest returns, encouraging the agencies instead towards a "fewer-bigger" approach' (50). This is important as RDAs are the main source of funding for rural economic development, and consequently exercise a significant influence over what does or does not get done. It is unclear how effective market towns can be in influencing the agendas and strategies of RDAs, but their RESs and Frameworks for Regional Employment and Skills Action (FRESA) remain key elements in determining local approaches and priorities, both directly and indirectly through their role in shaping the plans and actions of key delivery agencies.

It is also not entirely clear how market towns come to be identified for inclusion in the RDAs' programmes. So, for example, in the case of Yorkshire Forward, the RDA for Yorkshire and Humber in North England, the starting point is the rural towns identified in the RSS. Towns that fall within the 2,000–30,000 population band and that are 'stand-alone settlements outside of the urban hinterland' or 'remote settlements' are eligible to be considered against a number of factors, including prosperity, average income, house ownership and educational achievement, before their inclusion in the programme is discussed with partners (Yorkshire Forward 2006). However, the process is described by the RDA as 'a framework for internal use' (personal communication), so it is not possible to develop a clear idea how eligibility is decided.

In the same way that market towns vary in their attributes and problems, so too will policy approaches need to be tailored to meet varying local needs. While the Action Plans examined during the course of the case study work were far from formulaic, their approaches did frequently address a similar range of options, perhaps in part reflecting what seemed feasible. Most will recognise the range of issues identified elsewhere in this chapter, but their capability to translate the diagnosis into action is inhibited by a number of factors, including the limited powers and capacity of any one agency, and the limited ability to effectively engage all agencies in the policy implementation process.

In a town planning context, the recently introduced LDFs, with a focus on developing policy with a greater awareness of implementation issues, exemplify this concern. Policies in recent rural LDFs frequently refer to the priority to be given to market towns alongside aspirations for improving skills, developing business support facilities and maintaining environmental quality, along with detailed local policy elements designed to maintain and enhance local qualities. However, such aspirations are not readily in the control of the planning system or the local authority in any of its guises.

One area where some influence can be exercised is in the supply of affordable housing, as the provision of affordable housing has become recognised as a legitimate role for planning. With house prices increasing at a faster rate than in urban areas, and rural salaries lagging behind those elsewhere (see Chapter 2), affordable housing may become increasingly important to market towns. The provision of affordable housing, to match employment available, often in lower-paid industries, will become an important element in the pursuit of a sustainable communities strategy. At present, affordable housing can be more readily available in larger urban areas, generating commuting flows to work in the towns, sometimes mirroring flows out to work by those who have been able to exercise a lifestyle choice to live in the town and work elsewhere.

Conclusions

As has been established throughout this book, market towns are characterised by variety in their function, form and character, and this is reflected in their employment pattern and the factors (advantages and disadvantages) that go to shape their employment base. Some have fortunes that are mainly shaped by their employment pattern; for example the 20 per cent or so of towns identified as 'specialised employment' locations in Chapter 3. It is clear that many have potential to develop further as employment centres, maybe building on their environmental quality as a means of attracting entrepreneurs to set up and grow in the town. But, to realise this potential there are frequently issues to be addressed, as few businesses locate or succeed on the basis of being based in an attractive location.

This potential is perhaps reinforced by policy, in two ways. First, market towns initiatives by RDAs act to focus much of the available rural regeneration resource on the towns. Second, the sustainable development agenda, which seeks to concentrate most new rural development in places like market towns, which reinforces their role as service centres, employment centres and places for new housing development. However, for the sustainability objective to be met, the towns also need to be inhabited by individuals who behave sustainably and eschew the temptation to enjoy the attractions of market towns as a place to live while not working and shopping there.

But to succeed, the towns need to be able to mobilise a range of institutions and resources to focus on the mix of factors that they need to enhance to realise their potential. While frameworks exist by which these relationships and dialogues can take place, it is unclear as to whether market towns possess the capacity and capability to effectively influence agendas.

Notes

1   They also point to a significant difference between accessible and remote rural areas, with the former having a significant advantage.
2   For example, wage rates in hotels and catering – a key employer in tourism and an important source of employment in many market towns – are up to 50 per cent lower than the national average (ONS 2006).
3   The concept of a single, relatively self-contained rural labour market covering a locality is theoretical rather than real, with increasing mobility and labour market segmentation resulting in a number of sub-markets within any one area being a more accurate description of reality.
4   Wages in Alnwick, perhaps the most remote of the 11 case study towns, were lowest, at 63 per cent of national average (ONS 2006).
5   The six towns were Chard, Shepton Mallet, Bridgwater, Watchet/Williton, Wellington and Yeovil.
6   Such towns were identified as having high levels of employment in public administration, manufacturing, and distribution and retail.
7   This testing was undertaken using the chi-squared independence test.

Chapter 10

Visiting the shops

Rural service centre or visitor attraction?

Neil Powe and Trevor Hart

Introduction

As increasing prosperity and mobility have given most people more choices about where they shop, attracting shoppers has come to be seen more as a competitive activity between places, not just a competitive activity between retailers in one place. In this competitive environment, what do market towns have to offer, both residents and visitors? What is the nature of the competition they are facing and what is their capacity to respond?

The retail world seems to be becoming ever more dominated by a smaller number of larger retailers, mostly operating from larger centres. In such a world, small centres face a future of decline, unless they can identify niche markets unrecognised or abandoned by the increasingly dominant larger retailers. This can be achieved through promoting local distinctiveness in terms of merchandise mix, the shops themselves, streetscape and type/style of service given. Often being attractive places to visit, with many independent shops, market towns have potential to develop and capitalise on retail distinctiveness. To realise this potential requires creative responses from the retailers and key actors within the towns.

This chapter considers the competitive position of market towns to attract trade from town and hinterland residents and from visitors. Through survey evidence from four contrasting towns and a sample of city residents, it considers how far they are succeeding in their efforts to capture sufficient market share to maintain vitality and viability.

The retail environment

Up until the 1960s, the retail landscape was dominated by a traditional pattern of facilities and habits, and remained focused on the high street, where shoppers could find both the comparison and convenience goods they sought as well as a range of key services. However, this pattern was challenged in both elements of the retail sector. Retailers of 'bulky goods' sought sites away from the centre where they could both display and sell items such as carpets, furniture, white goods and DIY materials, taking advantage of cheaper sites and premises that incorporated large areas of parking to attract an increasingly mobile and affluent customer base. This move to larger, often out-of-town premises was echoed by food retailers, for many of the same motives. Their larger premises allowed them to expand not only the range of food lines on offer, but also to move into other areas of retailing in the same building. Particularly during the 1980s, these developments were facilitated by a more 'free-market' stance on planning policy for retail development, which only began to be reversed when the damage such an approach brought to existing retail centres became apparent.

Such changes in the style of retailing had significant impacts on all centres, large and small, but further changes also became apparent over this 40-year period. While there was increasing affluence and therefore spending power, the increased spending power was not uniformly distributed between parts of the retail sector. So, while total spending increased by 184 per cent over the period 1965–2005, most of this increase was devoted to durable and semi-durable goods, for example clothing, furnishings and household goods, with spending increasing by 663 and 519 per cent respectively (ONS 2005). In contrast, spending on non-durable goods went up by only 66 per cent, and an increasing proportion of this spending has been captured by large supermarkets. Both of these factors can be seen as having an impact on smaller centres such as market towns. First, their capacity to host 'comparison' shops is less; in England, 75 per cent of comparison sales (such as fashion and gifts) are now in the top 200 retail centres, compared to 50 per cent in the early 1980s (English Market Towns Forum 2002). Second, their scope to host larger convenience goods outlets is limited.

At the same time, a number of developments have been seen to influence the nature of the high street and the range of retail goods and services present. Factors such as the deregulation of the financial services sector prompted banks, building societies and other providers of financial products to seek to gain market share through developing their presence on the high street, leading to a concern that they provide 'dead' shop frontages, posing a threat to the vibrancy of town centres. More recently, the emergence of new products and services, the most obvious being mobile telephones, has led to further changes of the appearance of retail centres. The vitality and atmosphere of market town centres depends on them being able to compete for shares of such emerging sectors.

The impact of such trends on smaller centres as a whole in more recent years was considered by Baldock (2004), where it is clearly evident that smaller and local centres have lost out to larger centres in a number of areas of retailing. In particular:

- The increasing dominance of larger centres in food retailing is clearly demonstrated;
- Sales are being concentrated into a smaller number of units; given the increases in levels of spending noted above, these will be larger, more efficient units (higher turnover per square metre of floorspace);
- There is an evident pattern of decline across most sectors in smaller centres, except hair and beauty salons and charity shops, where the latter are often seen as a sign of a loss of vitality and viability for an existing centre.

Clearly, such aggregates conceal a wide variation between centres, with the variation and comparative success or failure determined by a number of internal and contextual factors. Places that have both a competitive range of shops and an attractive centre will be in a better position to succeed. Places that have something extra to offer, such as the distinctive heritage or unique features and attractions, can succeed in capturing some additional patronage from tourists. Places that are located in more affluent areas will be better placed to succeed if they can be managed in such a way as to capture the potential patronage offered by their hinterlands. Capturing customers and spending may also depend on successful place marketing activity, focused on establishing and maintaining an image of a place that is pleasant and interesting to visit, and which will meet a range of retail and leisure needs. The key question then is: how well are market towns placed to be competitive in this changing market?

The competitiveness of market towns

A central element of activity in the MTI has been carrying out 'health checks', which essentially attempt to assess the competitive strengths and weaknesses of towns. The health check approach has been along very similar lines to that suggested in *Vital and viable town centres: Meeting the challenge* and in subsequent planning policy advice, on how to go about assessing the vitality of a town centre (DoE 1994; NRPF 2000; ODPM 2005). This includes a number of key items: the retail 'offer', that is the range of uses in the centre, including retailer representation; the shopping environment, including the quality of the public realm (Plate 10; Plate 9), factors such as crime and safety, and numbers of vacant units; accessibility; 'footfall', indicating pedestrian flows past the shops; and views and opinions of the centres' users. Also relevant is the nature of the catchment for centres (and the characteristics of visitors and potential visitors) as this can help determine the potential type and volume of spending in the shops and services. Some key factors affecting the competitiveness of market towns are reviewed below.

Retail offer

The classification of market towns proposed in Chapter 2 and discussed in Chapter 3 suggests that there is a number of retail markets in which town centres may need to compete. Market towns must try to meet the needs of their hinterland populations, providing a 'service hub', as well as trying to satisfy a number of what might be more specialised needs of commuters, retired people and tourists. This potential multiplicity of retail roles was highlighted in the study town of Minehead, where four different types of shoppers were identified: people looking to meet basic needs; people, mostly in-migrants, looking for a range of higher-order goods; and two types of visitors whose needs differed (see Box 3.3). Given the size and catchment of the typical market town, it would appear inevitable that the range of retail choice is less than in larger urban areas, and that most towns will struggle to meet a wide range of needs. Indeed, the wider range of services provided in larger urban centres is perhaps a key motivation for those with cars 'bypassing' market towns. It is also a compelling reason for market towns to seek to differentiate themselves from competing centres in order to identify a market where they can mark out and maintain an advantage.

Towns that are seeking to act as a service hub for their hinterland need to offer a range of key facilities. In larger urban areas and in shopping malls, department stores frequently act as 'anchors' (Robertson 1997); such stores, usually run by local owners, can sometimes be found in larger market towns, but this is not the norm (Plate 11; Plate 12). More frequently observed would be a good-sized supermarket, to act as an 'anchor' for the town centre and as a means of capturing spending on food items and, in some cases, non-food items that would otherwise leak out to other centres. For example, a study of the town of Alnwick by Powe and Shaw (2004) showed that those using the supermarket in the towns for their main food shopping were also more likely to visit other shops and services in the town. As two edge-of-centre supermarkets have just been granted planning permission, the future for the town centre is uncertain (see Box 10.1). The data below illustrates the desire of local residents for an enlarged and improved supermarket. A similar desire for supermarkets, even if located out of town, was found in some of our other case study towns. For example, the development of two supermarkets in Todmorden was felt to encourage people to see the town as a place to meet a majority of their shopping needs, while in Crediton a proposal to build a new supermarket was seen as means to both stop leakage of local convenience spending to the nearest large supermarkets in Exeter, 15 miles distant, and to capture more trade from the hinterland.

Inserting a large supermarket into a market town is not a guaranteed 'win'. A study by the DETR (1998c) into the impact of new supermarkets built at edge-of-centre and out-of-centre locations in market towns identified a loss of market share from existing convenience

---

Box 10.1 Supermarkets in Alnwick

Later in this chapter it is shown that there have been calls for a new and better supermarket in Alnwick, which would also provide competition for the Morrisons store (formerly Safeway Stores plc) (the largest supermarket within the town at the time of writing). The issue of supermarkets in Alnwick has a long and controversial history. Summarising the issues as described by Cotterell *et al.* (2000), in 1993 an application was lodged for a development on the outskirts of Alnwick, which included a retail element. Outline planning was granted by Alnwick District Council in that year. Safeway subsequently became interested in the site as a replacement for their existing store in the town and acquired a freehold. In 1996 the Secretary of State consulted as to whether he should exercise his powers under Section 100 of the 1990 Town and Country Planning, and act to revoke or modify the planning permission. An inspector was appointed and retail use was deleted from the 1993 planning permission, partly because of the effect that development would have on the vitality and viability of the proposed retail development. There were concerns that the compensation required for the revocation of planning permission would bankrupt Alnwick District Council, but Barclay (2002) reports that Safeway's original claim for £4.6 million was reduced to a settlement of £2 million, which was paid by the council's insurers.

In 2006 Alnwick District Council issued planning permission, not contested by national government, for a Sainsbury's supermarket in a similar location to that of the proposed Safeway store. However, this time the agreement was coupled with a planning agreement (Section 106) with Sainsbury's ensuring the viability of a bus service to the site and providing up to £100,000 funding for projects to support the vitality and viability of the town centre (Vaggs 2006). Clearly there are strong local feelings on the subject, as well as a perceived need for a new supermarket. The data presented within this book suggests the new supermarket will 'claw back' trade to Alnwick, but may also have adverse effects on the town centre. Only in the longer term will the overall effect on the town emerge.

---

retailers of between 13 and 50 per cent. Associated impacts included a decline in the number of food retailers, an increase in vacant units and 'a noticeable deterioration in the built environment' (7). Impacts were not confined to the convenience sector but, reflecting the range of goods and services offered in larger supermarkets, could affect comparison and service outlets in the town centre. It was suggested that the more marginal retailers and centres are least able to resist these potential negative impacts. Where such developments are able to be sited within a market town's centre, the risk of such adverse impacts may be lower. Market towns, however, may not always have the necessary capacity to accommodate an in-town anchor store. For example, in a study of North Walsham (Norfolk, East of England), the Civic Trust (2000) found most retail units were small and not to meet the needs of national retailers. Indeed, a national electrical multiple moved out of the town because they were unable to display the range of stock they wanted. Supermarkets typically require very large sites and these are unlikely to be available in (often historic) market town centres.

An additional form of support for market towns' retail cores can come from their having the facilities to attract visitors. Visitor spending can support established local retail outlets or lead to new traders entering the market and extending the range of goods and services on offer in the town. Visitors may be attracted by a range of facilities nearby, such as historic buildings and other elements of 'heritage' within the town, or the distinctive nature of the shopping experience they offer.

Schiller (1994) suggests that this differentiation can be achieved where 'middle-class shoppers seem to prefer uncongested, attractive small towns to the hurly-burly of the big town high street and the soullessness of out-of-town shopping' (49). The New Economics Foundation (NEF) (2005) provides a further insight by considering the degree to which British settlements can be referred to as 'clone towns'. Clone towns are ones where 'the individuality of high street shops has been replaced by a monochrome strip of global and national chains' (10). The opposite is defined as a 'home town', which is 'a place that retains its individual character and is individually recognisable and distinctive to people who live there, as well as who visit' (15).

In NEF's methodology, the extent to which a settlement is labelled a 'clone town' depends upon the existence of independent shops, with a higher number of independent shops being associated with a lower likelihood of 'clone' characteristics emerging. From 103 towns investigated in Britain with between 5,000 and 150,000 population, 42 per cent were identified as clone towns, 34 per cent as home towns and 27 per cent as a mixture between the two. Of particular relevance to this chapter is the finding that places with higher populations are more likely to be classed as clone towns, and smaller towns, such as market towns, are more likely to be classed as home towns. The fact that there is great diversity between market towns may add to their attraction, with diversity being promoted by specialised goods such as local products or food, or developing a niche in a particular range of goods. Despite the importance of its research, the NEF (2005) did not consider the extent to which clone or home towns are preferred by shoppers. This is crucial because, if rural residents want well-known high street names when shopping, the different nature of shopping provided in market towns is going to be less likely to attract trade.

While the NEF (2005) points to a preponderance of independent traders as a potential advantage, it needs to be remembered that most independent traders are small enterprises and as such share the advantages and disadvantages common to all small businesses. Small businesses have been identified as driving improvements in innovation and productivity, but they are also seen as operating under a number of constraints, including a lack of skills generally and shortages of specific skills necessary for advancing technological and market penetration (SBS 2004). Rural small firms are typically smaller than urban SMEs and recently have been seen as losing their dynamism and lagging in the introduction of process technology and the use of the Internet. They have lower levels of internal resource to meet their development needs and they are less likely to have ready access to private or public sources of business support nearby to help remedy such internal weaknesses (Smallbone *et al.* 2002). Some of these weaknesses can be a disadvantage for a business when seeking to maintain a competitive position; a concentration of such disadvantaged businesses can compromise the competitiveness of a market town.

Interviews in our case study towns highlighted some issues related to locally-based small businesses. The lack of broader market awareness was seen to inhibit traders in developing a response to changing market contexts. In some cases, local shopkeepers were seen as lacking the dynamism necessary to help drive changes to capture and maintain market share. For example, they were seen as 'treading water' or 'seeing out their time', a problem that was compounded by a lack of succession planning.[1] Such traders can also have a dampening effect on local business institutions, which often play an important role in driving forward a transformation of a market town.

Achieving improvements will frequently require consensus and cooperation amongst retailers. Phillips and Swaffin-Smith (2004) suggest this may be difficult amongst a number of independent traders who may not be accustomed to working collectively. Indeed, Phillips and Swaffin-Smith (2004) also find that retailers were poorly represented within the MTI partnerships (see Chapter 4), making it more difficult for retailing initiatives to be implemented.

The fact that there is an absence of systematic understanding of the importance of visitors to the shopping economy of market towns has not discouraged the development of a range of marketing initiatives to attract visitors. These often rely on establishing a heritage and countryside-related image for the town, and highlighting key local attractions, including historic features, environmental quality and special attractions, such as the availability of local produce and farmers' markets.

However, success in developing an attractive range of shops and services for visitors does not necessarily benefit local residents. The higher returns that can be made by catering for the demands of visitors may result in shops selling basic convenience goods, where margins are traditionally low, switching to supplying gifts and other such items. So, for example, one of the strengths of Todmorden (a case study town) in contrast to nearby Hebden Bridge, which has a large number of visitors and shops catering for their needs, was stated by a resident to be that 'you can buy ordinary stuff here'. Indeed it is possible to find small towns where the impact of the development of tourism has been to drive out all basic services from the town.

Places to eat and an 'evening economy' are part of the attractions that visitors may well look for in a market town. Most towns will offer a variety of places to eat during the day, while the fact that an increasing number of pubs offer food means that few towns will have nowhere to eat in the evening. Some market towns have built a reputation as good places to eat, with Ludlow in Shropshire having developed a particular name as a place to go for top-quality restaurants, offering a choice of seven Michelin-listed restaurants. However, not everywhere can offer an evening economy to satisfy the needs or desires of visitors or residents. Some work by Hart and Strange (2000) found that the quality of the evening economy was a particular source of dissatisfaction among residents of three Yorkshire market towns.

A possible source of competitive advantage for market towns is to be found in the potential for independent traders to offer a more personal level of service as a means of attracting and retaining customers. Using social capital theory as a framework, Miller (2001) considered in detail the social environment in which rural retail is provided. When considering reciprocal relationships, Miller (2001) found that:

> rural consumers held expectations that local merchants would be fair and honest in their business dealing with community representatives (institutional reciprocity), and that, since the merchants usually knew their customers very well (interpersonal reciprocity), they would select products or services with the specific needs and wants of residents in mind (retail reciprocity)
>
> (Miller 2001: 487)

This 'embeddedness'[2] in terms of social and economic relationships was seen by Miller (2001) to be a competitive advantage for rural shops and was found to be statistically linked to in-shopping for home furnishing (small appliances, bedding, draperies etc.) and apparel (clothes, shoes and accessories). Creating a friendly and trusting environment where the customers are known by name to the shopkeepers, it is argued, is likely to lead to a loyal customer base, although the extent to which this is achieved within market towns will vary between towns and between retailers in those towns.

Developing a sense of affinity and loyalty for the market town has been central to customer loyalty card schemes, which echo those developed by large multiple retailers. Their success, however, has been questioned and their long-term effect is seen to be doubtful (Worthington 1998; Hallsworth and Worthington 2000). Similarly, Powe and Shaw (2004) found no such feelings of loyalty in Alnwick, with hinterland residents instead seeing their relationship with the town as purely instrumental. In contrast, village-level services were held dearly and seen to provide an added value in terms of an informal meeting place and to play an important role in community cohesion. There may not always be a strong relationship between feelings of loyalty or attachment and levels of spending: some work by Hart and Strange (2000) in Malton in Yorkshire suggested some distance between how much residents 'valued' a town and how much they actually used its facilities. However, if market towns are going to compete with larger urban areas, they need to provide an added value beyond a basic range of services, and the use of a variety of means to generate loyalty in their customer base is one weapon in their armoury.

Shopping environment

The environment that market towns offer is often seen as one of their key competitive strengths. As well as not having to suffer the disadvantages that can sometimes be associated with large urban areas, such as being very fast-paced and with risks of crime, they frequently offer calm and distinctive environments characterised by historic buildings, elements of 'local distinctiveness' in their street patterns and use of materials, and attractive countryside settings. Such features are key elements of marketing strategies, and their conservation and enhancement have emerged as components of Action Plans developed as part of work in the MTI. In many cases, towns invest in improvements for certain times of the year through schemes such as 'in bloom' and 'Christmas lights', as well as continually paying attention to the appearance of the shop fronts, displays, and sign posting and interpretation/information boards through the town. Adopting an approach followed in larger urban areas and having a town manager may be key to getting such important issues right[3] and reaping the benefits in increased trade.

The impact of public realm improvements was considered by Bromley et al. (2003), who found such improvements had provided limited success if implemented in isolation. For their case study town, environmental improvements led to disruption during implementation, general satisfaction as to the improvements in appearance, but limited effects on business, the most positive of which were localised to the immediate areas affected by the scheme. Bromley et al. (2003) do, however, identify a catalytic effect on private sector investment resulting from an increase in confidence and the potential for success that this implies.

Accessibility

The theoretical pattern of use of shopping and service facilities in market towns by residents of their hinterlands, that has underpinned several decades of planning policy, has been undermined by changes in mobility and has been shown by recent research to be unlikely to apply in practice (Shorten 2004). Indeed, Guy (1990) has shown increased car access to enable residents of small towns to out-shop more easily, and this is reflected in trends towards increased concentration of retail activity into large centres. The distance to large urban areas varies between market towns, and the quantitative results in Chapter 2 suggested that more remote towns (from both large urban areas and other towns) tended to be better serviced than 'commuter' towns located near large urban areas.

The link between 'out-working' and 'out-shopping', with commuters more likely to shop other than in their home market town, has been observed by empirical studies of rural residents (Pinkerton et al. 1995; Civic Trust 2000; Findlay et al. 2001; Courtney et al. 2006), but the different studies suggest different patterns of impact, with the work by the Civic Trust (2000) pointing to a link with all shopping categories, while others observed relationships with particular segments. Indeed, the results of our survey within Chapter 9 were also mixed, but on the whole suggested that where people worked made little different to where they shop. In summary the evidence suggests that more 'out-working' may lead to less trade for local shops, but how an individual sector would be affected remains unclear.

SERRL (2004) found that the 'functional attachment' to market towns was greater for their residents than those living in villages. Pinkerton et al. (1995) and the Civic Trust (2000) found that those living more centrally within settlements are more likely to shop locally. Hence, there is an expectation that town residents will create more trade per person than hinterland residents, and those living in the town centre may create more trade per person than those living on the outskirts of the town. However, this relationship is not universal or uniform between places and is likely to vary in terms of differences in the catchment populations and the nature of town centres.

Given the overwhelming importance of the car as a means of travel, the convenience, availability and cost of parking are important factors in determining the competitiveness of a market town. For Schiller (1994) the key issue for town centres is parking. Although market towns are usually located closer to rural residents than other shopping centres, out-of-town shopping elsewhere will tend to have ample and free parking that the market towns cannot always match. Where there is limited parking, a charge can be important in managing demand, but in a number of the case study towns, the cost of parking was seen as an annoyance and disincentive to visit the town, even though it was not expensive compared with larger urban centres.

The characteristics of the catchment population

The increased propensity to travel makes the definition of a market town catchment area and population problematic; the inclusion of a significant number of tourists and day visitors adds to the complexity. However, the characteristics of a 'catchment' population can influence the nature and level of patronage that a market town attracts. A number of factors have been considered, including age of residents, length of residence (for in-migrants) and incomes.

Relationships have been observed between age and shopping behaviour, and older people are sometimes found to be more likely to shop locally (Pinkerton *et al.* 1995) and less likely to visit the town in the evening (Richardson and Powe 2004; Powe and Shaw 2004). However, the pattern of findings is not uniform from all sources. Apart from Guy (1990), who found that length of residence affected the level of out-shopping for a range of comparison goods, little difference has been observed between shopping patterns of in-migrants and longer-term residents. Income data is rarely collected as part of surveys of market town residents, and official statistics of income levels are not available for small areas. Such survey data as has been collected (Pinkerton *et al.* 1995) did not show any significant relationship between income levels and out-shopping, but observation in the case study towns suggested some coincidence between low levels of pay and levels of vitality and vibrancy of the local retail core.[4]

For those limited in their mobility, there is likely to remain a dependence upon market town services, with lower service levels in hinterlands making transport links to market towns and/or outreach services essential. Rural bus services can be limited and demand is falling (Social Exclusion Unit 2003). Based on the results of Lovett *et al.* (2002; 2003), it is expected that those using the bus service to access market towns in the UK will only be located in larger villages and other towns. Indeed, Moseley (1996) found scheduled bus services to be largely irrelevant for the disadvantaged because of their infrequency and lack of door-to-door convenience. Investigating the accessibility of rural services for elderly and younger groups (both of which have lower levels of access to private cars), Williams and White (2001) found car sharing to be common, as a means of addressing problems of access to services. Generally speaking, the less mobile are likely to have lower levels of disposable income so market towns particularly reliant on the patronage of such groups may have a captive market but one that spends less.

Evidence from four market towns

Retail in the case study towns

Questionnaire surveys of town residents were undertaken in four towns, two of which are located close to large urban areas (Wymondham in Norfolk, East of England, located close

to Norwich; and Morpeth in Northumberland, North East England, located close to
Newcastle) and two located more remotely (Downham Market in Norfolk and Alnwick in
Northumberland). As described in Chapter 8, these towns also differ in terms of housing
growth and residential composition. They can also be characterised very differently in terms
of retail. Table 10.1 provides a profile of each town.

All of the case towns' historic centres originate from an agrarian past when the market
town was the commercial hub of its surrounding rural hinterland. However, the contemporary
importance of these historic linkages now varies between the towns but, in the case of

Table 10.1 Description of retail in surveyed towns

Morpeth	With a population of approximately 13,500, Morpeth is the largest of the towns considered. As such, it falls within the category 'medium-to-large town with good services' and, indeed, has the range of services you would expect in a town of its size. As well as a number of supermarkets located in the town's centre, range of national and regional chain stores as well as a number of independent stores (including a small department store (Plate 11)), a range of public houses and restaurants. The centrally located historic marketplace, bell tower and chantry, help provide an attractive location for shopping and tourism. In 2005 a survey revealed the convenience and comparison retail trade for shops in Morpeth town centre to be in decline (Powe 2005). However, a £30 million redevelopment of town centre shops and parking is currently underway that may regenerate the fortunes of the town's retail.
Wymondham	Wymondham is nearly as large as Morpeth, with a population of 11,000, and also labelled as a 'medium-to-large town with good services'. However, perhaps representing the size difference, the range of retail is not as great, with fewer national and regional chain stores. The attractive and historic town centre includes a market cross, abbey and provides a motivation for day visits from the nearby city of Norwich. In the absence of survey evidence, it is unclear how important the town's hinterland is to its custom. However, in terms of food shopping, there is a large supermarket on the edge of Norwich located not far from the town that is likely to attract much of the hinterland's trade.
Alnwick	Alnwick is a medium-sized market town (8,000), which was labelled as 'well serviced for its size' in Chapter 2. The town centre provides a reasonable range of services including a medium-sized supermarket, a few national and regional chain stores as well as a range of independent shops, pubs and restaurants. The town's more remote location has also helped maintain sufficient trade to support a cinema/theatre. The town also has a regionally notable second-hand book shop. Tourism and day visitors are important, with the town centre castle together with the recently developed water gardens being a key visitor magnet. Consequently, some of the retail provision is focused towards the recreational visitor. A town centre survey suggests that most trade comes from the town's residents and its hinterland (Powe and Shaw 2004).
Downham Market	The smallest of the towns considered, with approximately 7,000 residents, it was described in Chapter 2 as having 'below-average services'. Dominated by the nearby market town of King's Lynn, which provides a retail offer normally associated with a much larger town, Downham Market provides a very different independent-dominated retail offer in a compact area, which includes a medium-sized supermarket and a large independent furniture store (see Plate 12). There has been a recent environmental enhancement of the town, part of which has led to a relocation and renovation of the market (see Plate 14). A notable characteristic of the town, identified within Chapter 2, is the high proportion of population which is retired.

Alnwick, a survey by Powe and Shaw (2004) has shown them to be still important. Although there is a presence of multiple chain stores, these are relatively few, and the dominant form of retailer is the independent trader.

Survey results

The surveys revealed that the town centres are popular for main and top-up food shopping. Between 61 per cent and 74 per cent of those questioned in three of the towns identified the town centre as the location for their main food shopping. The exception was Wymondham, where nearly half did their main food shopping in the nearby city of Norwich, where there is a large supermarket on the edge near to Wymondham. However, the other towns also experienced some leakage (around 20 per cent) to nearby cities and towns.

Only a small percentage of residents (around 10 per cent) actually buy their clothes[5] or most of their non-food shopping in the market towns. The key reason for shopping locally was proximity to home.[6] Cities and other large urban areas account for most of the clothes shopping and non-food expenditure. The main reason for not shopping in the market towns themselves was given as a lack of choice of goods. However, a reasonable proportion of town residents (around half) do still shop locally for non-food products at least once a week. This suggests potential in that, if people are still visiting the town centres as least for 'odds and ends', they could potentially be encouraged to buy more, if the right inducement could be found. This will depend on what residents like about shopping in their market town centres and what is needed to encourage them to shop there more often.

Table 10.2 summarises what respondents said they liked about their towns. The most important feature was its closeness and convenience as a place to shop. An average of 25 per cent of people noted that the towns were friendly in terms of both the shopkeepers and people in the town. More specifically, comments related to 'meeting people you know' or the shopkeepers 'knowing you by name' or the personal service they provide. Also important are the specialist/independent shops (average of 18 per cent). The compact nature of the towns was also seen as attractive (average of 11 per cent), as an aid to elderly shoppers but generally in giving a simplified shopping experience. The traditional/historical nature of the towns was also important for some (average of 4 per cent). Others (average of 13 per cent) were satisfied with the variety/choice in the town centres, providing all their 'everyday' requirements.

Table 10.3 provides a summary of the improvements that respondents would like to see in the towns. Two main issues (in bold in the table), 'better services/wider variety of services' and 'parking' were identified. A need for more clothes shops and better supermarkets was

Table 10.2 What do residents like about shopping in the towns? (%)

Topic	Morpeth	Alnwick	Wymond-ham	Downham Market	Average
Close/convenient/handy	36	38	44	46	41
Friendly (shops and people)	16	33	24	27	25
Specialist/independent shops	22	22	15	12	18
Choice/variety	17	8	20	6	13
Compact/small town	9	12	8	13	11
Market town/tradition/history	4	3	7	3	4
Sample (those making a positive comment)	184 (57% of sample)	111 (52% of sample)	207 (80% of sample)	158 (68% of sample)	660 (64% of sample)

Note: Figures are for percentage responding to the questions, with more than one response per respondent allowed.

Table 10.3 How to encourage customers to visit the town centres more often (%)

Topic	Morpeth	Alnwick	Wymond-ham	Downham Market	Average
Better services/wider variety of services	55	74	65	79	68
Need more clothes shops	13	12	16	22	16
High street/chain stores/multiples	6	7	4	15	8
More independent shops	4	1	6	1	3
Better supermarkets	6	36	10	2	14
Places to eat and drink	3	2	5	7	4
Parking	45	25	20	16	27
Parking charges	37	6	11	14	17
More parking spaces	7	12	12	0	8
Fewer charity shops	15	6	10	6	9
Opening hours	1	1	2	0	1
Pedestrian access	2	2	3	1	2
Sample (those responding)	269 (83% of sample)	179 (84% of sample)	141 (54% of sample)	177 (76% of sample)	766 (74% of sample)

Note: Figures are for percentage responding to the questions, with more than one response per respondent allowed.

also noted. There were generally few national chain clothes stores, if any, located in the town centres and often no shops for particular age groups. Parking was an emotive issue accounting for an average of 27 per cent of responses. The problems varied between towns but the key issues related to parking charges and a lack of spaces, sometimes of particular types, such as short stay or disabled.

Visiting the town centre in the evening was popular, with an average of 55 per cent of the respondents having visited the town in the evening in the month prior to being interviewed. Table 10.4 provides a more detailed picture. Among a wide range of activities, the most popular were eating out, visiting public houses and bars, purchasing takeaway food and visiting the sports centre/gym. In the case of Alnwick, the only town with a permanent cinema/theatre (Plate 15), up to 40 per cent of residents visiting in the evening had visited the establishment in the month prior to the survey and it was popular with all age groups, and this may lead to wider benefits for the town centre from people using other facilities on their visits.

Table 10.4 Residents visiting the town centre in the month prior to interview (%)

Age Group	Morpeth	Alnwick	Wymondham	Downham Market	Average
18–24	89	75	86	50	75
25–34	89	56	64	56	66
35–44	65	69	53	63	62
45–54	73	76	53	58	65
55–64	46	58	46	56	51
65–74	20	55	26	28	32
75+	10	29	37	41	29
Sample	325	213	260	234	1032

Table 10.5 How to encourage residents to visit towns more in the evening (%)

Topic	Morpeth	Alnwick	Wymondham	Downham Market	Average
More choice	58	64	77	85	71
Restaurants	19	25	21	16	20
Cinema/better cinema	20	9	20	27	19
Intimidation	34	21	25	20	25
Rowdy/drunkenness	20	17	16	9	16
Increase police presence	7	4	7	7	6
Sample (those responding)	162 (50% of sample)	95 (44% of sample)	120 (46% of sample)	138 (59% of sample)	515 (50% of sample)

Note: Figures are for percentage responding to the questions, with more than one response per respondent allowed.

Table 10.5 highlights two key issues affecting people's willingness to make more frequent visits to the towns in the evening: a desire for more choice in terms of evening entertainments (average of 71 per cent); and a feeling of intimidation when visiting the town centre (average of 34 per cent). Of the specific types of evening entertainment that people would like, a cinema and a better selection of restaurants were by far the most commonly mentioned. Feelings of intimidation were equally common across age groups and whether the resident had recently visited the town or not.

Potential of attracting urban visitors

Having considered the 'core' town and hinterland trade, the potential for attracting visitors will now be explored through a survey of residents in the Tyneside conurbation. Although only a small proportion (roughly 5 per cent) of visitors to the Northumberland case studies came from Tyneside, their views on the qualities of market towns can act as proxies for the views of the wider potential customer and visitor base in urban areas that market towns seek to reach.

Newcastle and North Tyneside is a large urban area, with a population of around half a million. There are fourteen 'market towns' in the North East that are potential visitor destinations for urban residents from the North Tyne part of this conurbation: Alnwick; Amble; Barnard Castle; Berwick-upon-Tweed; Bishop Auckland; Corbridge; Crook; Haltwhistle; Hexham; Morpeth; Prudhoe; Rothbury; Stanhope and Wooler. The analysis in Chapter 2 categorised most of these towns as acting as visitor attractions. Generally the affluence of North East towns is below that of the English average for market towns. Views of residents were explored through two focus groups and a separate questionnaire survey.

Perceptions of market towns

Through the questionnaire survey, residents' ideas about what constituted a 'market town' were explored. Respondents were initially asked to choose from the list of country towns in the North East their top three in terms of what they consider to be the most typical market towns. Table 10.6 presents the results in order of popularity. From this list, clearly Hexham.[7] Alnwick and Morpeth have the strongest image, with Corbridge, Berwick-upon-Tweed and Rothbury also popular. These are all small rural towns, with historical rural hinterland linkages.

Most respondents had clear ideas about the meaning of the term 'market town'. Only 11 failed to give a meaning and a further six did not add to the dictionary definition.

Table 10.6 Choice of most typical and popular market towns

Town	First choice (%)	Chosen in top three (%)	Visiting (%)	Average no. visits (last 12 months)
Hexham	39	71	69	3.6
Alnwick	20	67	72	3.2
Morpeth	11	43	66	3.3
Corbridge	8	26	56	2.9
Berwick-upon-Tweed	7	18	31	2.4
Rothbury	6	26	40	2.3
Barnard Castle	3	12	30	1.6
Amble	2	6	38	2.8
Bishop Auckland	1	2	10	1.8
Wooler	1	9	22	2.1
Haltwhistle	1	4	18	1.3
Prudhoe	0	0	14	1.5
Stanhope	0	0	11	1.2
Crook	0	0	6	1.6
Sample	148	148	148	–

Widely-held ideas about market towns included: their historical character (32 per cent); their size (31 per cent); their rural location (29 per cent) and their role as rural service centres (20 per cent). Smaller numbers highlighted their linkages with agriculture (7 per cent) and the availability of local produce (9 per cent). The 'different from the city' nature of the shops was also noted by a number (15 per cent) of the respondents, coincident with the idea that the shops tend not to belong to a chain and be in some way 'specialist'. There were few negative comments about market towns with the main ones related to parking problems (mostly difficulties finding a space) (37 per cent), congestion in the towns (27 per cent), and a recent increase in chain stores, charity shops and limited opening hours (19 per cent).

Table 10.6 also shows the popularity of the country towns in terms of the percentage visiting in the last 12 months and the average number of visits made within that period. It is interesting to note that the top three typical 'market towns' are also the top three in terms of popularity, with Corbridge also proving popular (56 per cent) (see below for a description of Corbridge).

The methods used by respondents to find out about towns to visit and activities available varied, but the key methods were friends and family (41 per cent), the Internet (35 per cent), library/tourist information/tourist leaflets (21 per cent) and the local newspaper (21 per cent). The level of use of the Internet points to the importance of a town having an attractive and up-to-date website.

Why do people visit market towns?

The focus groups and the questionnaire results showed that there were two purposes for visiting market towns: as part of a day out in the country or as the main purpose of their outing, spending the whole day at the town. 45 per cent of questionnaire respondents saw visiting the towns as the main purpose of their day out. This suggests market towns can be seen as self-contained visitor attractions in their own right, and need to have sufficient activities to maintain the interest of visitors for the whole day.

The focus group discussions allowed these motivations to be explored in a little more detail. The 'different from the city' factor was a key attractant. Prosperity and safety are part of this, but also character in terms of history, pace of life and tranquillity, and the opportunity to buy or eat local food. This 'difference' was particularly noted for shopping, where participants suggested that they would buy the 'things that you just can't get in the city' or at least 'not the general run of the mill shopping'. By way of an illustration one participant said: 'I can go to Leeds, I can go to Manchester and it is the same shops. So why should I go there. I would rather go to these smaller places and stop and look at individual shops.' Shopping was seen as likely to be more expensive in market towns, so the shopping is not for bargains but instead for 'originality', 'authenticity' and 'quality'.

For those who were visiting the town as part of a day out, the location near the Northumberland National Park or the Northumberland Heritage Coast was significant, but this does not make its attractions insignificant. So, one participant stated: 'I might visit the town for a walk, so I wouldn't go there to shop particularly but whilst we are there we might do a bit of shopping. I really like market towns but I find them a bit boring if I stay too long.' Not everyone visiting the towns for a whole day goes just to shop, as exemplified by an older participant in a focus group: 'quite a few of them [market towns] are nicely preserved and have nice parks. I've got grandchildren so we go somewhere like Morpeth and we can go to the park and things like that can be a multi-attraction. You can go off and do some shopping and have something for the kids.'

What do visitors to market towns do?

The evidence in Table 10.7 suggests that the most common activity by urban residents in country towns is to purchase snacks/refreshments/meals and visiting gardens or historic buildings. A significant number also visited farmers' markets in the towns and the purchase of food – particularly local produce – was important. Overall there was a tendency towards purchasing convenience products (75 per cent) compared to comparison goods (59 per cent), with the comparison products noted tending to be small. However, the pattern of purchases underlined 'difference' as an important factor in the competitive position of the towns in capturing retail trade.

Table 10.7 Facilities visited in country towns

	% visiting in a country town	Which towns? (% of those using the facility)
Teashop or café	70	Alnwick (35), Hexham (35), Corbridge (33)
Public house	68	Corbridge (36), Hexham (31), Morpeth (26)
Garden or park	66	Alnwick (69), Morpeth (24), Hexham (14)
A meal in a restaurant	63	Hexham (29), Alnwick (27), Corbridge (27)
Castle or other historic building	60	Alnwick (65), Hexham (17), Barnard Castle (15)
Craft/art shops	51	Corbridge (36), Alnwick (29), Hexham (28)
Specialist food shop	50	Corbridge (43), Morpeth (26), Hexham (21)
Book shop	44	Alnwick (65), Hexham (32), Morpeth (25)
Clothes shops	41	Hexham (44), Alnwick (30), Morpeth (30)
Spent the evening	40	Corbridge (25), Alnwick (24), Hexham (22)
Regular market	37	Hexham (39), Alnwick (24), Morpeth (19)
Farmers' market	30	Hexham (45), Alnwick (18), Morpeth (14)
Antique shops	29	Hexham (40), Corbridge (20), Rothbury (20)
Museum	28	Barnard Castle (48), Alnwick (14), Hexham (12)
Festival or fair	25	Alnwick (49), Hexham (22)
Garden centre	25	Morpeth (45), Hexham (19), Alnwick (16)

The activities listed in Table 10.7 were largely undertaken in the top four towns identified in Table 10.6, with Corbridge performing particularly strongly. Corbridge has been very successfully developing a niche in quality boutique shops, food shops, coffee shops and restaurants, where some nineteenth-century decorated shop fronts still survive, emphasising 'difference'. Corbridge, with a population approximately 3,000, and located in close proximity to the larger town of Hexham, would appear to have been successful in establishing a distinct identity and function. In contrast, the larger town of Morpeth (population 13,500) appears as something of an underachiever in attracting visitors, with the majority of its trade coming from residents of the town and its hinterland. Its efforts to improve its competitive position underline a number of issues that emerged from the literature.

In response to current difficulties in Morpeth, major redevelopment work of the central marketplace took place in 2003 and is soon to be used again as a location for an improved market. This should be an important attraction for leisure shoppers and, more generally, enhance the identity and 'traditional' appeal of the town. However, the disruption caused by this development has affected trade and the more functional shopper using their rural service centre. More recent efforts have focused on this 'core' business, with a parking scheme being introduced offering free parking for residents of the borough council at non-peak times. A £30 million scheme to regenerate the town centre has been granted planning permission, which will radically change an existing shopping arcade as well as providing new retail units, extending an existing medium-sized shopping area, create more spaces and change the parking in the town as well as the bus interchange. This scheme is likely to provide extra high street multiple retailers in the town, which reflects the desires of its residents. However, in order to maintain the interest of the leisure shopper it will be important that the traditional feel of the town is not lost and the independent/specialist shops remain. The balancing of the needs and wishes of visitors and the local catchment area will be important in determining the future of the town.

Conclusion

This chapter has considered the competitive position of market towns, with regard to their role as rural service centres as well as leisure shopping locations. Surveys of residents have been conducted in four market towns, two of which are located close to larger urban areas and two more remotely located. The results have demonstrated a sizeable leakage of retail expenditure out of the towns, particularly in terms of comparison goods, with large urban areas being the main beneficiaries. Consideration of the night economy has demonstrated its importance to all age groups, with eating out and visiting pubs being the most popular activities. This research is complemented by an urban survey, in the North East of England, which considered the behaviour and attitudes of urban residents to market towns. Attracted by their 'difference from the city', the term 'market town' was found to have a clear and positive meaning that is of relevance to the marketing of these towns.

There would appear to be two types of customer: those hoping to do their main shopping in the market town and those looking for something 'different from the city'. Clearly there are some overlaps between these groups. However, they beg the question as to what extent the town's identity is generated from it being a rural service centre or a leisure shopping location. For those wishing to continue doing their main comparison-shopping in larger urban areas, they probably see town centres in terms of a place for the occasional leisure shopping experience, where they do something different from the norm. For those hoping to do more shopping in the town centres they may be encouraged by its natural advantages in terms of its location, but also the friendly nature of the town (shops and people) and its compact/small size. For such residents, there is a desire for greater choice and variety within the shops, particularly high street chain stores. In the case of the occasional leisure shopper, it is the specialist/independent shops that are appealing and, indeed, their tastes are unlikely to be much different from those living in larger urban areas. This dichotomy was also observed when respondents were asked what could be improved to encourage them to shop more in the town. The results strongly suggest that the desire for more clothes shops, high street/chain stores/multiples and bigger and better supermarkets was stronger than the need for more independent shops. As such, these are the needs of the 'core' shoppers. Leisure shoppers remain a minority but important group and any changes to appease the 'core' shoppers should not detract from the overall appeal of the town providing a shopping experience that is different from the city.

In terms of the evening economy, market town centres were found to be important locations to most residents and, as with their rural service centre role, the issue most commonly noted was a need for a wider range and quality of entertainment/establishments. The range and quality is likely to be better in larger urban areas, but as with shopping, market town centres have the natural advantage of location as well as hopefully providing different and friendlier forms of entertainment. Given the concerns raised in terms of feelings of intimidation, this may not always be the case.

Increased in-migration, commuting, consumer expectations, ageing populations and pressures to reap economies of scale are likely to continue into the future. Although some role for non-food retail is likely to remain, due to the frequency of purchase, the physical distance is likely to be more of a deterrent for food shopping and evening entertainments. Through good location of supermarkets there may be potential for linked trips. The range of comparison goods in market towns is inevitably going to be less than in shopping centres within larger urban areas. However, there is potential for attracting the leisure shopper and, for key retail sectors, the friendly and more personal service that can be provided within independent shops may also attract loyal custom. Providing a 'difference from the city' and maintaining convenience is likely to provide a future for market town centres.

Success in any of these missions requires creative responses from traders and towns alike. Whether they have the resource to create and implement such a response will determine their futures.

Notes

1. Harding (2004) identified rural entrepreneurs as being older than their urban counterparts.
2. See Granovetter (1985) for a discussion of embeddedness.
3. See Paddison (2003) for an example of how a town centre manager successfully helped the regeneration of a Scottish market town.
4. Comparison of wage rates offered in local employment bureaux, employment structures and associated income levels, range/type of local retail outlets.
5. Clothes shops were singled out for consideration as they are non-food products that everyone buys.
6. This question was not asked within the earlier Morpeth survey.
7. Alnwick and Morpeth have been previously described in detail. Hexham (see also Chapter 6), with a population of approximately 11,000, is situated in the Tyne Valley. It is a gateway to the Northumberland National Park. It lies in the Newcastle-to-Carlisle corridor (two cities in the North of England) carrying both road and a passenger/freight railway. Tourism plays a central role in the life of the town, capitalising on the area's Roman heritage and abbey, which dates back to 647 AD.

Part 3

What prospects for market towns?

The third and final part to this book asks the question: what are the prospects for market towns? Part 3 effectively provides the discussion and conclusion for the book, but is separated into two chapters. Drawing from 11 case study towns, Chapter 11 considers the challenges facing the towns; strategies adopted to improve the towns; developments occurring within the towns and their experiences with the MTI. In terms of these findings, Chapter 11 also considers their prospects for the future.

Reflecting on the wide-ranging coverage of this book, Chapter 12 describes the characteristics of market towns and the challenges they face. In the light of these findings a vision is then set out and how this vision can be better implemented is then considered. The chapter and book ends with some speculation in terms of the likely future for market towns.

Chapter 11

Drivers for change in the case study towns

Trevor Hart and Neil Powe

Introduction

As part of the research for this book 11 towns have been visited, where discussions were held with key actors (e.g. town clerk, town manager, planners, local organisations etc.) and the relevant policy material has been reviewed. The towns were selected as examples of the five functional roles of towns identified in Chapter 2, as well as attempting to cover a range of locations and contexts; the towns are profiled in Chapter 3. This chapter considers these case study towns in terms of: the strategies adopted to improve the towns; the developments occurring within the towns; and their experiences with the MTI. The results provide confirmation for the more general analysis provided in Chapters 2 and 3, and provide an opportunity to consider factors affecting the likely future for these towns and for market towns generally.

Town improvement strategies

Key actors in most of the towns had some sense of vision for their future. The vision for Wymondham, for example, was 'a forward looking market town with a strong sense of its own history, seeking sustainable growth for the future' (Sawyer 2003: 1). This was then broken down into key issues that the town's partnership hoped to address, with a focus on both residents and visitors. In the case of Keswick, the vision was along similar lines, also with a particular need for change not to adversely affect the town's character. The vision may also relate to the application of current initiatives. For example, in Richmond a number of efforts have focused on realising the benefits of the town's many heritage assets.

In some towns, however, determining a vision was difficult as they faced an uncertain future, with no clearly obvious strength on which to focus a strategy. Although the role of visitor attraction is important to a number of towns it is not a panacea. For example, although both the towns of Todmorden and Crediton feel they have some potential, they are not really 'on the way' to any major attractions and they do not have a profile as a major attraction in their own right. The lack of a master plan for town regeneration, particularly when there are no realistically achievable projects headlined, inhibits development of broad commitment to regeneration. For example, in Todmorden, the town square was thought to be crying out for some form of plan to guide effort, but such guidance is partial and focused on other spaces. Other missed opportunities were also identified within the towns, partly as a result of difficulties in finalising planning and implementation strategies. An exception is Keswick, which commissioned the production of a master plan document, which can help ensure that the vision is consistently delivered throughout the town.

But, for most places, a central part of the town strategies is attracting visitors, whether town and hinterland residents, day-trippers or holiday makers and parking is a key issue affecting visitors to most towns. For example, parking charges have been recently increased in a number of the towns. Although the charges are not high compared with those often charged within large urban areas, they are more expensive than out-of-town locations, which often provide free parking. The increases in charges observed were sometimes seen to be sufficient to encourage potential visitors to go elsewhere. In a number of towns frictions were observed between the traders' wish for free and adequate parking, and district councils' seeing parking as a source of revenue. While this might possibly be an aid to funding improvements in the town there were thoughts that the levels of charges may be driven by a desire to balance costs between market towns and larger urban areas within the same local authority boundary.

The commuter town of Wymondham provides an unusual case, where parking had been free, but the town centre car parks had been used as if they were 'park-and-ride' sites, with car sharing from Wymondham car parks reducing the cost of parking within Norwich. This meant the spaces were occupied throughout the day. The simultaneous introduction of a parking charge and an actual park-and-ride facility on the outskirts of Norwich was seen to free up spaces for genuine shoppers. The use of short-term car parking close to the shops is, however, generally regarded as good practice, avoiding the all-day use of those working in the towns.

A different example is provided by Keswick, where outline plans exist for underground car parking in the town. As space is severely restricted in the town centre, this is felt to provide a viable but expensive alternative, replicating a model that is common in continental Europe (Keswick Area Partnership Ltd. 2006). Being a tourist town, the large car parks are considered to be 'bleak and empty places' in the winter months, and underground parking enables space to be more productively and attractively used (Keswick Area Partnership Ltd. 2006: 106). However, concerns with flooding in the town may scupper these plans.

A key factor attracting people to the towns is the quality of the public realm. Indeed, this issue would seem to have had attention in all the case study towns. Consistent with the findings of Bromley *et al.* (2003), there was a general perception that improvements to the public realm add to confidence in the town and increase private investment. In Richmond, for example, improving the public realm was central to the vision for realising the benefits of the town's many heritage assets, with lighting being used to improve the visibility of buildings; bins and signage developed in a consistent style, avoiding clutter; and property improvement grants being made available to reinstate traditional painted shop frontages (see Plate 13).

A common problem was getting the many businesses, perhaps too focused on their own enterprise, to act together to improve the shopping environment.[1] In Keswick a unique form of cooperation – a Business Improvement District – has been set up, which should ensure better collaboration between town centre businesses, and is likely to lead to an increase in funding available for schemes to improve the area (see Box 11.1). Another example is provided by Haslemere, where the high street in the town is dominated (perhaps with the exception of a very discrete Woolworths) by a range of family-owned, up-market shops selling high-quality goods, often expensive. These shops have come under pressure in recent years from competitors within the sub-region. One of the contributions the Haslemere MTI has made recently is that of working with local shopkeepers on a customer loyalty scheme. 'Haslemere Rewards' uses a card incorporating chip technology. This system allows up to 48 separate companies to operate their own rewards and discounts through the chip, with the option of donating rewards to a local school. Customers have to buy the card, as it was felt that they would then value the card scheme. The Haslemere MTI

Box 11.1 Keswick's Business Improvement District

In the absence of a chamber of commerce in Keswick, it was felt that something was needed to improve the 'offer' of the town as a visitor attraction. In order to raise more funding than would normally be achieved through a chamber of commerce, Keswick Area Partnership has helped set up England's first rural Business Improvement District (BID). Like a chamber of commerce, the scheme acts within a defined area and has the aim of improving the trading environment. However, once in the BID there would be compulsory payment through business rates (1 per cent is proposed), which would fund schemes to be decided upon through the voting of members. This compulsory nature of contributions is expected to raise more funds and ensure greater participation of its members.

The scheme is in its first year, and although initial signs are good, it is too early to judge its success. It will clearly be interesting to follow how successful the scheme is in achieving its objectives. The scheme has initially been set up for a five year period, with funding divided equally between the Keswick Area Partnership and businesses for the first 2 years, and then it will become self-financing for the remainder of the project.

---

received an award for this scheme in the 2006 Action for Market Towns Awards and has been successful in encouraging firms to work together. Fiercely independent, many local traders had to be encouraged to sign up to a more collective approach in some of the initiatives. Clearly, the loyalty card scheme would not have worked without their commitment.

The use of events leaflets was a common means of trying to attract town and hinterland residents. These were sometimes delivered or made available at a number of information points within the towns, with a wide variety of events publicised. Cultural attractions have proved to be particularly important, with theatres perhaps the most popular in appeal. The Playhouse in Alnwick (Plate 15), which doubles as both a cinema and theatre, was discussed in Chapter 10. Richmond and Keswick provide two further examples. Richmond has an original Georgian theatre in the centre of the town, which has been restored and developed. As well as providing an important tourist attraction, the theatre has proved to be popular amongst town and hinterland residents, and is an iconic element in the presentation of the town's Georgian heritage. Following a long-drawn-out process to gain planning permission, an impressive 'Theatre by the Lake' has been built, located on the edge of Keswick and Derwent Water (Plate 16). Like the theatre in Richmond, this has proved to be both a commercial success and created a great deal of local pride, attracting visitors from throughout the county of Cumbria.

In Chapters 9 and 10, proximity to the countryside was seen to be important for those living in and visiting market towns. Some towns have tried to capitalise on this link. For example, Wymondham and Morpeth have both tried to encourage visitors to the towns through publicising improvements to the fabric and facilities, and through highlighting the potential for countryside walks by production of guided walk leaflets. In this way the towns can be simultaneously marketed as both a visit to the countryside and a visit to the town.

Other examples can be found of towns adopting a multi-faceted approach to marketing. Ghost and historic pub walks in Richmond capitalise on the history of the town and events that have taken place. In Alnwick, the problem is not attracting visitors but rather ensuring that visitors visit the town centre in addition to the headline attractions associated with

Alnwick Castle, which are on the edge of town. A 'road train' has been set up, which runs through town to link different facilities (between the Alnwick Gardens and Castle). However, this scheme has not yet proved to be as successful as planned.

Food festivals were found in a number of towns. These aided in marketing the towns through emphasising their linkages with hinterlands and countryside, often through references to local produce. Chapter 10 pointed out how such linkages are seen to be important by urban visitors. For example, Haslemere Food Festival was organised in autumn 2006 by a team assembled by the MTI coordinator, and was the third event to highlight 'all that is good' about the town. The first of these was held in 2005 and featured the town's history and literary associations for which it won the Action for Market Towns Best Regional Project Award. The Food Festival provided opportunities for local businesses and local farmers to make statements about the quality of their produce and the way in which it feeds into the local businesses. Reflecting the growing interest in organic produce, the Festival provided an excellent opportunity for local producers to introduce local people and visitors to an interesting product range.

Developments within the towns

Problems and issues in developing housing and employment in the towns have been reviewed in earlier chapters, highlighting the range of inter-related factors to be addressed and the constraints and limitations to be faced in so doing, so here the focus is on other types of development – retail development and community uses.

Retail development

Shopping is seen as the central feature of a market town and, in all MTI programmes and the case study towns, improving or maintaining the retail offer was the major focus of attention. Shops are felt to give purpose and vitality to the town, and are an essential element in fulfilling the role of a service hub. Developing or maintaining competitiveness involves many elements, as the review in Chapter 10 demonstrated, but in many of the towns a key element was seen to be the ability to offer supermarket shopping of a standard that could compete with nearby urban centres or their edge-of-town retail parks. However, a supermarket in a market town can be something of a two-edged sword in that, rather than retain trade in the town, it can also attract trade away from local shops, and, as the range of goods sold by supermarkets increases, so does the range of local shops that are vulnerable to its competitive pressure. The issue is usually thrown into relief by the fact that the only sites in a market town that can accommodate the size of store and associated parking are on the edge of the town and not always well connected to the rest of the retail core.[2]

The location of supermarkets is an area of much debate in the literature. This is particularly the case in Alnwick, where results in Chapter 10 illustrate the residents' aspirations for competition for the existing supermarkets and the need for a larger supermarket within the town. However, in the absence of an available location within the town centre there has been much debate over the balancing of 'clawed back' trade from larger urban areas and the potential effects on trade for businesses located within the historic town centre. Box 10.1 provides details of the outcome, and the resultant effect on the town centre will be the subject of future research. In the case of Todmorden, an edge-of-town supermarket is viewed favourably as to be clawing back more trade than affecting the town centre. As Box 11.2 suggests, town centre retail has a different form than often observed within market towns, which can be viewed as a reason for its success.

Improving the public realm

Another form of development commonly occurring within towns is improvement to the fabric of the town centre. Such schemes range from small-scale 'cosmetic' improvements

---

Box 11.2 Todmorden Market

In the centre of Todmorden is a retail market that has been expanded under the MTI (Plate 17). The traditional indoor market has been supplemented by the development of a group of outside market stalls, built at a cost of £600,000. The market is felt to act like an 'anchor store' for the retail core of the town, and on the Saturday that it was visited it seemed quite busy if not thronging. The market draws people into the town from surrounding urban areas (Rochdale, Oldham). These visitors are not 'tourists' such as are attracted to nearby Hebden Bridge, but more people varying their shopping pattern and coming to some of the specialist stalls. It is nominally open seven days a week (which is unique for the area), but not all stalls function on all days and the outdoor extension opens only Wednesday to Sunday. A flea market on a Thursday is popular and attracts extra trade.

Shoppers explained that the market can cater for almost all their needs and that there was a good range of shops in the market as whole. A balanced selection of traders seemed to bear this out with the added attraction of a number of stalls selling specialist items or locally produced meats and cheeses.

The market is owned by Calderdale Council, which gathers rent from the operation. Even though a large amount has been spent on the market extension, work is felt to be needed to the old market hall. Its design, with a high glass roof, means that it is very hot at any time of the year when the sun shines, so air conditioning is felt to be necessary by the market traders. The gas heating system is also felt to be in need of renewal as extreme cold in some parts of the hall affects stock and makes retention and recruitment of staff difficult.

There are two supermarkets on the edges of town that are felt to be an advantage rather than a drain on trade from local independent retailers – they stop people going further afield to shop and they therefore use local traders and services on their visit – a largish Morrisons adapted from an established Safeway store on the west of the town and a recent Lidl on the east. Competing supermarkets are a distance away in other settlements so, together with the choice available in the market, these stores add a dimension to the town that helps it maintain a competitive range of retail provision.

---

to much larger-scale redevelopments of significant sites, but at any scale schemes may lead to improved confidence and additional private investment. The towns of Morpeth, Crediton and Downham Market provide examples of significant expenditure on town centre improvement.

Morpeth was discussed in Chapter 10, with the substantial redevelopment causing disruption at a difficult time for the town centre's retail provision, but the longer-term benefits should be positive as the improved marketplace is an important attraction for leisure shoppers and, more generally, enhances the identity and 'traditional' appeal of the town. A Marks & Spencer 'Simply Food' outlet has recently taken a key site near the marketplace and a future development is planned on the nearby Sanderson Arcade as part of a £30 million scheme to regenerate the town centre (Plate 18).

Primarily funded by Mid Devon District Council and the South West Regional Development Agency, Crediton has seen an improvement to the town square costing somewhere in the region of £2.6 million (Plate 19).[3] This scheme was seen as providing an improved venue for farmers' markets, open air theatre and concerts, and as a catalyst to bring in both businesses and tourists. It also adds significantly to the visual appeal of the town square. At present, however, it seems to be something of an underused space when the monthly farmers' market or other cultural events are not taking place. It also seems to lack proper integration with the surrounding buildings. However, with time, usage may increase and, with a further scheme improving the high street, there is hope that this will contribute to improving the town's fortunes. It is seen as providing an additional cachet for the town and features prominently on the Mid Devon District Council's website.

In 1998 the Downham Market Regeneration Partnership commissioned the Civic Trust Regeneration Unit to prepare a regeneration strategy for Downham Market. The study found that the 'town, and in particular the town centre, was not robust. But there is the basis of a strong commercial centre sufficient to warrant measures to ensure its viability' (Local Area Framework 2005: 26). This has led to a number of town centre enhancements relating to: traffic calming; improvements to the street scene (see Plate 14); conservation of historic features (see again Plate 14); the improvement and upgrading of business premises; and the provision of interpretation/visitor signage and public art features. Innovative use has been made of stainless steel, copper and stone, with local schools being involved within the design of carvings made (see stone blocks on the left-hand side of Plate 14). Table 8.3 (Chapter 8) notes that 19 per cent of residents in the town survey mentioned regeneration as a key change occurring within the town. Responses were mixed but a sizeable majority were in favour of the works undertaken, noting particularly that the scheme had modernised the town without losing its traditional features. As was the case in Morpeth, the scheme created much disruption and, reflecting this, a local trader brought out a 'Downham Market Regeneration Blues 2004' calendar with photos illustrating the effects on the town. Although the regeneration impact was seen as positive, concerns were raised at the time of construction as to whether the loss of trade would lead to business closure and whether trade would return.

Community developments

Community facilities are part of the glue that binds a town together, and improvement to community facilities frequently features as part of the menu of activities in a town's 'action plans'. A number of the case study towns provided examples of initiatives to improve the provision of community facilities. For example, Todmorden was about to build a new health centre and had promoted, through a community partnership, the development of a new cricket pavilion that was widely used as a recreational resource. In addition, a range of community spaces and uses were being developed alongside the Rochdale Canal, which passes through the town (Plate 20).

Some community facilities aim to meet the needs of particular groups, and in a number of cases there was an emphasis on projects serving the needs of the towns' youth communities. The Minehead EYE project provides an interesting example of such a facility. There had been a long-standing desire for a skate park and this had been under consideration by the district council. The idea was developed through the Market and Coastal Towns Initiative (MCTI) and, although the MCTI has ended, the Youth Working Group has continued to campaign for youth provision to be developed in the town. Its work included the collection of over 800 user surveys and a 1,000-signature petition, and the young people involved in the project held a skate-demonstration day on the seafront in Minehead to show the need for a youth facility. This led to West Somerset District Council agreeing in principle to allocate land for the scheme, and a site was identified in October 2006. The planning of the scheme is likely to extend into 2007 (May 2006) but when it is complete it will meet identified local needs and include sport and leisure, media, music and arts facilities. This project illustrates what can be achieved when there is a strong local will but sadly also shows that persistence is required to make progress.

A less ambitious, though still successful project is the Youth Café in Oswestry. As with the proposed facilities in Minehead, the Youth Café was also identified as part of the action plan for the town. The Youth Café provides a safe, clean and friendly environment in the town centre, where young people aged 11 years and over from Oswestry and the surrounding area can meet together. The facility appears to provide a key point for youth information as well as staging regular entertainment and providing help for the young unemployed. Since it was first set up through a grant from the SRB, the café has seen the numbers using the facility increasing, the facility now also including commercial users. The user satisfaction levels have remained high and a project coordinator has been employed to ensure the continuation and expansion of the project.

Role of the Market Towns Initiative (MTI)

The MTI has been the subject of evaluations at national and local level. A national evaluation was undertaken for the Countryside Agency in 2004 (Countryside Agency 2004b) but other evaluations have taken place at a more local level; an example of the latter is the Yorkshire and Humber Assembly's scrutiny of Yorkshire Forward's operation of the MTI and its successor, the RMT programme (YHA 2004), which stressed the need for better evaluation of market towns programmes. Essentially, all such evaluations are more focused on the processes rather than the outcomes as, for many towns, it is too early to attempt to measure outcomes or the true effectiveness of the interventions. For many of the case study towns, the MTI was but the most recent example of an 'initiative' to address issues facing the town. So in the case of Richmond there had been a number of business-driven partnerships and local authority-inspired reviews and programmes; it is currently part of the Beacon Towns Programme. The multiplicity of initiatives can sometimes contribute essential infrastructure on which the MTI can build, as well as providing a contribution to shaping a succession strategy when the MTI process – and funding – is complete.

The national evaluation of the MTI (Countryside Agency 2004b) concluded that a high percentage of those involved found it a useful means of raising the profile of the town and as acting as a focus for bringing about change. Many have focused on smaller-scale projects, such as enhancement schemes and community projects, maybe because 'issues such as affordable housing, economic decline and agricultural reform are considered to be difficult for the MTI to tackle' (Countryside Agency 2004b: 18). To make progress with these larger issues, it is important to be able to gain access to additional funds, principally by influencing the programmes and strategies of other organisations. Efforts in this direction are more likely to be successful if the MTI is well-aligned with the programmes of key agencies (Langdon-Davies 2006).

The key resource for many market towns was the funding to be able to appoint a dedicated officer to drive the MTI process forward (YHA 2004); such funding is less widely available under some of the new incarnations of MTI. In the absence of such an officer, some difficult stages of the process can devolve on existing community organisations, many of which will lack the knowledge and resources to effectively influence the programmes and policies of key funding bodies. The ability to fund activity will vary between localities, depending both on the attitudes of key local players and the funding available in the locality. In Crediton it was pointed out that the resources available there differed greatly from that which could be accessed in Cornwall, where funds were available from the Objective 1 programme to fund both a project officer and development projects (Langdon-Davies 2006).

A key element of the MTI – and perhaps an output in its own right – is the development of partnership working. It not only shapes the achievements of the MTI but also can lay the foundations for continued activity to benefit the town. The contribution of MTI to partnership development was identified by both evaluations noted above, with the national evaluation pointing to the difficulties and stresses that can be involved in partnership working.

Most of the case study towns entered the MTI when the Countryside Agency still had a role in its management. Interviews with key actors in the towns suggested that, generally, they found the Countryside Agency to be very supportive and, as may be expected, staff had a good understanding of rural issues. RDAs were also found to be supportive but some partnerships took time to adjust to their different style of working. For example, RDAs tend to be more output-driven, focusing on economic issues, with less easy access to funding for community projects than was the case when the Countryside Agency had a substantial role.

All of the towns visited were able to identify positive impacts from their involvement in the MTI or its successors, though there were sometimes frustrations with the processes involved. Consistent with the objectives of the MTI, many local concerns have been raised and those projects seen to have the highest priority were often funded. The role of the partnership coordinator (or similar job title) was confirmed as being central to this process by all of the case study towns. Other achievements relate to the development of a collective vision for the towns and improving the extent to which businesses are working together to achieve the vision. It is unlikely that the loyalty card scheme in Haslemere, the BID in Keswick, the Youth Café in Oswestry, public realm improvements in Richmond and many other projects would have happened when and how they did in the absence of the MTIs and the accompanying coordinators. As with all programmes with time-limited funding, there are problems with retaining coordinators throughout the life of the project – they need to move on to the next job and the next project, and many echoed the concern of the Yorkshire and Humber Assembly (YHA 2004) in being unsure where they would go after the funding from the MTI came to an end.

The future for market towns

When considering the future for the case study towns – and all 200+ towns in the MTI reviewed as part of this research – an immediate issue is the nature and quality of their succession strategy for life after the MTI. Experience in the case study towns varied, with some unearthing a range of other mechanisms to fund staff to take the programme forward, to others being forced back on existing local community groups to take responsibility for their individual areas of interest. A crucial factor was the quality of engagement that could be generated with key bodies such as LSPs, the local authority and the RDA, and what commitment these might have to the success of the market town. As would be expected, experience here was variable but with no clearly identified route to success to be followed.

However, this is to take very much a process-focused view of the future, and one which does not address more fundamental questions related to the future of market towns in fulfilling the roles identified for them in this book. As part of the interviews in case study towns, key actors were asked where their town would be in 10 to 20 years' time. By and large, their views can be summarised as 'where we are now, but doing a little better'. So, many suggested there is likely to be little change, where the challenges currently being faced are likely to remain the same and are unlikely to be fully addressed. Instead, policy was seen as an ongoing process of merely alleviating fundamental concerns raised, such as: the extent of commuting and 'out-shopping'; mismatch between house prices and local wages and related issues of affordability; extent of in-migrants retiring in the towns; and lack of employment. Most key actors also expressed the need for change to occur without detracting from the character of the town, where the strongest such feelings were expressed within towns with planned housing expansion.

History is littered with examples of failed forecasts. In the context of planning, evidence from SERRL (2004) in mapping the pattern of interactions in rural communities suggests that limited capacity exists to forecast secular trends or the nature of responses to them. It is perhaps the latter that have been more influential in shaping the nature of market towns, in that behavioural changes have been substantial and in many ways counter to the direction underpinning policy design. However, a review of some of the key variables can help define the range of options open for market towns.

Demographic changes have helped shape the present roles of some market towns. An ageing population with increased disposable income has facilitated movements to market towns for retirement – one of the five roles identified for the towns in this book – as well as increasing the size of the group that finds much to admire in the towns as places to visit. A continuation of the trend towards an ageing population suggests that these forces will remain an influence for some time yet and that market towns will continue to face pressures on their housing stocks from those seeking to fulfil their dreams of rural retirement, and continue to enjoy a growth in day and staying visitors. Both these trends suggest a boost to the prosperity of towns that are able to tap into this growing segment, but also suggest a continuation of a number of negative pressures, such as those affecting housing affordability and demands for expensive social services. However, such a future is based on a number of assumptions and particularly that tomorrow's 50- and 60-year-olds will share the preferences of today's cohort. Life in the countryside has not always been an aspirational goal, and a continuation of this status may be challenged by the success of the urban renaissance turning urban living into the lifestyle choice of tomorrow. Such a development may be partly driven by structural factors, such as the changing composition of households.

Many of the recent trends have been made possible by changes in the cost and ease of travel. Dramatic changes in the costs of mobility will be required to bring them back up to the levels of the relatively recent past, but much of the current debate around elements of environmental sustainability suggests that trends for ever cheaper travel are about to be reversed. While this might be seen as a force for slowing the trend towards more dispersed patterns of employment and service purchase in relation to place of residence, it is the case that many of those exercising these types of residential preferences are among the more affluent, and if they continue to value highly the benefits offered by rural living they may well strive to continue this pattern of life based on intensive movement until the cost of travel starts to take a very large proportion of their disposable income. The more immediate impact of increased travel costs will be on the less affluent, and the main impact of policy based on increasing the cost of travel will be on more vulnerable groups and will act to widen social differences and increase social exclusion. Whether these are able to be limited by the development of more innovative forms of travel (or service delivery) and by achieving some form of modal shift is yet to be proved. How far patterns of access might be affected by the further development of modes of service delivery more strongly based on ICT is unclear, but recent impacts seem to have been supporting forms of employment more loosely related to the physical location of other facilities while improving access – for some groups – to a wider range of services.

It has been established that the fortunes of market towns reflect those in the national and regional economies. Indeed, prosperous regions frequently support market towns and a prosperous nation produces the increased wealth that eases the exercise of residential preferences for an increasing number. In considering how far wider economic trends will continue to fuel or make possible a continuation of past trends it is salutary to remember that, at the national level, most economic forecasts made by government look only at the relatively short term. So it is probably only possible to be to any degree confident about distributional impacts of changes in economic fortunes, with the most likely impact of a reversal of positive economic trends being increased disparities in wealth between individuals and places, the result of a process of cumulative causation, expressed simply as the already advantaged are likely to suffer less than the already disadvantaged.

However, a possibility that should be considered is the future role of market towns in relation to agriculture. The origin of market towns was as a distribution and exchange centre for agricultural products. But agriculture is likely to be subject to a number of forces for change in the future. Growing world competition for food is likely to change both availability and prices, with rising transport costs for imported foods adding to upward pressure on prices. Such trends may well begin to give a renewed importance to domestic agricultural output and thus to the status of the industry and its principle resource, land. In addition, pressures to produce new crops, such as bio-fuels, will contribute to these pressures and may give market towns a new role, as centres for fuel production and distribution. Although such arguments are to a degree speculative, they point to the possibility that new economic drivers may emerge to shape the future of market towns, and emphasise the need for the towns and the regulatory regimes within which they operate to be alert and adaptable to major secular changes.

The key underpinning for many market towns is their role as service centres, for both public and private services. In both sectors, change will reflect broader economic trends, but also market and management strategies. To some extent, the pattern of private services is a response to more or less liberal public policy frameworks, and this is discussed below, but they are also shaped by advances in delivery processes and strategies to capture or shape markets. How the independent traders, such an important element of service provision in market towns, will react to changing competitive environments – or what will be the nature of these changing environments – is hard to define. Some recent research from the United States (Stanyon 2006) suggests that independents could be well placed to capitalise on developing preferences for more personalised services, better value and a growing attachment to locality, but more intense competition from multiples is likely to come in the more successful towns.

The pattern of public services is shaped by polices on management and delivery. Past trends have tended towards favouring more centralised delivery, in pursuit of economy and limited perceptions of effectiveness, but more recent debates have focused on the scope for increased devolution in decision making. However, the history of devolved approaches in the public sector is one of tensions between developing local structures and stronger central financial control. The resolution of such potential conflicts in favour of market towns may, in part, be found in the success – or otherwise – of the policy of rural proofing but it is hard to find evidence as to how this innovation from the Rural White Paper (MAFF and DETR 2000) is actually working – or indeed may work in the future.

Policy more generally, and particularly policy influencing future patterns of development, can be seen as favouring market towns over other rural locations, insofar as planning guidance[4] sees the route to sustainability as being through locating most new development in service centres such as market towns. The success of this policy approach would see new residential, service and employment development being focused on the towns, acting to reinforce existing patterns of provision and cement the roles the towns currently perform. However, where market towns sit within emerging policy paradigms, such as the developing focus on the city region, is unclear, and would depend on how far the 'rural' is able to exercise influence in these arenas where the city is by far the weightiest player – perhaps another case where the impact of some form of rural proofing will be important.

How far it is possible to develop and implement a sustainable development agenda depends on both having the right policy and on inducing the right behaviour. Past neo-liberal manifestations of planning policy that have given greater freedom to the market to shape development patterns – such as the 1980s regime that oversaw the development and growth of out-of-town shopping – would suggest that regulation is an important tool in the achievement of sustainable patterns of development and behaviour. It is a matter of speculation how far longer-term trends such as global warming alter both behaviour and policy priorities. Insofar as such longer-term trends add to the priority given to the pursuit of what are seen to be sustainable patterns of development, it may be seen as favouring development in market towns. However, the future success of market towns is shaped to a significant extent by the way that individual towns and the stakeholders within them respond to changing circumstances. To this extent, many of the lessons to emerge through the MTI programme and its successors will continue to be relevant.

Notes

1   Many comments were also noted that businesses lacked the will and desire to innovate. As independent traders many of the owners were thought to be seeing out their last years prior to retirement.

2   An example of an exception to this is provided by a town in the SERRL (2004) study. In Marlborough, a sizeable branch of Waitrose is situated in the middle of the main shopping street, but here it proved possible to locate adequate car parking behind the street frontage, which is carefully blended in with local vernacular.

3   The apparent high cost of the scheme is perhaps explained by the cost of relocating existing uses on the site.

4   Current planning guidance, in the form of Planning Policy Statements 1 and 7, interpret sustainable development in a way that requires local plans to focus new development in rural areas in a small number of larger settlements.

Chapter 12

Market towns

Roles, challenges and prospects

Trevor Hart and Neil Powe

Introduction

This book has explored the roles, challenges and prospects for market towns that, up to now, have been defined in policy in terms of their size (between 2,000 and 30,000) and their role in servicing a surrounding rural hinterland. There are over 1,000 such towns in England. Market towns have been shown to act as rural employment and service centres, visitor attractions, and key locations for the development of new housing, including affordable housing. Less concretely but no less importantly, they are perceived by many as desirable places to live in and to visit, reflecting their position as an exemplification of the rural idyll.

Although this gives market towns a certain strength, many are struggling to re-invent themselves in the face of increased mobility and other changes challenging their role as rural service centres. There are also other pressures to be handled, including ageing populations and having to accept high levels of development, which can threaten the very qualities that give them tangible and cultural advantages. In many ways they are a microcosm of rural life, but policy has given them a pivotal role maintaining functional rural communities and at the same time promoting sustainable patterns of development and living in rural areas. As well as being subject to change, they may also have a role as agents of change.

Building on the analysis in this book, this final chapter reflects on the characteristics of market towns and the challenges they face. In the light of these reflections, a vision is suggested that seeks to maintain or capture a competitive position, encourage a sustainable, self-contained lifestyle and promote the development of cohesive and mixed communities. Factors affecting how such a vision can be delivered are then considered before finally the chapter and book concludes with some thoughts about the likely future for market towns.

Characteristics of market towns

While the analysis in this book shares the conclusions of others' work, that there is no such thing as a stereotypical market town, it has provided the basis on which an analysis of market towns can be conducted. All market towns perform a variety of roles, and if they are to become part of a quest for sustainable rural development, it is necessary that they do so, but the emphasis between the roles will vary between places. So, by focusing on a range of town characteristics, the analysis has succeeded in identifying the main functional roles they perform and to build from this a basis for understanding similarities and differences between towns. This in turn can provide a useful input to subsequent analysis of challenges and opportunities, for evaluating the impact of policy measures and highlighting what might be best practice in similar circumstances.

Market towns will clearly be influenced by their location, regional context, and economic and social characteristics, as well as policy, and all of these have been found to be important determinants of their success. Reflecting these contextual factors are the roles market towns play within the settlement hierarchy. The analysis has identified five main functional roles, which can be described in the following terms:

- *Service centres*: most towns were found to be providing some form of service function, but a number of market towns were found to be particularly well serviced for their size and with the capacity to perform strongly as rural service centres.
- *Visitor attractions*: attracting a mixture of day-trippers and holiday makers, these towns tend to be remote from other urban areas and often located near the coast or national parks. They rely on the spending of visitors to support and extend the services on offer to an above-average level.
- *Employment centres*: towns that have one dominant employer or sector of employment, such as defence or manufacturing, are a distinct group, with typically younger populations and more contained work patterns.
- *Housing commuters*: with increased mobility and people able to make 'lifestyle' rather than functional decisions about where they live, a number of towns are becoming commuter towns.
- *Housing the retired*: due in part to inadequate services in smaller rural settlements, attractive market towns (often small, remote and affluent) are becoming popular locations for retirement for older people who like to have easy access to some important services.

So, while all successful market towns will offer a range of services and facilities, most will have an identifiable emphasis towards some function, and what the above roles represent are the dominant and in some ways defining roles that towns have been found to perform. These five functional roles provide a basis from which to explore the key challenges facing market towns and the way they function.

Key challenges

The key challenges that towns have been found to face fall largely into five groups: maintaining a competitive retail offer; adapting to the impact of increased personal mobility; effectively servicing elderly and disadvantage groups; maintaining mixed communities through the provision of affordable housing and managing the impact of housing growth. Each of these is considered in turn below.

Maintaining retail competitiveness

Retailing is a highly competitive sector, and a number of trends have been identified that are challenging the position and function of market towns and small settlements generally. First, there has been a spatial shift in the location of comparison shopping, with purchases becoming increasingly concentrated in larger centres. Second, the role of multiples is becoming more and more dominant. Third, in convenience goods shopping, the four or five major supermarkets are taking an increasing share of expenditure and are becoming a determining feature in the success of centres. Indeed, their influence is becoming more pervasive as they extend the range of goods and services they sell. How market towns deal with these trends and major players is and will be very influential in shaping their retail futures.

It has been pointed out that there are two types of retail visitor to market town centres: those hoping to do their main shopping and leisure shoppers looking for something 'different from the city'. This gives a market town two markets to attack but begs the question as to what extent the town's identity is formed by being a traditional rural service centre or by acting as a leisure shopping location. For town and hinterland residents, convenience and personal service may be dominant attractants, but for those doing their main shopping in larger urban centres, the market town may remain a place for the occasional leisure shopping experience, where they do something different from the norm, or a place for 'top-up' shopping, like the suburban corner shop. For outside visitors to the town, leisure shopping is likely to dominate and they will be primarily or exclusively seeking 'something different from the city'. The type and range of shops may not be suitable for both types of customer. Indeed, the presence of high street multiples may detract from the quality of experience that market towns provide but be essential if local patronage is to be retained. Balancing these requirements and maintaining a distinct identity is a key challenge.

A second dimension relates to the capacity of the town centres and the sites for development that they can offer. The lack of large shops and multiples within market town centres is a key motivation for out-shopping by rural residents, leading to a leakage of trade from the towns. However, these often historic town centres may not have the sites available to match modern requirements, particularly for supermarkets. Permitting edge-of-centre or out-of-town sites may 'claw back' lost trade from larger urban areas. However, the close location of such competition may seriously affect town centre shops and lead to a loss of vitality for these centres. Balancing these two possibly competing demands is a further challenge that many market towns are currently facing. If edge-of-town developments occur, town centres may need to re-invent themselves, providing a different form of service.

The impact of greater personal mobility

The cost of motoring falling as a proportion of disposable income has encouraged and facilitated a change in 'lifestyle' that has meant that market town and hinterland residents have become more inclined to shop, work and be entertained elsewhere. In the case of towns that act as rural employment centres, it has facilitated increased commuting into the town for work. This has led to rural road usage (particularly on 'A' roads) increasing much faster than within urban areas, which in turn has added an additional challenge to the compact and quiet characteristics that are a foundation of the towns' success. As such, the towns have to both accommodate additional moving traffic and find additional parking spaces.

It has also had implications for the trade for town businesses and may also have affected the degree of attachment to the town by local and hinterland residents. Primary research has shown that although the extent to which residents engage with their town does vary between different types of respondents, the greatest variation is found between different towns. Key determinants of difference between towns in performance are related to the importance of the town within the local area, the range and location of services, the availability of employment and proximity to other urban areas. This suggests a more selective approach to settlement planning is perhaps required.

Tools available to tackle this challenge directly are limited. A logical approach, and one that is sometimes espoused in policy, is to improve public transport, as this both limits environmental impacts of traffic and may reinforce the role of towns as a local service hub through the structuring of public transport routes. Unfortunately, it is difficult to put in place a public transport system that meets current needs to both work and shop, but it is also hard to change habits and patterns of life that have been built up around highly flexible personal mobility. It is also hard to develop the appeal of public transport in a way that effectively competes with the cachet attached to the private car. This would suggest that increased personal mobility is likely to remain a challenge that towns will have to learn to live with in the short-to-medium term and they will need to develop strategies to compete with other locations in a more mobile world.

Providing for the less well-off/less able rural residents

There are perhaps two groups for whom market towns are an attractive option as a place to live: older, often retired people who enjoy the lifestyle they offer; and the less well-off, who may be better able to find affordable housing there. With declining levels of village services, market towns have become increasingly important for the less mobile in rural areas. In addition, market towns are the places where the majority of new rural housing is built, both for purchase and the majority of rural social rented housing, cementing their attraction for these two groups. The question then arises, is a town focused on meeting the needs of (say) retired people still able to attract other groups, to live and shop?

In terms of resources to help meet the needs of elderly or less well-off residents, the 'intermediate' position of market towns, somewhere between the truly rural and truly urban, may mean that they miss out on the government support they require. As such, these towns may face 'urban' problems of disadvantaged households and communities and economic decline, without access to the regeneration funding regimes that are available only to larger towns and cities. With ageing populations there is an increasing need for social and medical care, but not all market towns can offer the private or public services that meet their needs. Very few towns have appropriate hospital facilities, for example. They may also offer problematic physical environments for less able and mobile residents, as few historic environments are well adapted to the needs of this group. If something approaching a full range of services for the elderly should be available, the fact that such work tends to offer lower wages adds to difficulties, either of increased commuting into the towns or of demand for affordable housing.

Providing affordable housing

Although in-migration can increase the overall affluence of the towns and trade for local businesses, external demand for housing significantly affects prices in the local residential property market. With house prices increasing at a faster rate than in urban areas and rural wages and salaries lagging behind elsewhere, affordable housing may become an increasing concern if the towns are to continue as centres for the provision of services and for other forms of employment.

Maintaining mixed communities and the supply of workers needed to staff local services and businesses is crucial for the viability of towns. With larger urban areas often having clusters of affordable housing, low-paid employment growth in market towns may lead to reverse commuting (urban to rural), which does little to contribute to self-containment or the local economy of the towns. In the case of remoter towns more innovative solutions to housing employees may have to be developed in order to sustain local businesses and services. These problems have been observed to occur particularly in tourist towns, where work tends to be low-waged or seasonal and there is a sizeable external demand for housing. However, these problems are more pervasive and extend into other sectors beyond tourism.

Managing the impact of housing growth

Planning policy has focused much housing growth in market towns and the current emphasis of policy will continue this pattern of development. In Chapter 8 it was pointed out that, in pressured areas such as the East and South East of England, market towns may be allocated more housing than required for what some see as their local needs, while in less pressured areas such as in the North of England housing allocations for market towns may be regarded

151

as insufficient to maintain the vitality of the towns. In both regions, market towns face challenges in maintaining the very features that make the towns attractive and successful whilst accommodating high rates of growth or pressures on available housing stock.

High levels of housing growth have been shown to lead to an imbalance between population growth and the supply of services and infrastructure that a growing population demands. In the longer term this extra population may be advantageous as the towns can capture the benefits of growth, but in the shorter term problems may arise and the scope is limited for the towns to act as self-contained sustainable communities. However, although the increased in-migration that results from housing growth is likely to lead to more commuting, the long-term effect may be more positive. Indeed, high rates of in-migration and growth in self-employment often co-exist. Concerns have also been raised that population growth leads to the loss of the small-town feel and community spirit, again eroding a key strength and competitive advantage of market towns.

In less pressured areas such as in the North of England, a key emphasis of planning policy is often to address urban problems, including areas of low housing demand in run-down areas of old industrial cities, by directing most housing development to these areas as part of housing-led regeneration. However, low demand in the cities does not mean that there is low demand for housing throughout a region. Areas of high and low demand can coexist over quite small spaces. In such areas, market towns are still seen as attractive places to live but the low allocation of housing outside the urban areas adds to the housing pressures and problems experienced by market towns. At the same time, problems of deprivation exist in some market towns but they are also disadvantaged in competition for funds to deal with their pockets of need.

So, managing growth in housing demand in slower-growing regions may prove as problematic for market towns as managing growth in a region of high growth, particularly in the absence of a more sophisticated understanding of housing markets being developed to inform planning policy. In both cases, the challenge of achieving sustainable development and sustainable living is equally difficult but maybe for a different mix of reasons.

Vision for market towns

A number of potential strategies exist for market towns, ranging from holding their own, through achieving incremental improvement, to radical repositioning. Key actors interviewed as part of the research for the book were generally found to be determined to maintain the vital functions of providing services, employment and housing but at the same time hoping to achieve some degree of improvement. Although providing perhaps the most realistic positive outcome, such an approach runs the risk of failing to focus on or fully understand what the key objectives for the towns should be. In some cases the towns developed and adopted a clearly focused vision, based on a move towards developing as sustainable communities, in terms of the following:

- *Competitive towns*: there is a need for towns to maintain a competitive position attracting customers and investment, and developing indigenous businesses. To move in this direction, the towns need to have an attractive public realm, be marketed in terms of a positive image and identity, have good accessibility and adequate facilities for expansion. In terms of employment it is important that the local labour force has sufficient skills to support business and that there is a socially mixed community enabling a range of employment opportunities to be filled. Adequate locally based business support should be provided and business-aware policies developed by key public sector agencies.

- *Sustainable towns*: a primary goal of market towns is providing the co-location of employment, housing and services to minimise car use and social exclusion within rural areas, and help support local services. A key aspect of achieving such a self-contained lifestyle is engagement of residents within the towns, in terms of working, shopping, enjoying entertainment and participating within community activities. Engagement is also important for businesses and other organisations based within the town.
- *Cohesive towns*: this is an articulation of cultural and social objectives for market towns, supporting the development of a common sense of affinity and belonging for the towns and working towards being self-supporting in terms of a strong community engagement while at the same time developing an understanding of difference in residents. The achievement of cohesive and mixed communities makes community engagement and understanding of difference important.

Delivering futures for the towns

As there is variety in the towns, so there is likely to be different futures emerging for different towns. However, all will need to build from their analysis and visions towards effective implementation of policies and programmes designed to get them to become the places they want to be. This means that policies and mechanisms will need to mobilised and shaped to meet the needs of the towns, and that key actors, locally and further afield, will need to be marshalled to work with local communities to implement policies and plans. Although analysis and evaluation of policies and processes has not been the main focus of the research for this book, a number of valuable lessons have emerged from the case study work and this provides a basis for considering what policy mechanisms are likely to work for market towns.

Organisations at the town level

Town partnerships provide the basis from which all towns have proceeded to develop and implement strategies and plans for improvement. They should have the knowledge to develop an understanding of the issues that face the town as well as an appreciation of the context in which policy implementation will need to take place. However, they can also be handicapped by narrow vision borne of insularity and lack the resources to tackle the complex web of policies and agencies that command the resources necessary to implement policy. For such reasons, a market town officer, dedicated to the task and bringing outside knowledge and expertise, has been seen to make a real difference, bringing a focus for actions, time and expertise, and an ability to act as advocate with key players.

In other parts of Europe, chambers of commerce would be the driver of such initiatives, but chambers in England rarely command the resource and status of their continental counterparts. Although they are often active members of town partnerships, they are rarely able to substitute for the input that would be provided by a full-time market town officer. In addition to their usual involvement with 'town in bloom', Christmas lights, marketing, and the like, chambers can also help bring together the many small businesses more used to seeing each other as competition than striving for a common cause. Through programmes such as the Business Improvement District in Keswick, chambers may prove to be more useful in generating finance and communal effort and come to play a larger part in market town regeneration activities.

Town councils (or sometimes parish councils) form the most local tier of government. This was recognised in the Rural White Paper (MAFF and DETR 2000) and from this point efforts have been made to develop their capabilities and the part they play in rural governance. Town councils can take on responsibility for a range of functions affecting the quality of life in towns, as well as playing a central role in activities that are important to town improvement strategies. They also fulfil a crucial role where, as elected bodies, they can be seen to have perhaps a degree of democratic legitimacy and a stronger mandate for action. However, they are sometimes handicapped in carrying out their potential role to the full by lack of resources. For example, Woods (2006) points to the small proportion of local councils having full-time staff, a finding confirmed in our case study visits. There are mechanisms for improving their resource base, including the operation of local services, such as car parking, drawing down delegated functions from principal authorities under the 'Quality Councils' initiative, and they can also be nominated as the recipient of planning gain (Section 106) using the funds in a manner appropriate to the development. In addition to a role in implementation, local councils have a part to play in influencing policy, in local plans (LDFs) and decisions on development proposals through their role in being consulted on planning applications, but in these circumstances, they can be one voice among many.

Higher-level organisations

Although in touch with local needs, organisations at the town level need to work with organisations at higher levels, such as local authorities and RDAs to access resources to implement plans and projects. These and other tiers of governance exercise an influence over policy and resources vital to the success of market towns in developing and implementing their improvement strategies.

Local authorities, at the district and county level, have a mix of powers, resources and expertise to assist market towns in developing and implementing their strategies. In addition to capacity and capability in their key areas of expertise, their role of developing policy and the nature of those policies can affect the future of market towns. This extends beyond planning policies, which have been discussed in the text, to plans and strategies for a number of key services – education and social services are but two examples – that affect the functioning of rural communities. In making decisions over policy and service levels, friction can sometimes be observed between town councils and local authorities, where the wider objectives of local authorities may not be in tune with the sometimes more parochial bodies operating within the towns. There may be some distance between what the town sees as a priority and the view of the local authority, which has a more strategic basis or which is driven by a more politically expedient decision process reflecting the distribution of population and votes within the authority.

As has been identified at several points in the text, the role of local authorities in framing planning policies directly influences the location and availability of housing, business work space and retail, and through LDFs influence the delivery of rural settlement policy and, it is to be hoped, sustainable development. These are activities that directly act to shape the future of market towns. More pragmatically, they are also important in the negotiation of planning gain through Section 106 agreements, influencing resources gained for market towns through the planning process, and as such they can have a key role to play in the implementation of the visions of town partnerships. At the policy level, a poorly-located supermarket, too much or too little housing and insufficient possibilities for business can severely affect the fortunes of towns. Tight regulation, such as provided by environmental or conservation designations, can act to inhibit necessary development, but of course they also act as guardians of the qualities that make market towns special.

At a regional level, a number of agencies can have an influential role. The body responsible for producing the RSS will influence the planning framework within which local policy is developed but it is also likely to have a role in influencing other key regional strategies. First among these is the RES and the work of the RDAs. As RDAs are the main providers of funding and drivers of policy for market towns, successful towns will need to work well with their RDA. Questions have been raised in earlier chapters about the nature of the rural focus of RDAs, but up to now all have demonstrated a commitment to rural areas and market towns in particular, if with something of a bias towards harder economic outputs. A continuation, and preferably widening, of this support will be key to the future progress of market towns, and be crucial in terms of keeping experienced staff and maintaining the momentum within the towns. Also important will be an effective engagement with the Regional Housing Strategy, influencing directions of development in social housing, vital to the success of towns in promoting and achieving mixed communities and addressing issues of affordable housing. Perhaps a less immediate sense, it is also important for towns to be aware of the role of the Regional Sustainable Development Framework, insofar as it acts as an overarching framework for other regional strategies and influences the stance on the important issue of how sustainable development is achieved in a locality.

At a national level, it is clearly important to have a suite of policies and programmes that recognise the importance of market towns, both in the direction that is set for the provision of centrally funded and directed services affecting life in rural communities, and in the levels of resources that are made available for the delivery of services. Achieving these sorts of objectives is the role of rural proofing, but just how effective this is is very hard to measure. The Rural White Paper (MAFF and DETR 2000) and a number of successor documents have indicated a commitment to rural areas on the part of government, but what this amounts to and how market towns are affected is not completely clear. Clearly, there are a number of vocal rural lobbies working on behalf of rural communities generally and of market towns specifically, but as market towns are a relatively new area of policy intervention is not possible to produce any robust evaluation of the effectiveness of these interventions.

Finally, in this fragmented state there are many non-departmental public bodies (sometimes know as QUANGOs), which are responsible for the delivery of services that are key to the success of market towns, through exercise of control over the pattern and quality of service delivery. Two examples might be Primary Care Trusts, responsible for the planning and delivery of health services, and Learning and Skills Councils responsible for the delivery of skills and training. There is a considerable literature pointing to concerns over accountability in such bodies (see, for example, Day and Klein 1987; Weir and Hall 1994; Hart *et al.* 1996) and the difficulty of understanding and influencing their decision-making processes. The same judgement may be made in relation to the various regional bodies and strategies reviewed above. Taken together with the array of other organisations considered, there emerges a challenging task of influence and partnership working to be mastered by market towns and their advocates. The difficulty of performing this task effectively has been reviewed in Chapter 4, and our researches have only served to confirm both the challenge it represents and the importance of doing it successfully.

Future prospects

The recent history of market towns shows a fluctuating pattern of success and failure in economic activity and it is inevitable this will continue to be the case. In a changing environment, market towns remain a logical place in which to plan for sustainable rural communities. Although those living in the towns can do a great deal to help themselves, their future also very much depends on external factors.

Market towns do not operate in a vacuum: they are operating in a broad and competitive market for investment, employment and trade, as well as being affected by social trends and government policy. However, it is likely that some of the characteristics of market towns can act to shape those forces and outcomes in a particular way, with their often attractive and historic character making them desirable places to work, live and visit.

Trends in the cost and nature of transport have been central to understanding the challenges that market towns face. Future changes in the cost of private transport as a proportion of disposable income are likely to have a considerable effect on the links between the town and hinterland residents, in terms of shopping, employment, entertainment and community activities as well as affecting the numbers wishing the migrate into the areas. Although the willingness to travel can be shaped through a number of channels, the ability of market towns to play a large part in this shaping must be limited. Improved communication technology can have some effects on the need of individuals to travel, but people still have to meet and goods still need to be transported. Public transport solutions are likely to remain less attractive than movement by personal transport.

Government policy will also have important effects on market towns. The nature of planning policy, levels of expenditure on rural services and the availability of regeneration funding all provide examples of how impacts might be generated. Having an 'intermediary' position in terms of many aspects of government policy, being neither truly rural nor truly urban, is unlikely to help them raise funding for regeneration and social support or to be considered within rural proofing exercises, however effective these may be.

A further factor affecting towns is the growth of housing, with rapid expansion occurring in the last 40 years. Villages have become small towns and small towns become larger. Although a continued expansion may be seen as positive, improve vitality and services, and provide regeneration opportunities, it is inevitable that the character of these towns will continue to change. Part of such change will be a weakening of their identity as part of a rural idyll and also perhaps as 'market towns', where the importance of their hinterland linkages may become diluted.

Trends in retail, with an increasing dominance of multiples and public desires for a wider range of products, easily accessed, are likely to continue and present an enduring challenge to market towns. Although planning has been restricting the out-of-town development that had continued the undermining of the position of market towns, recent developments in the national planning policy review (Barker 2006) shows that developing conceptions of competitiveness and 'market failure' may reopen the debate on the distribution of retail development. The constraints of historic town centres, built for smaller populations and a different style of retailing, are likely to pose continuing challenges for market towns in resolving the conflict between environment and competitive retail provision. For the independent traders that help define market town identity and offer an aspect of competitive advantage, there are succession and other issues to be faced.

To succeed, the towns need to be able to mobilise a range of institutions and resources to focus on the mix of factors that they need to enhance to realise their potential. While frameworks exist by which these relationships and dialogues can be built, it is unclear as to whether market towns possess the capacity and capability to effectively influence agendas. As such, the prospects for market towns remain uncertain. They need to continue to evolve, inventing new roles. However much they strive to improve, there are perhaps some trends easier to predict. It is likely market towns will continue to be seen as wanting by some groups and comfortable and satisfying by others. Linkages with their rural hinterland may continue to weaken, threatening the achievement of rural sustainability, but they will remain important. They will continue to provide something 'different from the city' and act as visitor attractions and be seen as key rural locations for housing growth and 'affordable housing'. Above all it is hoped they will remain an important part of our heritage, culture and way of life.

Appendix 1
A short history of market towns

Neil Powe and Trevor Hart

The pattern of settlements we see today is the product of a long history of development and change. The origin of many of our towns and villages is to be found in their agrarian past, reflecting historical functional roles. Researching the period 1000–1540, Dyer (2002) suggests the main reason for the market towns' existence 'lay in the buying and selling activities of the ordinary people of the hinterland' (15), with the hinterland containing many more people than the towns themselves (on average the hinterland had a population of 10,000 people, whereas the population of the towns averaged only 800 people). As such, the pattern of towns could be seen to reflect 'the amount of time it may take to come to the market from an outlying [agricultural] area, dispose of the produce, and to complete the journey home before dark.' (Platt 1976: 75). For example, Chalklin (2001) reports that in the 1650s market towns were servicing hinterlands of between 3 and 6 miles. Howkins (1991) suggests that by the 1851 census the average was still only 6 miles. With mobility improvements, the number of accessible towns increased, eventually blurring the pattern of relationships and service areas described by Christaller (translated Baskin 1966) or nucleated settlement (Dickinson 1942). The typical characteristic of a market town, of having more services and facilities than one would expect for its size, remains.

Chalklin (2001) identifies that, in 1650, settlements with as few as 500 people were providing what he termed 'urban functions' for their rural hinterlands. By the late Victorian times the range of shops and services had increased. But the trajectory of development was not constant. Indeed, Howkins (2003) suggests that in the late Victorian period there was a decline in village-based services, for example, boot and shoe makers, tailors and even some types of food, with this trade being gained by the larger market towns. Howkins (1991) describes how market towns had become centres for social gathering, religious, political and leisure organisations, as well as providing identity to rural dwellers. For example, people from Hexham in Northumberland would refer to it as 'Hexhamshire' or from Banbury in North Oxfordshire as 'Banburyshire'. The local press added to the sense of place, with papers being dominated by local news, often providing stories in a local dialect, which reinforced ideas of a better rural way of life (Howkins 1991).

Beyond their role of servicing their immediate hinterland, throughout the medieval times towns began to specialise. For example Dyer (2002) reports how Beccles in Suffolk specialised in fish, Thaxted in Essex in knifes and Bridport in Dorset in robes. Changes in processes accompanying the development of industrialisation had its impacts, leading to more specialisation within the economy. Mechanisation was occurring in production, putting pressure on local handcraft businesses dependent on their local market. In other towns, mining and industrialisation were providing a new focus for economic and social life. Changes were also occurring in agriculture. While large-scale mechanisation was some time off, in late Victorian times new cattle markets were being custom-built away from the old marketplace (Howkins 1991), often creating a division between 'shopping' and 'going to the market'. More recently, as a result of changing methods of cattle sales and purchase and a tightening of health and safety legislation, cattle markets are being centralised in only a small percentage of towns, further changing the relationship between the visit to market and the visit for shopping.

Although travel to market towns has been difficult in the past, linkages between towns improved with the creation of turnpike trusts, and then later the railways (Chamberlin 1983). With the growth of rural bus services in the 1930s, once-a-year trips to large towns and urban areas for a fair could be increased to perhaps four or five times a year with the intention of shopping. The 1930s saw the early spread of the chain store from the cities and suburbs to the market towns, with Sainsbury's being an early pioneer in the South of England (Howkins 2003). This provided competition for existing independent older established businesses. These were the early signs of changes that were to continue until recent times, such that there has been a concentration of retail activity into larger urban areas and a loss of trade for independent traders to multiples.

For market town centres, the early improvements in mobility provided perhaps the golden era for the market town, where access had improved so that new goods became available to market town shops and it was easier to travel in from the rural hinterland. However, post-World War II increases in car ownership brought increased competition from the larger urban areas. This provided a challenge for market town traders used to a captive market. For example, by 2002 in England 75 per cent of comparison sales (such as fashion and gifts) were in the top 200 retail centres compared to 50 per cent in the early 1980s (English Market Towns Advisory Forum 2002).

A further factor affecting market towns has been the changing form of local government. In rural England there had traditionally been a three-tier system of local government: county council, middle tier (often rural or urban district councils), and parish and town councils. The headquarters of local authorities can provide employment vital to the prosperity of the local economy, as well as providing a service 'anchor' for the town: the middle and lower tiers have been more commonly found in market towns. Keith-Lucas and Richards (1978) suggest 'rural districts', as they were called, were often based on the poor law unions of parishes for the hinterland around towns and 'urban district' councils represented the towns. The urban districts had often been formed when the towns were made responsible for their own sanitary services. With the improvements in transport and linkages between market town and hinterland, Keith-Lucas and Richards (1978) suggest the dual rural and urban district status became less workable. For this and other reasons, local authorities were viewed to be too small for their purpose and, following the Local Government Act of 1929, they were reduced in number. More radical changes were not to occur until 1974 (following the 1972 Local Government Act), when the essence of the present-day system was set in place.

Prior to 1974 there were 1,250 middle-tier councils (urban and rural district councils), which were replaced with 369 district councils following the 1972 Act. The number of upper-tier county councils was also reduced. While the implications of this change for market towns have not been systematically studied, a couple of examples can illustrate impacts. Wymondham in Norfolk was elevated from a parish council to an urban district council in 1935, but then lost out in 1974 when South Norfolk District Council was established and its headquarters were set up in another settlement. In Wymondham today there is only a town council. Alternatively, Stroud District Council in Gloucester was formed from four district councils and two urban councils, providing increased employment to the town and also a focus in terms of public services present in the town.

What is clear is that many of these market towns continue to act as a focal point for trade and services for their rural hinterlands. Indeed, in many cases strong linkages between market towns and their hinterlands have existed for centuries. Such relationships have become the basis for policies controlling and guiding development in rural areas. However, the traditional patterns of activity that defined and supported these roles are being challenged by a number of factors, particularly by increased personal mobility resulting from the cost of motoring falling as a proportion of disposable income (DfT 2005).

Appendix 2

A short guide to the English development planning system

Trevor Hart

A government guide for the public has described the planning system as being 'about how we plan for, and make decisions about, the future of our cities, towns and countryside' and having the task 'to balance different views and often make difficult decisions' (DCLG 2004). The 1990 Town and Country Planning Act established something called a plan-led system, which means that the basis for making such decisions are the policies set out in the adopted development plan. The 2004 Planning and Compulsory Purchase Act made some changes to the way development plans are made and structured, and an outline of this system is given below.

Development plans

Development plans are a prepared by unitary and district local authorities in England. Under the 2004 Act, development plans consist of two elements:

- Each region (such as the North East of England) prepares a Regional Spatial Strategy (RSS) which sets out things such as how many homes are needed to meet the future needs of people in the region, or whether the region needs a new major shopping centre or an airport. RSSs are drafted by the Regional Planning Body and provide a framework and context for the preparation of plans focusing on the more local level, as well as being formally part of the 'plan-led' system of documents on which decisions on proposals for development are based.
- At a local level, there are Local Development Frameworks (LDFs). These are 'folders' or collections of documents that set out how a local area may change over the coming years. LDFs are prepared by the local planning authority – the unitary or district council – for the area concerned. As is the case for the RSS, there are opportunities provided for public involvement in the plan making process.

The structure of the new plans is different from the previous system and the approach and purpose of the plan itself is also said to be radically new. The concept of 'spatial planning' is intended to be at the heart of the new planning system. Previously, the focus of the planning system was mainly regulatory. The government's aim is that the new spatial planning system of RSS and LDF should be wider and more inclusive. The new process requires the local authority and other agencies to work much more closely together, and to coordinate their activities to achieve agreed objectives. For example, the LDF needs to take account of the intentions of agencies concerned with education, transport and health and the LDF provides a major opportunity, in conjunction with these agencies, to coordinate all these activities as they affect the different parts of a local authority area. In short, the plan is also intended to have a greater concern for implementation than has previously been the case.

One of the key purposes of the new LDF will be to give a spatial expression to the Community Plan (CP). The main underlying principle of the CP is that it should deal with the issues that local communities feel are important to their economic, social and environmental well-being. The CP sets out a long-term community vision for an area, and is based on the principles of community involvement, sustainable development and promoting diversity. It defines the shared vision of the Local Strategic Partnership (LSP), a partnership of public and private organisations and community groups.

Regional Spatial Strategies (RSSs)

In terms of what might be considered to be important for market towns, RSSs provide the arena in which levels of growth appropriate for a region are debated and decided, and policies for how that growth should be distributed in the region are put in place. In some cases towns are identified in the strategies that will take on the roles of market towns, though the term 'market town' may not be used describe them. All RSSs are prepared in line with government policy guidance, much of which is set out in the 24 Planning Policy Statements. These include its policy concerning sustainable development, which seeks to focus new development in rural areas on selected settlements. This is expressed in PPS7 as 'away from larger urban areas, planning authorities should focus most new development in or near to local service centres where employment, housing (including affordable housing), services and other facilities can be provided close together' (ODPM 2004a: 6).

The RSS may also assume a role in guiding the work of the RDA in developing and delivering its policies for market towns. So, in the Yorkshire and Humber region, the towns on which the RDA will focus in future for its Renaissance Market Towns programme will be drawn from the 63 towns identified as service centres for rural areas in the recently prepared RSS (Yorkshire Forward 2006).

Local Development Frameworks (LDFs)

The LDF is often described as being best thought of as a folder, which contains a number of documents, each of which is briefly explained below.

A Local Development Scheme (LDS), which is reviewed at least annually, sets out the documents that will be contained within the LDF, their broad contents and the timetable for their preparation. The main documents that go to make up the rest of the contents of the 'folder' comprise the following:

- The *Core Strategy* – sets out the spatial vision for the area over the whole plan period, together with key spatial objectives and strategic policies. All other LDF documents must be in conformity with the Core Strategy.
- *Development Policies* – a set of policies that guide the granting of planning permission and apply across the whole local planning authority area. Implementing these policies will be one of the main ways of achieving the Core Strategy.
- *Allocations* – which detail all the area designations and site-specific proposals for new development, relating to the Core Strategy; these are frequently organised on a sub-area basis.
- *Proposals Map* – which shows the location of the site-specific allocations, and other designations and constraints, on an Ordnance Survey map base (with large-scale inset maps).

- *Statement of Community Involvement* (SCI) – the proposals for the involvement of all interested parties, including the general public, which the council establishes both for the making of the LDF documents, and for consultations about individual planning applications.

Except for the SCI, all the above documents are termed Development Plan Documents (DPDs), as they constitute part of the development plan (with the RSS) and each is subject to formal processes of preparation, which include examination by an independent inspector, whose report is binding on the council.

In addition, Supplementary Planning Documents (SPDs) are frequently produced to go into the LDF folder. These provide additional guidance relating to the policies identified in DPDs. There has been an increase in the use of such documents in recent years, in an attempt to strike a balance between giving detailed guidance on important topics or sites and producing main planning policy guidance that is not overburdened by detail. They can cover a range of topics – such as affordable housing and designing out crime – or focus on important sites in the locality where a particular standard or pattern of development is thought necessary. Examinations are not held into SPDs, but they are subject to detailed public consultation (as identified in the Statement of Community Involvement), which contributes to their achieving a status necessary to exercise influence over decisions on development proposals.

For market towns the key element of the plan is the definition of a settlement hierarchy in the core strategy, along with detailed allocations of housing growth and other forms of development in the main settlements. Again, policies will be developed in line with the pursuit of sustainable development as outlined above, focusing most development on a number of larger rural settlements. Often, such settlements will be defined a 'service centres' or something similar, but many plans will include policies dealing specifically with market towns, and particularly with their role in local economic development. So, for example, in the LDF for Hambleton District in North Yorkshire, it is stated that:

> It will be important for the LDF, through its Core Strategy, and through its Allocations and Development Policies DPDs, to give sustained and expanded support for the market towns initiatives work – covering each Service Centre as appropriate, and for other proposals that will support the regeneration and role of these towns. Examples will also include transport schemes that provide environmental benefits, reduction of congestion and better links between the market towns and their hinterlands.
>
> (Hambleton DC 2005: 33)

The plan then goes on to detail policy proposals to give effect to these aspirations, through a range of measures designed to maintain and improve economic and environmental conditions for communities in the five main centres in the district.

Bibliography

Adams, D. and Watkins, C. (2002) *Greenfields, Brownfields and Housing Development*, London: Blackwell Publishing.

Affordable Rural Housing Commission (ARHC) (2006) Not titled. Available at: www.defra.gov.uk/rural/housing/commission/ (accessed 8 December 2006).

Age Concern (2003a) *Older People – Their Transport Needs and Requirements*, Norwich: Age Concern.

Age Concern (2003b) *Adding Quality to Quantity: Older People's Views on Quality of Life and its Enhancement,* London: Age Concern.

Age Concern (2006) *The Age Agenda 2006*: *Public Policy and Older People*, London: Age Concern.

Alnwick District Council (2003) *Alnwick Wide District Plan Review (Jan. 2003), Issues Paper, number 5: Housing*. Available at: www.alnwick.gov.uk/an/webconnect.exe/AO2/View/?Site=1798 (accessed 8 December 2006).

Alnwick District Council (2004) *Urban Capacity Study for Alnwick District Wide, Local Plan Review*. Available at: www.alnwick.gov.uk/supporting/released/2006–4/7396/UrbanCapStudyPrintML2004 Activefile.doc (accessed 8 December 2006).

Alnwick District Council (2005a) *Alnwick District Council Comments on Consultation Draft of Regional Spatial Strategy (01/05)*, Alnwick: Alnwick District Council.

Alnwick District Council (2005b) *Building the Future of our District: Core Strategy Development Plan Document: Preferred Options Draft*. Available at: www.alnwick.gov.uk/an/webconnect.exe/AO2/View/?Site=1798 (accessed 8 December 2006).

Audit Commission (2004). *Older People – Independence and Well-Being: The Challenge for Public Services*, London: Audit Commission.

Bailey, T.C. and Gatrell, A.C. (1995) *Interactive Spatial Data Analysis*, Harlow: Longman.

Baker, R. and Speakman, L. (2006) 'The older rural consumer', in Lowe, P. and Speakman, L. *The Ageing Countryside: The Growing Older Population of Rural England*, London: Age Concern England.

Baldock, J. (2004) *The Role and Vitality of Secondary Shopping,* Research for the National Retail Planning Forum. Available at: www.nrpf.org/BCSC_files/frame.htm (accessed 8 December 2006).

Banister, C. and Gallent, N. (1998) 'Trends in commuting in England and Wales – becoming less sustainable?', *Area*, 30: 331–43.

Banister, D. (1999) 'Planning More to Travel Less', *Town Planning Review*, 70(3): 313–338.

Barclay, C. (2002) *Third Party Rights of Appeal in Planning*, House of Commons Library, Working Paper, 02/38.

Barker, K. (2003) *Review of Housing Supply: Securing Our Future Housing Needs (Interim Report – Analysis)*, London: TSO.

Barker, K. (2004) *Review of Housing Supply – Delivering Stability; Securing Our Future Housing Needs*, HM Treasury.

Barker, K. (2006) *Barker Review of Land Use Planning: Final Report – Recommendations*, Norwich: TSO.

Berry, B.J.L. (1976) 'The counterurbanization process: urban America since 1970', *Urban Affairs Annual Review*, 11: 17–30.

Bate, R., Best, R. and Holmans, A. (eds) (2000) *On the Move: The Housing Consequences of Migration*, York Publishing Services.

Bevan, M., Cameron, S., Coombes, M., Merridew, T. and Raybould, S. (2001) *Social Housing in Rural Areas,* Coventry: Chartered Institute of Housing/Joseph Rowntree Foundation.

Bevan, M. and Croucher, K. (2006) 'Delivering Services to People in Rural Areas', in Lowe, P. and Speakman, L. (eds) *The Ageing Countryside, The Growing Older Population of Rural England,* London: Age Concern.

Blackburn, R. and Curran, J. (1993) 'In search of spatial difference: evidence from a study of small service sector enterprises', in Curran, J. and Storey, D. (eds) *Small Firms in Urban and Rural Locations,* London: Routledge.

Bolton, N. and Chalkley, B. (1990) 'The rural population turnaround: a case study of North Devon', *Journal of Rural Studies*, 6: 29–43.

Bosworth, G. (2006) *Counterurbanisation and Job Creation: Entrepreneurial In-Migration and Rural Economic Development*, Centre for Rural Economy Discussion Paper Series No. 4, Centre for Rural Economy, University of Newcastle upon Tyne.

Boyle, P. and Halfacree, K. (1998) *Migration into Rural Areas*, London: Wiley.

Bramley, G. (1995) *Circular Projections: Household Growth, Housing Development and the Household Projections,* London: Council for the Protection of Rural England.

Bramley, G. (2007) 'The sudden rediscovery of housing supply as a policy challenge', *Housing Studies,* 22(2): 221–41.

Breheny, M., Gordon, I. and Archer, S. (1997) *Can Planning for a More Compact City Secure Sustainable Levels of Urban Travel in the London Region?* Department of Geography, University of Reading.

Bromley, R., Hall, M. and Thomas, C. (2003) 'The impact of environmental improvements on town centre regeneration', *Town Planning Review*, 74(2): 143–64.

Buller, H., Morris, C. and Wright, E. (2003) *The Demography of Rural Areas: A Literature Review*, Gloucester: CCRU.

Bunce, M. (1982) *Rural Settlement in an Urban World*, London: Billing and Sons.

Butler, H., Morris, C. and Wright, E. (2003) *The Demography of Rural Areas: A Literature Review*, Countryside and Community Research Unit and University of Gloucestershire: Cheltenham.

Butt, R. (1999) 'The changing employment geography of rural areas', in Breheny, M. (ed.) *The People: Where Will they Work?,* London: TCPA.

Cabinet Office & Strategy Unit (2005) *Improving the Prospects of People Living in Areas of Multiple Deprivation in England*, London: Strategy Unit.

Caffyn, A. (2004) 'Market town regeneration: challenges for policy and implementation', *Local Economy*, 19(1): 8–24.

Cameron, S. (2006): 'From low demand to rising aspirations – housing market renewal within regional and neighbourhood Regeneration Policy', *Housing Studies*, 21(1): 3–16.

Campbell, H., Ellis, H., Henneberry, J., Poxon, J., Rowley, S. and Gladwell, C. (2001) *Planning Obligations and the Mediation of Development,* RICS Foundation: London.

Castle Morpeth Area Committee (2005) *Report of the Assistant Director (Environmental Services) View: Shaping the North East – Submission Draft of the Regional Spatial Strategy for the North East*. Available at: www.northumberland.gov.uk/%5Cdrftp%5C10866.doc (accessed 8 December 2006).

Castle Morpeth Borough Council (2002a) *Castle Morpeth Urban Capacity Study*, Castle Morpeth Borough Council. Available at: www.castlemorpeth.gov.uk/an/webconnect.exe/AO2/View/?Doc=9872&Site=999 (accessed 8 December 2006).

Castle Morpeth Borough Council (2006) *The Dransfield £30m Retail Development for Morpeth Town Centre*. Available at: www.castlemorpeth.gov.uk/an/webconnect.exe/AO2/View/?Doc=9891&Site=1650 (accessed 8 December 2006).

Chalklin, C. (2001) *The Rise of the English Town 1650–1850*, (New Studies in Economic and Social History), Cambridge: Cambridge University Press.

Chamberlin, R. (1983) *The National Trust Book of the English Country Town*, Exeter: Webb & Bower.

Champion, A. (ed.) (1989) *Counterurbanisation: The Changing Pace and Nature of Population Deconcentration*, London: Edward Arnold.

Champion, A. (1998) 'Studying counterurbanisation and the rural population turnaround', in Boyle, P. and Halfacree (eds) *Migration into Rural Areas: Theories and Issues,* London: John Wiley, 21–40.

Champion, T. and Fielding, A. (1992) *Migration Processes and Patterns: Volume 1. Research Progress and Prospects,* London: Belhaven Press.

Champion, T. and Shepherd, J. (2006) 'Demographic change in rural England', in Lowe, P. and Speakman, L. (eds) *The Ageing Countryside: The Growing Older Population of Rural England,* London: Age Concern, 29–50.

Chaplin, R., Martin, S., Royce, C., Saw, P., Whitehead, C. and Yang, J. (1995) *Housing Associations, Private Finance and Market Rents in England's Rural Districts*, Cambridge University Land Economy Department.

Chapman, P. (1998) *Poverty and Exclusion in Rural Britain*, York: Joseph Rowntree Foundation.

Christaller, W., trans. C.W. Baskin (1966) *Central Places in Southern Germany*, Englewood Cliffs, NJ: Prentice Hall.

Civic Trust (2000) *Small Town Vitality: The Impact of New Housing*, London: The Civic Trust.

Cloke, P. (1979) *Key Settlements in Rural Areas*, London: Methuen.

Cloke, P. (1983) *An Introduction to Rural Settlement Planning*, London: Methuen.

Cloke, P. (2006) 'Conceptualizing rurality', in Cloke, P., Marsden, T. and Mooney, P.H. (eds) *The Sage Handbook of Rural Studies*, London: Sage.

Cloke, P., Milbourne, P. and Thomas, C. (1994) *Lifestyles in Rural England,* Rural Development Commission.

Collis, C. Berkeley, N. and Fletcher, D.R. (2000) 'Retail decline and policy responses in district shopping centres', Town Planning Review, 71(2): 149–68.

Commission for Integrated Transport (CfIT) (2001) 'Rural transport: an overview of key issues'. Available at: www.cfit.gov.uk/docs/2001/rural/rural/key/index (accessed 8 December 2006).

Commission for Rural Communities (CRC) (2005a) *The State of the Countryside 2005*, Wetherby, W. Yorks.: Countryside Agency Publications. Available at: www.ruralcommunities.gov.uk/publications/crc05stateofthecountryside2005 (accessed 25 January 2006).

Commission for Rural Communities (CRC) (2005b) *Keswick – A Market Town in the Lake District National Park*, London: CRC. Available at: www.ruralcommunities.gov.uk/files/CRC09Keswick.pdf (accessed 1 October 2006).

Commission for Rural Communities (CRC) (2005c) *Rural Proofing Report 2004–5*. London: Commission for Rural Communities.

Commission for Rural Communities (CRC) (2006a) *Challenging Government to Meet Rural Needs: Rural Proofing Monitoring Report 2006*, London: Commission for Rural Communities.

Commission for Rural Communities (CRC) (2006b) *Is the Countryside Sustainable? State of the Countryside Report 2006*, London: CRC.

Commission for Rural Communities (CRC) (2006c) *Our Evidence to the Affordable Rural Housing Commission*. Available at: www.ruralcommunities.gov.uk/publications/ourevidencetothearhc (accessed 8 December 2006).

Commission for Rural Communities (CRC) (2006d) *Choice of Jobs in Rural England, Rural Economics – Bulletin 1*. Available at: www.ruralcommunities.gov.uk/files/CRC21-RuralEconomiesBulletin1Choice ofJobs.pdf (accessed 8 December 2006).

Cotterell, A., Briscoe, J. and Edwards, M. (2000) 'Alnwick District Council v. The Secretary of State for the Environment, Transport and the Regions and Safeway Stores plc and others', *Journal of Planning and Environment Law*, May, 474–97.

Counsell, D., Haughton, G.F., Allmendinger, P. and Vigar, G. (2006) ' "Integrated" spatial planning – is it living up to expectations?', *Town and Country Planning*, 75(9): 243–45.

Countryside Agency (1999) *The State of the Countryside 1999*, Wetherby, W.Yorks.: Countryside Agency Publications. Available at: www.countryside.gov.uk/Publications/articles (accessed 25 February 2005).

Countryside Agency (2000) *Market Towns Initiative: Operating Guidelines for Local Partnerships 2000/2001, Yorkshire and Humber Region*, Wetherby, W.Yorks: Countryside Agency Publications.

Countryside Agency (2003) *The State of the Countryside 2003*, Wetherby, W.Yorks.: Countryside Agency Publications. Online. Available at: www.countryside.gov.uk/Publications/articles/Publication_tcm2–4322.asp (accessed 25 January 2006).

Countryside Agency (2004a) *The State of the Countryside 2004*, Wetherby, W.Yorks: Countryside Agency Publications. Available at: www.countryside.gov.uk/Publications/articles (accessed 8 December 2006).

Countryside Agency (2004b) *Assessment of the Market Towns Initiative*, Cheltenham: Countryside Agency.

Countryside Agency (2004c) 'Housing and support needs of older people in rural areas', London: Countryside Agency.

Countryside Agency (2004d) *Developing Indicators of the Effect of Geodemographic Factors on Cost and Performance of Public Services Sector for the Countryside Agency*, Cheltenham: Countryside Agency.

Courtney, P. and Errington, A. (2000) 'The role of small towns in the local economy and some implications for development policy', *Local Economy*, 15: 280–301.

Courtney, P., Agarwal, S., Rahman, S., Errington, A. and Moseley, M. (2004) *Determinants of Relative Economic Performance of Rural Areas*, London: DEFRA.

Courtney, P., Mayfield, L. and van Leeuwen, E. (2006) 'Contemporary functions of small and medium sized towns: a study of rural consumption patterns in the UK and Netherlands', paper presented at *Agricultural Economics Society 80th Annual Conference*, Paris.

Cousins, L. with Clive Miller & Associates and Roger Tym & Partners (2004) *Innovative Market Towns Labour Market Strategies: Baseline Study,* Taunton: Somerset County Council.

Croden, N., Costigan, P. and Whitfield G. (1999) *Helping Pensioners: Evaluation of the Income Support Pilots*, DSS Research Report 105, Leeds: CDS.

Crook, T., Curry, J., Jackson, A., Monk, S., Rowley, S. Smith, K. and Whitehead, C. (2001) *The Provision of Affordable Housing Through The Planning System*, Joseph Rowntree Foundation: York Publishing Services.

Crook, T., Rowley, S. and Jackson, A. (2002) *Planning Gain and Affordable Housing*, Joseph Rowntree Foundation: York Publishing Services.

Dahms, F. and McComb, J. (1999) ' "Counterurbanization", interaction and functional change in a rural amenity area – a Canadian example', *Journal of Rural Studies*, 15: 129–46.

Davies, J. (2003) 'Partnerships versus regimes: why regime theory cannot explain urban coalitions in the UK', *Journal of Urban Affairs*, 25(3): 253–69.

Davies, W.K.D., Townsend, I. and Ng, L. (1998) 'The survival of commercial hierarchies: rural service centres in Western Victoria, Australia', *Tijdschrift voor Economische en Sociale Geografie,* 89: 264–78.

Dawson, J. and Errington, A. (1998) *The Bude Survey: A Baseline Study of Bude and the Surrounding Rural Area*, Plymouth: Market Towns Research Group.

Day, P. and Klein, R. (1987) *Accountabilities: Five Public Services*, London: Tavistock.

Dean, K.G., Shaw, D.P., Brown, B.J.H., Perry, R.W. and Thorneycroft, W.T. (1984) 'Counterurbanisation and the characteristics of persons migrating to West Cornwall', *Geoforum*, 15: 177–90.

Department for Transport (DfT) (2005) *Transport Trends*, London: DfT. Available at: www.dft.gov.uk/stellent/groups/dft_transstats/documents/divisionhomepage/035611.hcsp (accessed 8 December 2006).

Department for Transport (DfT) (2006a) *Transport Statistics*, London: TSO.

Department for Transport (DfT) (2006b) *Public Transport Statistics Bulletin* 2006, London: TSO.

Department of Communities and Local Government (DCLG) (2004) *Creating Better Places to Live: A Guide to the Planning System in England.* Available at: www.communities.gov.uk/index.asp?id=1144503 (accessed 8 December 2006).

Department of Communities and Local Government (DCLG) (2006a) Planning Policy Statement 3: Housing. Available at: www.communities.gov.uk/index.asp?id=1504592 (accessed 8 December 2006).

Department of Communities and Local Government (DCLG) (2006b) *A Framework for City-Regions,* London: ODPM.

Department for Environment, Food and Rural Affairs (DEFRA) (2004a) *Review of the Rural White Paper: Our Countryside: the Future*, London: DEFRA. Available at: www.defra.gov.uk/rural/rwpreview/ (accessed 8 December 2006).

Department for Environment, Food and Rural Affairs (DEFRA) (2004b) *Rural Definition and Local Authority Classification.* Available at: www.defra.gov.uk/rural/ruralstats/rural-definition.htm#defn (accessed 8 December 2006).

Department for Environment, Food and Rural Affairs (DEFRA) (2006a) *Rural Services Review*, London: DEFRA

Department for Environment, Food and Rural Affairs (DEFRA) (2006b) *Public Update on Implementation of Lord Haskins' Rural Delivery Review – Report 2006,* London: DEFRA.

Department of the Environment (DoE) (1994) *Vital and Viable Town Centres: Meeting the Challenge,* London: HMSO.

Department of the Environment (DoE) and Ministry for Agriculture, Fisheries and Food (MAFF) (1995) *Rural England: A Nation Committed to a Living Countryside*, London: Cm3016 HMSO.

Department of the Environment, Transport and the Regions (DETR) (1998a) *Building Partnerships for Prosperity*, London: HMSO.

Department of the Environment, Transport and the Regions (DETR) (1998b) *Guidance to the Regional Development Agencies on Rural Policy*, London: DETR.

Department of the Environment, Transport and the Regions (DETR) (1998c) *The Impact of Large Food Stores on Market Towns and District Centres,* London: HMSO.

Department of the Environment, Transport and the Regions (DETR) (1999) *Projections of Households in England to 2021*, London: DETR.

Department of the Environment, Transport and the Regions (2000) *Planning Policy Guidance 3 (Cancelled): Housing*. Available at: www.communities.gov.uk/index.asp?id=1143941 (accessed 8 December 2006).

Department of the Environment, Transport and the Regions (DETR) (2001) *Planning Policy Guidance 13: Transport*. Available at: www.communities.gov.uk/index.asp?id=1144015 (accessed 8 December 2006).

Department of the Environment, Transport and the Regions (DETR) and Department of Health (DoH) (2001) *Quality and Choice for Older People's Housing: A Strategic Framework,* London: DETR.

Department of Health (DoH) (1998) *Our Healthier Nation: A Contract for Health*, London: DoH.

Department of Health (DoH) (1999) *Saving Lives: Our Healthier Nation*, London: DoH.

Department of Health (DoH) (2003) *National Booking Programme: Access, Booking and Choice*, London: NHS Modernisation Agency.

Department of Health (DoH) (2005) *Independence, Well-being and Choice: our Vision for the Future Social Care of Adults in England,* CM6499, London: The Stationery Office.

Department of Transport, Local Government and the Regions (DTLR) (2001) *Planning: Delivering a Fundamental Change*. Available at: www.communities.gov.uk/index.asp?id=1143142 (accessed 8 December 2006).

Department of Work and Pensions (DWP) (2005) *Opportunity Age*, London: DWP.

Dickinson, R.E. (1942) 'The social basis of physical planning', *Sociological Review*, 34: 51–67 and 165–82.

Dixon, S. (2003) *Migration within Britain for Job Reasons*, Labour Market Trends April 2003, London: ONS.

Dyer, C. (2002) 'Small places with large consequences: the importance of small towns in England, 1000–1540', *Historical Research*, 75: 1–24.

DTZ Pieda (1998) *The Nature of Demand for Housing in Rural Areas*, London: DETR.

Eardley, D. (1999) *Discover Derbyshire – Wirksworth and the Surrounding Area,* Solar Press.

East of England Development Agency (EEDA) (2004) *A Shared Vision: The Regional Economic Strategy for the East of England*, EEDA.

East of England Regional Assembly (EERA) (2004) *The East of England Plan: Draft Revision to the Regional Spatial Strategy (RSS) for the East of England*. Available at: www.eera.gov.uk/category.asp?cat=452> (accessed 8 December 2006).

East of England Regional Assembly (EERA) (2005) *Regional Housing Strategy for the East of England 2005–2010*. Available at: www.eera.gov.uk/category.asp?cat=461 (accessed 8 December 2006).

English Market Towns Forum (2002) *Conclusions of Seminar*, 21 February.

ENTEC, Three Dragons and Nottingham Trent University (2002) *Delivering Affordable Housing Through Planning Policy*, London: DLTR.

Ermisch, J. (1990) *Fewer Babies, Longer Lives: Policy Implications of Current Demographic Trends*, York: Joseph Rowntree Foundation.

Errington, A., Bennett, R. and Marshall, B. (1989) *Employment and Training in Rural Areas*, Salisbury: Rural Development Commission.

Evandrou, M. (1997) *Baby Boomers*, London: Age Concern.

Evans, A. and Hartwich, O. M. (2005a) *Unaffordable Housing: Fables and Myths*, Policy Exchange. Available at: http://policyexchange.moodia.co.za/Publications.aspx?id=61 (accessed 8 December 2006).

Evans, A. and Hartwich, O. M. (2005b) *Bigger Better Faster More: Why Some Countries Plan Better Than Others*, Policy Exchange. Available at: www.policyexchange.org.uk/Publications.aspx?id=161 (accessed 8 December 2006).

Evans, A. and Hartwich, O. M. (2006) *Better Homes, Greener Cities*, Policy Exchange. Available at: www.policyexchange.org.uk/ (accessed 8 December 2006).

Experian (2003) *Mosaic Group and Type Descriptions*, London: Experian.

Farquharson, H. (2006) '76 year old council tax rebel prepared for jail', *This is Local London*. Available at: www.thisislocallondon.co.uk/news/boroughpolitics/councilnews/display.var.896100.0.76yearold_council_tax_rebel_prepared_for_jail.php (accessed 8 December 2006).

Farrington, J., Shaw, J., Richardson, T., Maclean, M., Bristow, G., Halden, D. and Leedal, M. (2004) 'Putting accessibility policy appraisal into practice', *Town and Country Planning*, 73(6): 196–98.

Farthing, S., Brown, C., Nadin, V. and Smith, I. (2005) 'Transport issues in small town and rural regeneration', *Town and Country Planning*: 74(6), 198–201.

Findlay, A., Short, D. and Stockdale, A. (2000) 'The labour market impact of migration to rural areas', *Applied Geography*, 20: 333–48.

Findlay, A.M., Stockdale, A., Findlay, A. and Short, D. (2001) 'Mobility as a driver of change in rural Britain: an analysis of the links between migration, commuting and travel to shop patterns', *International Journal of Population Geography*, 7: 1–15.

Fløysand, A. and Jakobsen, S-E. (2007) 'Commodification of rural places: a narrative of social fields, rural development, and football', *Journal of Rural Studies*, 23(2): 206–221.

Fothergill, S. and Gudgin, G. (1982) *Unequal Growth: Urban and Regional Employment Change in the UK*, London: Heinemann.

Fotheringham, A.S., Brunsdon, C. and Charlton, M. (2000) *Quantitative Geography: Perspectives on Spatial Data Analysis*, London: Sage.

Frey, W.H. (1993) 'The new urban revival in the United States', *Urban Studies*, 30: 741–4.

Gallent, N. (1997) 'Planning for affordable rural housing in England and Wales', *Housing Studies*, 12(1): 127–137.

Gallent, N. (2005) 'Regional housing figures in England: policy, politics and ownership', *Housing Studies* 20(6): 973–88.

Gallent, N. and Bell, P. (2000) 'Planning exceptions in rural England: past, present and future', *Planning Practice and Research*, 15(4): 375–84.

Gilder, I. (1984) 'State planning and local needs', in Bradley, T. and Lowe, P. (eds) *Locality and Rurality: Economy and Society in Rural Regions*, Norwich: Geo Books.

Gilg, A. (1996) *Countryside Planning: The First Half Century*, London: Routledge.

Gillespie, A. (1999) 'The changing employment geography of Britain', in Breheny, M. (ed.) *The People: Where Will They Work?* London: Town and Country Planning Association.

Glaister, S., and Graham, D. (2006) *National Road Pricing: Is it Fair and Practical?* Social Market Foundation: London.

Glasgow, N. and Brown, D. (2006) 'Social integration among older in-migrants in non-metropolitan retirement destination counties: establishing new ties', in Kandell, W. and Brown, D. (eds) *Population Change and Rural Society*, Dordrecht, Netherlands: Springer Verlag.

Glennerster, H., Lupton, R., Noden, P. and Power, A. (1999) *Poverty, Social Exclusion and Neighbourhood: Studying the Area Bases of Social Exclusion*, London: LSE.

Granovetter, M. (1985) 'Economic action and social structure: the problem of embeddedness', *American Journal of Sociology*, 91(11): 481–510.

Gray, D. (2004) 'Rural transport and social exclusion', *Built Environment,* 30(2): 172–181.

Gray, D., Shaw, J. and Farrington, J.H. (2006) 'Community transport, social capital and social exclusion in rural areas', *Area*, 38: 89–98.

Green, A.E. (1997) 'A question of compromise? Case study evidence on the location and mobility strategies of dual career households', *Regional Studies*, 37: 641–57.

Green, A.E. (1999) 'Employment opportunities and constraints facing in-migration to rural areas in England', *Geography*, 84: 34–44.

Green, A.E. (2006) 'Employment and the older person in the countryside', in Lowe, P. and Speakman, L. (eds) *The Ageing Countryside: The Growing Older Population of Rural England*. London: Age Concern England.

Green, A. E. and Hardill, I. (2003) *Rural Labour Markets, Skills and Training*, Warwick: Institute of Employment Research.

Gudgin, G. (1990) 'Beyond farming: economic change in rural areas of the United Kingdom,' in ACORA, *Faith in the Countryside*, Worthing: Churchman Publishing.

Guy, C.M. (1990) 'Outshopping from Small Towns', *International Journal of Retail & Distribution Management*, 18(3): 3–14.

Gwilliam, M. (1998) *Urban Renaissance: The Role of Conservation,* paper to the RTPI Summer School, University of York.

Halfacree, K.H. (1994) 'The importance of "the rural" in the constitution of counterurbanization: evidence from England in the 1980s', *Sociologica Ruralis*, 34: 164–89.

Hall, P., Gracey, H., Drewitt, R. and Thomas, R. (1973) *The Containment of Urban England*, London: Allen & Unwin.

Halliday, J. and Coombes, M. (1995) 'In search of counterurbanisation: some evidence from Devon on the relationship between patterns of migration and motivation', *Journal of Rural Studies*, 11: 433–46.

Hallsworth, A. and Worthington, S. (2000) 'Local resistance to larger retailers: the example of and the food superstore in the UK', *International Journal of Retail & Distribution Management*, 28(3): 207–16.

Hambleton District Council (2005) 'Local development framework: core strategy preferred options', *Consultation: July–August 2005,* Hambleton DC, Northallerton.

Hansard (2004) HC Deb (2003–4) Col 640W *Market Towns Initiative,* 1 March 2004.

Harding, R. (2004) *Global Entrepreneurship Monitor: United Kingdom 2003,* London: London Business School.

Harper, S. (2006) *Ageing Societies*, London: Hodder Arnold.

Hart, T. (1996) 'Rural Training & Enterprise Councils – local people influencing local decisions?', in Curry, N. and Owen, S. (eds) *Changing Rural Policy in Britain*, Cheltenham: Countryside and Community Press.

Hart, T. and Strange, I. (2000) *Towns in Transition: Reconstructing Roles for Market Towns*, presented to International Planning History Society Conference, Helsinki, Finland.

Hart, T., Haughton, G. and Peck, J. (1996) 'Accountability and the non-elected local state: calling Training & Enterprise Councils to local account', *Regional Studies*, 30(4): 429–441.

Haskins, C. (2003) *Rural Delivery Review: A Report on the Delivery of Government Policies in Rural England*, London: DEFRA.

Hass-Klau, C. (1986) *Can Rail Save the City*? Ashgate: Aldershot.

Haughton, G. and Counsell, D. (2004) *Regions, Spatial Strategies and Sustainable Development*, London: Routledge.

Healey, P. (1997) *Collaborative Planning: Shaping Places in Fragmented Societies*, Basingstoke: Macmillan.

Hepworth, M., Pickavance, L. and Ziemann, B. (2004) *The Knowledge Economy in Rural England*, London: Local Futures.

Higginson, M. (2005) *Tyne Valley Rail Study, Tyne Valley Rail Partnership: Hexham*. Available at: www.tyne dale.gov.uk/residents/showpdfagenda.asp?meetid=553&agendaid=3 (accessed 8 December 2006).

Holmans, A. (2001) *Housing Demand and Need in England 1996–2016,* London: Town and Country Planning Association.

Holmans, A., Monk, S. and Whitehead, C. (2004) *Building for the Future*, Shelter.

Holmans, A. and Whitehead, C. (2005) 'Housing the next generation. Household growth, housing demand and housing requirements,' *Town and Country Planning*, 74 (10): 301–04.

Holmans, A., Stephens, S. and Fitzpatrick, S. (2007) 'Housing policy in England since 1975, *Housing Studies'*, 22 (2): 147–62.

Howkins, A. (1991) *Reshaping Rural England: A Social History 1850–1925*, London: Routledge.

Howkins, A. (2003) *The Death of Rural England: A Social History of the Countryside Since 1900*, London: Routledge.

Imrie, R. (1996). *Disability and the City,* London: Chapman.

Imrie, R. and Hall, P. (2001) *Inclusive Design: Designing and Developing Accessible Environments*, London: Spon.

Johnson, K.M. and Beale, C.L. (1995) 'The rural rebound revisited: small towns and country homes are growing rapidly in the 1990s', *American Demographics*, 17(7): 46–60.

Joseph, A.E. and Cloutier, D.S. (1991) 'Elderly migration and its implications for service provision in rural communities: an Ontario perspective', *Journal of Rural Studies*, 7: 433–44.

Keeble, D. and Tyler, P. (1995) 'Enterprising behaviour and the urban-rural shift, *Urban Studies*', 32(6): 975–97.

Keith-Lucas, B. and Richards, P.G. (1978) *A History of Local Government in the Twentieth Century*, London: Allen & Unwin.

Keswick Area Partnership (2006) *Keswick Town Centre Masterplan*, produced by Willie Miller Urban Design for Keswick Area Partnership

King's Lynn and West Norfolk Borough Council (1998) *King's Lynn and West Norfolk Local Plan: Written Statement*. Available at: http://online.west-norfolk.gov.uk/local_plan/contents_written.htm (accessed 8 December 2006).

King's Lynn and West Norfolk Borough Council (2006) *Local Development Scheme*. Available at: www.west-norfolk.gov.uk/pdf/LDS%20Summary%202006.pdf (accessed 8 December 2006).

King's Lynn and West Norfolk Borough Council and Partners (2005b) *King's Lynn Urban Renaissance Strategy: Urban Plan*. Available at: http://www.west-norfolk.gov.uk/Default.aspx?page=22789> (accessed 8 December 2006).

Kirkwood, T. (2006) 'Opening address to launch the Newcastle 85+ study', Newcastle: Newcastle University.

KPMG (2000a) *Market Town Regeneration in the West Midlands*, Birmingham: Advantage West Midlands/Countryside Agency.

KPMG (2000b) *Shortlisting Report*, Birmingham: Advantage West Midlands/Countryside Agency.

Krueger, R.A. (1994), *Focus Groups: A Practical Guide for Applied Research*, Thousand Oaks, CA: Sage.

Ladd, H. F. (1992) 'Population growth, density and the costs of providing public services', *Urban Studies,* l29(2): 273–95.

Land Registry (2006) *Property Prices*. Available at: www.landreg.gov.uk/propertyprice/interactive/ppr_ualbs.asp (accessed 1 October 2006).

Langdon-Davies, T. (2006) 'Crediton MCTi – history, lessons learned, and the future', presentation to Local Strategic Partnership.

Law, C.M. and Warnes, A.M. (1976) 'The changing geography of the elderly in England and Wales', *Transactions of the Institute of British Geographers*, 1(4): 453–71.

Leather, P. (1997) 'Providing liveable environments for an increasingly elderly population', paper given to the conference 'How shall we live?'. Mimeo available from Town and Country Planning Association, 17 Carlton House Terrace, London SW1Y 5AS.

Levett-Therivel Sustainability Consultants (2005) *What are Sustainable Rural Communities: Think Piece for the Commission for Rural Communities*. Available at: www.ruralcommunities.gov.uk/files/Sustainable%20Communities%20Thinkpieces.pdf (accessed 8 December 2006).

Lincolnshire County Council (2004) *Draft Structure Plan,* Lincoln: LCC.

Liu, A.Q. and Besser, T. (2003) 'Social capital and participation in community improvement activities by elderly residents in small towns and rural communities', *Rural Sociology*, 68(3): 343–65.

Llewelyn Davies Yeang (2006) *Quality of Place The North's Residential Offer Phase 1 Report,* Newcastle: Northern Way Sustainable Communities Team.

Local Area Framework (2005) *Local Area Framework Fens Area 2005/06*. Available at: www.gos.gov.uk/goee/docs/193516/193520/198138/Fens_LAF_September_2005.DOC (accessed 8 December 2006).

Lovett, A., Haynes, R., Sünnenberg, G. and Gale, S. (2002) 'Car travel time and accessibility by bus to general practitioner services: a study using patient registers and GIS', *Social Science & Medicine*, 55: 97–111.

Lovett, A., Sünnenberg, G., Dockerty, T., Bore, A. and Haynes, R. (2003) 'Public transport and accessibility to services in two districts of East Anglia', in Higgs, G. (ed.), *Rural Services and Social Exclusion*, European Research in Regional Science, 12, London: Pion.

Lowe, P. (ed.) (1999) *The Rural Economy of North East England*, Research Report, University of Newcastle upon Tyne: Centre for Rural Economy.

Lowe, P., Bradley, T. and Wright, S. (1986) *Deprivation and Welfare in Rural Areas,* Norwich: Geobooks.

Lupton, R. (2001) *Places Apart: The Initial Report of CASE's Area Study*, London: LSE.

Maidment, R. and Thompson, G. (eds) (1993) *Managing the United Kingdom: An Introduction to Political Economy and Public Policy*, London: Sage.

Main Street (2005) *What is the Main Street Approach to Commercial District Revitalization?*. Available at: www.mainstreet.org/content.aspx?page=3&section=2 (accessed 8 December 2006).

Marsden, T., Franklin, A. and Kitchen, L. (2005) *Rural Labour Markets: Exploring the Mismatches*, Cardiff: Wales Rural Observatory.

May, E. (2006) *An Update in Respect to Young People's Projects*. Available at: www.westsomersetonline. gov.uk/minutes/Agenda%20item%209.%20%206.11.06.pdf (accessed 8 December 2006).

McLaughlin, B.P. (1986) *Rural England in the 1980s: Rural Deprivation Study Summary of Findings,* Department of the Environment/Rural Development Commission.

Martin and Voorhees Associates (1980) *Review of Rural Settlement Policies 1945–1980,* Martin and Voorhees Associates, London, for the Department of the Environment.

Miller, N.J. (2001) 'Contributions of social capital theory in predicting rural inshopping behaviour', *The Journal of Socio-Economics*, 30(6): 475–493.

Ministry for Agriculture, Fisheries and Food (MAFF) and Department of Environment, Transport and the Regions (DETR) (2000) *Our Countryside: The Future. A Fair Deal for Rural England* (Cm 4909), London: DETR.

Mitchell, C.J.A. (2004) 'Making sense of counterurbanization', *Journal of Rural Studies*, 20: 15–34.

Mitchell, C. (2006) 'Safe mobility for older people', *Generations Review*, 16: 33–36.

Monk, S. and Whitehead, C. (1999) 'Evaluating the economic impact of planning controls in the UK: some implications for housing', *Land Economics*, 75(1): 74–93.

Monk, S., Dunn, J., Fitzgerald, M. and Hodge, I. (1999) *Finding Work in Rural Areas: Bridges and Barriers*, York: York Publishing Services.

Monk, S., Crook, T., Lister, D., Rowley, S., Short, C. and Whitehead, C. (2005) *Land and Finance for Affordable Housing. The Complementary Roles of Social Housing Grant and the Provision of Affordable Housing through the Planning System*, Housing Corporation and Joseph Rowntree Foundation.

Moseley, M.J. (1996) 'Accessibility and care in a rural area – the case of Tewkesbury Borough', *Research, Policy and Planning*, 14: 19–25.

Moseley, M. (2003) *Local Rural Development: Principles and Practice*, London: Sage.

Moseley, M. (2005) *The Future of Services in Rural England – A Scenario for 2015*, Final Report to DEFRA, Countryside & Community Research Unit, University of Gloucestershire.

Murdoch, J. and Abrams, S. (2002) *Rationalities of Planning: Development versus Environment in Planning for Housing*, Aldershot: Ashgate.

Murdoch, J. and Day, G. (1998) 'Middle class mobility, rural communties and the politics of exclusion', in Boyle, P. and Halfacree, K. (eds) *Migration into Rural Areas Theories and Issues*, Chichester: John Wiley & Sons.

Murdoch, J., Lowe, P., Ward, N. and Marsden, T. (2003) *The Differentiated Countryside*, London: Routledge.

National Assembly for Wales (2002) *Dynamic Smaller Towns: Identification of Critical Success Factors. Final Report*, Bristol: University of the West of England and Roger Tym & Partners.

National Audit Office and Audit Commission (2005) *Building More Affordable Homes: Improving the Delivery of Affordable Housing in Areas of High Demand*, London: The Stationery Office.

National Health Services in England (2006) Available at: www.nhs.uk/England (accessed 8 December 2006).

National Retail Planning Forum (NRPF) (2000), 'Town centre vitality and viability: a review of the health check methodology', London: NRPF.

Newby, H. (1980) *Green and Pleasant Land? Social Change in Rural England*, London: Penguin.

New Economics Foundation (NEF) (2005) *Clone Town Britain Survey*. Available at: www.new economics.org/gen/news_clonetownbritainresults.aspx (accessed 8 December 2006).

Noble, M. (1979) *Change in the Small Towns of the East Riding of Yorkshire*, Beverley: Hedon and District Local History Society.

Norfolk County Strategic Partnership (2005) *Norfolk Ambition Annual Report 2004/5*. Available at: www.ncsp_annualreport.norfolk.gov.uk/pages/housing.htm (accessed 8 December 2006).

North East Regional Assembly (NERA) (2005) *View: Shaping the North East*, Regional Spatial Strategy for the North East Submission Draft, June 2005. Available at: www.eera.gov.uk/category.asp?cat=452 (accessed 8 December 2006).

North Norfolk District Council (2004) *Housing Strategy 2003/4*. Available at: www.northnorfolk. org/files/ffphousingstrat.pdf (accessed 8 December 2006).

Northern Way Steering Group (2004) *Moving Forward the Northern Way*. Available at: www.the northernway.co.uk/documents.html (accessed 8 December 2006).

Northumberland County Council (2006) *Performance Plan*. Available at: http://pscm.northumberland. gov.uk/pls/portal92/docs.2559.PDF (accessed 8 December 2006).

Northumberland County Council and Northumberland National Park (2003) *Northumberland County and National Park Joint Structure Plan Review: First Alteration, Deposit Plan*, Northumberland County Council and Northumberland National Park.

Ofcom (2006) *Media Literacy Audit: Report on Media Literacy among Older People*, London: Ofcom.

Office for National Statistics (ONS) (2005) *National Accounts: Household Final Consumption Expenditure Goods and Services 1948–2005*. Available at: www.statistics.gov.uk/statbase/Product.asp?vlnk=8256&More=Y (accessed 8 December 2006).

Office for National Statistics (ONS) (2006) *Annual Survey of Hours and Earnings*, London: ONS.

Office of the Deputy Prime Minister (ODPM) (2003a) *Sustainable Communities: Building for the Future*, London: ODPM.

Office of the Deputy Prime Minister (ODPM) (2003b) *Sustainable Communities in the North East: Building for the Future*, London: Department for Communities and Local Government. Available at: www.communities.gov.uk/index.asp?id=1139904 (accessed 8 December 2006).

Office of the Deputy Prime Minister (ODPM) (2003c) *Sustainable Communities in the East of England: Building for the Future*, London: Department for Communities and Local Government. Available at: www.communities.gov.uk/index.asp?id=1139884 (accessed 8 December 2006).

Office of the Deputy Prime Minister (ODPM) (2004a) *Planning Policy Statement 7: Sustainable Development in Rural Areas (London, Office of the Deputy Prime Minister)*. Available at: www.communities. gov.uk/index.asp?id=1139884 (accessed 8 December 2006).

Office of the Deputy Prime Minister (ODPM) (2004b) *Planning Policy Statement 12: Local Development Frameworks (London, Office of the Deputy Prime Minister)*. Available at: www.communities. gov.uk/index.asp?id=1143847 (accessed 8 December 2006).

Office of the Deputy Prime Minister (ODPM) (2004c) *Making it Happen: The Northern Way*, London: ODPM.

Office of the Deputy Prime Minister (ODPM) (2005) *Planning Policy Statement 6: Planning for Town Centres*. Available at: www.communities.gov.uk/index.asp?id=1143820 (accessed 8 December 2006).

Office of the Deputy Prime Minister (ODPM)/HM Treasury (2005) *The Government's Response to the Barker Review*. Available at: www.hm-treasury.gov.uk/pre_budget_report/prebud_pbr05/assoc_docs/prebud_pbr05_adbarker.cfm (accessed 8 December 2006).

One North East (2006) *Regional Economic Strategy (RES) 2006 – Leading the Way*. Available at: www.onenortheast.co.uk/lib/liReport/9653/Regional%20Economic%20Strategy%202006%20-2016.pdf (accessed 8 December 2006).

Ove Arup & Partners with Innovacion (2006) *The North's Residential Offer: Policy and Investment Review Phase 1 Report*, Newcastle: Northern Way Sustainable Communities Team.

Owen, S. (1996) 'Sustainability and rural settlement planning', *Planning Practice and Research*, 11(1): 37–49.

Owens, S. (1995) 'Land use planning as an instrument of sustainable development', *The Globe*, 3: 6–8.

Paddison, A. (2003) 'Town centre management (TCM): a case study of Achmore', *International Journal of Retail & Distribution Management*, 31(12): 618–27.

Paradis, T.W. (2000) 'Conceptualizing small towns as urban places: the process of downtown redevelopment in Galena, Illinois', *Urban Geography*, 21: 61–82.

Pearce, B. (2004) 'Affordable housing through the planning system – does it make housing more or less affordable,' *Town and Country Planning*, 74(4): 132–37.

Performance & Innovation Unit (PIU) (1999) *Rural Economies*, London: Cabinet Office.

Phillips, D.R., Vincent, J. and Blacksell, S. (1987) 'Spatial concentration of residential homes for the elderly: planning responses and dilemmas', *Transactions of the Institute of British Geographers*, 12 (1): 73–83.

Philips, M. (1993) 'Rural gentrification and the process of class colonisation', *Journal of Rural Studies*, 9(2): 123–140.

Phillips, M. and Swaffin-Smith, C. (2004) 'Market towns – victims of market forces?', *International Journal of Retail & Distribution Management*, 32(11): 557–68.

Pinkerton, J. Hassinger, E. and O'Brian, D. (1995) 'Inshopping by residents of small communities', *Rural Sociology*, 60: 467–80.

Platt, C. (1976) *The English Medieval Town*, London: Secker & Warburg.

Powe, N.A. (2005) 'Evaluation of Trading Conditions in Morpeth', Morpeth for Castle Morpeth Borough Council and Morpeth & District Chamber of Trade, unpublished document.

Powe, N.A. (2007) 'Population change in country towns: exploring the implications for rural Norfolk, England', unpublished manuscript.

Powe, N.A. and Shaw, T. (2003) 'Market town centres: exploring the service role through visitor surveys', *Planning Practice and Research*, 18: 37–50.

Powe, N.A. and Shaw, T. (2004) 'Exploring the current and future role of market towns in servicing their hinterlands: a case study of Alnwick in the North East of England', *Journal of Rural Studies*, 20: 405–18.

Powe, N.A. and Whitby, M. (1994) 'Economies of settlement size in rural settlement planning', *Town Planning Review*, 65(4): 415–34.

Reade, E. (1987) *British Town and Country Planning*, Open University Press.

Reichholf, J. (2004) *Der Tanz um das Goldene Kalb*, Der Ökokolonialismus Europas.

Renkow, M. and Hoover, D. (2000) 'Commuting, migration, and rural-urban population dynamics', *Journal of Regional Science*, 40: 261–87.

Rhodes, R. (1995) *The New Governance: Governing Without Government*, Swindon: ESRC.

Richardson, R. Bradley, D. Jones, I. and Benneworth, P. (1999) 'The North East' in Breheny, M. (ed.) *The People: Where Will they Work?* London: TCPA.

Richardson, R. and Powe, N.A. (2004) 'Service implications of population growth in market towns', *Planning Practice and Research*, 19(4): 363–73.

Robertson, K.A. (1997) 'Downtown retail revitalization: a review of American development strategies', *Planning Perspectives*, 12: 383–401.

Rogers, R. (2006) *Towards a Strong Urban Renaissance*. An independent report by members of the Urban Task Force chaired by Lord Rogers of Riverside.

Rogerson, R.J. (1999) 'Quality of life and city competitiveness', *Urban Studies*, 36(5–6): 969–85.

Rogerson, P.A. (2001) *Statistical Methods for Geography*, London: Sage.

Rugg, J. and Jones, A. (1999) *Getting a Job, Finding a Home: Rural Youth Transitions*, Bristol: Policy Press.

Rural Development Commission (1999) *Rural Housing*. London: Rural Development Commission.

Satsangi, M. and Dunmore, K. (2003) 'The planning system and the provision of affordable housing in rural Britain: a comparison of the Scottish and English experience', *Housing Studies*, 18: 201–17.

Sawyer, A. (2003) *Wymondham: A Market Town Health Check Report,* Wymondham Development Partnership.

Scase, R. and Scales, J. (2002) *Regional Futures and Neighbourhood Realities*, London: National Housing Federation.

Schiller, R. (1994) 'Vitality and viability: challenge to the town centre', *International Journal of Retail & Distribution Management*, 22(6): 46–50.

Seniors Network (2006) *Pensioners Parliament 2006*. Available at: www.seniorsnetwork.co.uk/npc/blackpool2006.htm (accessed 8 December 2006).

Shepherd, J. and Congdon, P. (1990) 'Small town England: population change among small to medium sized urban areas, 1971–1981', *Progress in Planning*, 33, 1–111.

Shorten, J. (2004) 'New light on country life', *Town & Country Planning*, 73: 186–91.

Shorten, J., Brown, C. and Daniels, I. (2001) *Are Villages Sustainable? A Review of the Literature*, Cheltenham: Countryside Agency.

Shucksmith, M. (1990) *Housebuilding in Britain's Countryside*, London: Routledge.

Shucksmith, M. (2000) *Exclusive Countryside? Social Inclusion and Regeneration in Rural Areas*, Joseph Rowntree Foundation: York Publishing Services.

Shucksmith, M. and Best, R. (2006) *Homes for Rural Communities. Report of the Joseph Rowntree Foundation's Rural Housing Policy Forum*, Joseph Rowntree Foundation: York Publishing Services.

Shucksmith, M. and Watkins, L. (1988) 'The supply of land for rural housing', in Winter M (ed.) *Who Can Afford To Live In The Countryside?* Cirencester: Royal Agricultural College.

Shucksmith, M., Watkins, L. and Henderson, M. (1993) 'Attitudes and policies towards residential development in the Scottish countryside', *Journal of Rural Studies*, 9(3): 243–55.

Shucksmith, M., Henderson, M., Raybould, S., Coombes, M. and Wong, C. (1995) *A Classification of Rural Housing Markets in England*, London: HMSO.

Smallbone, D., North, D., Baldock, R. and Ekanem, I. (2002) *Encouraging and Supporting Enterprise in Rural Areas*, London: Small Business Service.

Small Business Service (SBS) (2004) *A Government Action Plan for Small Business: The Evidence Base DTI London*. Available at: www.sbs.gov.uk/SBS_Gov_files/corporateinfo/sbs_evidence.pdf (accessed 8 December 2006).

Smith, D.P. and Phillips, D.A. (2001) 'Socio-cultural representations of greentrified Pennine rurality', *Journal of Rural Studies*, 17: 457–69.

Smullian, M. (2006) 'Sustainability drive hurts rural housing', *Planning,* 1 September: 14–15.

Social Exclusion Unit (1998) *Bringing Britain Together: A New Strategy for Neighbourhood Renewal*, Command Paper 4045, London: Cabinet Office.

Social Exclusion Unit (2001) *A New Commitment to Neighbourhood Renewal: National Strategy Action Plan*, London: Cabinet Office.

Social Exclusion Unit (2003) *Making the Connections: Final Report on Transport and Social Exclusion*, Social Exclusion Unit. Available at: www.socialexclusionunit.gov.uk/publications.asp?did=228 (accessed 8 December 2006).

Social Exclusion Unit (2004a) *Jobs and Enterprise in Deprived Areas*, London: ODPM.

Social Exclusion Unit (2004b) *Breaking the Cycle: Taking Stock of Progress and Priorities for the Future*, London: ODPM.

Social Exclusion Unit (2006) *Sure Start to Later Life: Ending Inequalities for Older People*, London: SEU.

South East Regional Research Laboratory (SERRL) (2004) 'The role of rural settlements as service centres', prepared for the Countryside Agency by Land Use Consultants, SERRL and Emma Delow.

South Norfolk Council (2003) *South Norfolk Local Plan* (adopted version). Available at: www.south-norfolk.gov.uk/planning/287.asp (accessed 8 December 2006).

SQW (2006) *Developing Entrepreneurship and Innovation in Rural Areas of West Yorkshire,* Leeds: Yorkshire Forward.

Standing Advisory Committee on Trunk Road Assessment (SACTRA) (1999), *Trunk Roads and the Generation of Traffic*, London: HMSO.

Stanyon, J. (2006) *Challenges of the Future: The Rebirth of Small Independent Retail in America*, Washington, DC: NRF Foundation.

Stead, D. and Banister, D. (2006). 'Decoupling transport growth and economic growth in Europe', in Jourquin, B., Rietveld, P. and Westin, K. (eds) *Towards Better Performing Transport Networks*, pp. 136–156. London: Routledge.

Stephens, M., Whitehead, C. and Munro, M. (2005) *Lessons from the Past, Challenges for the Future for Housing Policy: An Evaluation of English Housing Policy 1975–2000*, ODPM.

Stockdale, A. (2005) 'In-migration and its impacts on the rural economy', in Hill, B. (ed.) *The New Rural Economy: Change, Dynamism and Government Policy*, The Institute of Economic Affairs, London.

Swain, C. (1997) 'Economic and social trends in small towns', in *Action for Market Towns, Market Towns: Options for a Share in the Future*, Suffolk: Action for Market Towns.

Tarling, R., Rhodes, J., North, J. and Broome, G. (1993) *The Economy of Rural England*, Salisbury: Rural Development Commission.

Tetlow, R. (2006) *Continuing Care Retirement Communities: A Guide to Planning*, York: Joseph Rowntree Foundation.

Thomas, C.J. and Bromley, R.D.F. (2002) 'The changing competitive relationship between small town centres and out-of-town retailing: town revival in South Wales', *Urban Studies*, 39: 791–817.

Thompson, D. (1995) *The Concise Oxford Dictionary*, 9th edn, Oxford: Clarendon Press.

Town & Country Planning Association (TCPA) (2002) *New Towns and New Town Extensions*, Town & Country Planning Association.

Townroe, P. and Moore, B. (1999) 'The East of England', in Breheny, M. (ed.) *The People: Where Will they Work?* London: TCPA.

Transport 2000/Countryside Agency/Citizens Advice Bureau (2003) *Rural Transport Futures: Transport Solutions for a Thriving Countryside,* London: Transport 2000.

Tynedale Community Partnership (2003) *Tynedale Community Plan*, Hexham: Tynedale DC.

Vaggs, V. (2006) *Sainsbury's Planning Permission Approved,* website of Councillor V. Vaggs. Available at: www.councillor.info/alnwick/vvaggs (accessed 8 December 2006).

Vincent, J. (2003) *Old Age*, London: Routledge.

Walker, A. (1978) *Rural Poverty*, London: Child Poverty Action Group.

Walker, A. (2004) 'The ESRC *Growing Older* research programme 1999–2004', *Ageing and Society*, 24 (5): 657–676.

Walker, A., O'Brian, M., Traynor, J., Fox, K., Goddard, E. and Foster, K. (2003) *Living in Britain: Results from the 2001 General Household Survey*, London: The Stationery Office.

Ward, N. (2006) 'Rural development and the economies of rural areas', in Midgely, J. (ed.) *A New Rural Agenda*, Newcastle: IPPR North.

Warnes, A.M. and Law, C.M. (1984) 'The elderly population of Great Britain: locational trends and policy', *Transactions of the Institute of British Geographers*, 9 (1): 37–59.

Warnes, T. and McInerney, B. (2004) *The English Regions and Population Ageing,* London: Age Concern.

Waverley Borough Council (2006) Community Strategy. Available at: www.waverley.gov.uk/lsp/theme4.asp (accessed 8 December 2006).

Weir, S. and Hall, W. (eds) (1994) *Extra Governmental Organisations in the United Kingdom and their Accountability*, London: The Charter 88 Trust.

Wigglybus (2006) The Wigglybus Website. Available at: www.wigglybus.org.uk/ (accessed 8 December 2006).

Williams, A.S. and Jobes, P.C. (1990) 'Economic and quality-of-life considerations in urban-rural migration', *Journal of Rural Studies*, 6: 187–94.

Williams, C. and Ferguson, M. (2005) 'Recovering from crisis: strategic alternatives for leisure and tourism providers based within a rural economy', *International Journal of Public Sector Management*, 18: 350–66.

Williams, C. and White, R. (2001) 'Evaluating the role of the social economy in tackling rural transport problems', *Planning Practice and Research*, 16: 337–48.

Williams, J. (2000) 'Tools for achieving sustainable housing strategies in rural Gloucestershire', *Planning Practice & Research*, 15(3): 155–74.

Whitehead, C. (2005) *Using the Land Use Planning System to Provide Affordable Housing*, Dept of Land Economy, University of Cambridge. Available at: www.cchpr.landecon.cam.ac.uk/ (accessed 8 December 2006).

Wilcox, S. (2005) *Limits to Working Households' Ability to Become Home Owners*, Joseph Rowntree Foundation: York Publishing Services.

Wong, C. (1998) 'Determining factors for local economic development: the perception of practitioners in the North West and Eastern regions of the UK', *Regional Studies*, 32(8): 707–20.

Wong, C. (2001) 'The relationship between quality of life and local economic development: an empirical study of local authority areas in England', *Cities*, 18(1): 25–32.

Wong, C. and Madden, M. (2000) North West Regional Housing Need and Demand – Final Report, DETR.

Woods, M. (2006) 'Rural politics and governance' in Midgeley, J. (ed.) *A New Rural Agenda*, Newcastle upon Tyne. IPPR North.

Worthington, S. (1998) 'Loyalty cards and the revitalisation of the town centre', *International Journal of Retail and Distribution Management*, 26(2), 68–78.

Wymondham Town Council (undated) *Local Development Framework – Response from Wymondham Town Council*. Available at: www.wymondham-norfolk.co.uk/towncouncil/minutes/LDF_07%2002 %2006.pdf (accessed 8 December 2006).

Yarwood R. (1996) 'Rurality, locality and industrial change: a micro-scale investigation of manufacturing growth in the district of Leominster', *Geoforum*, 27: 23–37.

Yorkshire and Humber Assembly (YHA) (2004) *Scrutiny Enquiry 5: Market Towns Initiative and Renaissance Market Towns Programme*, Wakefield: YHA.

Yorkshire Forward (2006) *Renaissance Market Towns Handbook*, Leeds: Yorkshire Forward.

Index

Numbers in **bold** type indicate figures, tables and boxes.

accessibility 9, 34, 61, 95, 158; motorways 35; *see also* buses; cars; parking; public transport; railways

Action for Market Towns 5, 50, 52, 139–40

Advantage West Midlands 110

affluence 9, 15, 20–1, **22–4**, 30, 71, 91, 118–19, 145, 151

affordable housing, and ageing population 14, 71, 110; in commuter towns 110, 114; importance of 117; and planning 87–9, 117; shortage of 2, 32, 38, 49, 78–80, 82, 92, 103, 151; *see also* deprivation; house prices; in-migration

Affordable Rural Housing Commission 83, 86

ageing population 4, **13, 15, 16–17**, 18, 21, 145, 148; care 77–8; care homes 72, 78; and employment 106; government's ambivalence to 79; housing 25, 28–9, 36, 149; and immigration 34, 36–7, **38**, 73, 89, 95; mobility impairment 75–7; and political awareness 71; as positive social influence 71, 78; and self-employment 71; tax burden 71; and VAT on fuel 71; *see also* retirement

agriculture 12, **40**, 44, 130, 145–6, 157; governmental support 81

Alnwick 6, 7, **22**, 30, **31, 98, 129**; castle **31**, 102, 139–40; characteristics **39, 126**; classic market town 90; commuter town **36**, 97; employment 101, **111**; engagement 101; expansion 98; hinterland 38; house prices 40; housing allocation 99; housing policy 104; in-migration 101; Royal Air Force base 20, **98**;

specialised employment 40; supermarkets 120, **121**; theatre 139; tourism **31**, 102

Amble 12, **22**, 129

analysis; *see* cluster analysis; descriptive analysis; regressive analysis

architecture 29, 34, 50, 76, 109, 124

Areas of Outstanding Natural Beauty 40, 87, 110

attractions 9, 15, **16**, 25, 28, 32–3, 102, 131–2, 137, 149

Aylsham **24**

baby boom 69, 71

banks 6, 12–14, **21**, 30, **31**, 110, 119; branch closure 63

barn conversions *see* building conversions

Barnard Castle **22**, 66, 129

Beacon Towns 52, 143

Beccles **24**

Berkhamsted **23**

Berwick-upon-Tweed 12, **22**, 90, 129, **130**

bio-fuel 146

Bishop Auckland 12, 129

border towns 12

Brandon **24**

Brightlingsea **23**

Broughton Astley 66

BSE 50

building conversions 71

building societies 12, 14, 119

Burnham-on-Crouch 20, **23**

buses 36, 63, 65, 112, 125, 158; disabled access 77; free off-peak travel 72; increase in

frequency 59; school buses 65; *see also* transport
Business Improvement District 138, **139**
Business Link 110
business services 13, 106, 110
Butlins 33, 40, 110
bypasses **40**, 60, 62, 64, 68

Calder Valley 52
Cambridge 40, 97, 100–1, **112**
campsites 14, **17**
cars; bio-fuel 146; 'bypassing' shopping in market towns 120; in case studies 74; dependence on 59, 65, 80, 150, 156; dominant mode of transport 28, 30, 111, 125; employers demand ownership of 78; falling cost of 1, 28, 60, 108, 145, 150, 155; fuel prices 60, 71; increase in ownership 59–60, 79; insurance 78; lift giving 62–3; necessity of owning 61; reducing use of 46, 109, 153; sharing 63, 125; *see also* congestion; mobility, growth in; parking; transport
Carterton 66
castles **31**, 32, **34**, **98**, **126**, **131**, 140
categorisation 12–14, 18–20, 42, 48, 82, 86
catering 6, 13, 15, **16–17**, 18, 38
Catterick Garrison 34, 110
cattle markets *see* livestock markets
census *see* Population Census
charity shops 119, **128**, 130
Chatteris **23**
childcare 106
Christmas lights 124, 153
cinemas **31**, 74, **126**, 128–9, 139
cities, escape from 29
Civic Trust 2, 50, 95, 101, 121, 124; Regeneration Unit 142
'classic' market town 21–2, 28, 148
classification 11, 18–25, 27, 42, 82, 120
'clone towns' 122
clothes shops 14, **17**, 21, 76–7, 119, 123, 127, **128**, **131**, 133
cluster analysis 3, 9, 13, **21**, 38; defined **19**
coalfield towns 12, 82, 89–91; out-commuting 114; unemployment in 105
Community Strategies 53, **55**
commuting **22–4**, 30, 32, 62, 85, 144; and choice in job market 106, 108; commuter towns 25, 28, 97, 111; cost of 35; distance 15, **17**, 18; in East 21; and engagement 25, 35; and environment 91; and housing 35–6, 83, 100, 114, 149; and in-migration 35, 97–8,

109; linked to income 35; to London 38, 40, **98**, 100, 101, 113; in North East 20; and proximity to urban areas 35; and public transport 38, **41**; and retirement 70; *see also* cars
competition; between market towns 152; on high street 146; in labour market 153; from out-of-town shopping 46, 49, 66; from urban areas 18, 38, 118, 150
congestion 61–2, 66, 95, 102, 110, 130, 150; single biggest issue for market towns 64, 66; *see also* parking
Conservative Party 72, 82
Corbridge 129–32
council housing 41, 45–6, 90, 92, 102
Council Tax 71
counter-urbanisation 1, 70, 82, 112
Countryside Agency 12, 19, 20, 35, 47, 52, 54, 72, 116, 143–4
Crediton 7; characteristics **39**; closure of food factory 110; house prices 41–2; supermarkets 120; town centre improvements 141–3
Crook **22**, 129
cycling 59, 62, 67–8; networks 61, 64, 68

Debenham **24**
decline 2, 40, 44–9, 75, 89–90, 118–19, 151; *see also* regeneration
definitions 5, 9, 11–12, 14–15; dictionary 12, 129
DEFRA 2, 52–4, 72, 82–3, 90
demographics 19, 51, 66, 69–71, 81, 145; *see also* ageing population; retirement
dentists 75
Department of Communities and Local Government 88
Department of Environment, Food and Rural Affairs *see* DEFRA
Department of the Environment 89
department stores 76–7, 120, **126**
deprivation 9, **22–4**, 108, 116, 151
Dereham **24**
desirable, market towns seen as 1, 28–9, 86; *see also* quality of life
'difference from the city' 12, 114, 130, 132, 150, 156
disabled access 75–7, 79, 125, 128; *see also* mobility
Diss **24**
distribution 13
district councils **31**, 78, 99, 110, 138, 153, 158
diversity 3, 7n1, 13, 66, 122

doctors 12, 14–15, **16**, 37; and driving licences 75; *see also* hospitals; NHS
Downham Market 6, 7, **24**, 35; characteristics **39, 98, 126**; commuter town 111; employment 101, **112**; housing allocation 100; and King's Lynn 38, 97; regeneration 142; regeneration partnership 142; retirement **126**; town centre improvements 141
dual income households 35, 67, 109

East of England 20–4, 83, 93–4, 96–9, 102–4, 114; East of England Development Agency 96; prosperity 97
economy, structure of 5, 9, 43, 106–7
Edward I 7n1
elderly people, housing 88, 151; transport 2, 61, 68, 151; *see also* ageing population
Ely **23**
employment centres, market towns as 4, 43, 48, 105, 110
employment, declining 30, 105; greater opportunities in urban areas 35; growth in 106–7; in ICT 106; in market towns 108–12, 149; in rural areas 105–8, 151; in services 106; structure 13
engagement with community 25, 35, 37, 100–2, 109, 112, **113**, 150, 153
entrepreneurs 73, 107, 109, 112, 115, 117
environment 29, 44, 46; and cars 59–60, 66–7, 145; environmental capacity 47; environmental issues privileged above social 86, 87, 109; global warming 146; urban containment benefits 91; *see also* surroundings; sustainable communities
Estate Action 89–90
estates, newly built 71

family 70, 74, 79, 84, 131, 138
financial services 35, 106, 119; *see also* banks; building societies
food festivals 140
foot and mouth disease 32, 42n10, 50, 116
Frameworks for Regional Employment and Skills Action 116
fuel prices 60, 71
future for market towns 1, 3, 4, 30, 107, 137, 145, 152–6

gender 61, 106, 109
Gosforth 7
graduates 107
green belt 40, 86–7, 110

Guisborough 22
gyms 128

Halthwhistle 22, 129
Harleston **24**
Haskins Rural Delivery Review 52, 90
Haslemere 7; characteristics **39**, 110; customer loyalty scheme 138–9, 144; food festival 140
Haughton, Graham 47, 93–4
Haverhill **24**
health care *see* doctors; hospitals; NHS
Hebden Bridge **41, 141**
heritage 3, 12, 21, 28–9, 32–3, 66, 76, 95–6, 98, 109–10, 115, 121, 156
Hexham 20, **22**, 73–9, 129, 132, 157; shops 74; transport hub 73
hinterlands *see* rural hinterlands
history of market towns 3, 12, 29, 89, 98, 109, 114, 131, 137–40, 155, 157–9; *see also* heritage
home-based work 18, 106
HOPe 88
hospitals 77, 88, 151, 155; difficult to access 63, 72–3, 75; *see also* doctors; NHS
hotels 13, 15, **16, 38**, 40; and self-employment 18
house prices 4, 14, **17**, 83; and distance from cities 29; increase in 29, 40–1, 78, 83, 151; and Ministry of Defence 34; and proximity to London 21; as pull factor 29; *see also* affordable housing, shortage of; housing
housing, allocation 4, 91–2, 94–6, 98–9, 103–4, 151; availability 29, 94–6; commuters and 35–6; difference between towns and hinterlands 81; for the elderly 88; expansion 28, 102, 152, 156; 'right to buy' 45, 84; surplus 96; *see also* affordable housing, shortage of; council housing; house prices
Housing Corporation 87–8, 92
Housing Market Renewal Pathfinder 91, 96
Hunstanton 38

ICT 49, 68, 106–7, 111–12, 145; *see also* Internet; mobile telephones; websites of market towns
'in bloom' schemes 124, 153
in-migration 4, 13–15, **16–17**, 18, 28–9, 94; and ageing populations 36–7, **38**, 73, 95; and changes character of towns 95, 151; commuting 35, 97–8, 109; and employment 101; and house prices 49, 91, 151; and local politics 95; and out-shopping 95; positive effects 109; and public administration 33;

and self-employment 15, 36, 109, **111**, 152; and unemployment 29, 38–40

income 1, 35, 61, 83, 97; *see also* cars; dual income households; housing

Index of Multiple Deprivation 90

industry 12, 40; decline in **41**, 94, 110, 114; history 89, 157; *see also* coalfield towns; manufacturing

intermediate position of market towns 2, 12, 89, 114, 151

Internet 49, 52, 68, 79, 106, 122, 130; *see also* ICT; websites of market towns

intimidation 65, **129**, 133

Jobcentre Plus 106, 110

Jobseeker's Allowance 41

Joseph Rowntree Foundation 86

Keswick 7, **32**; Business Improvement District 138, **139**, 144, 153; characteristics **39**; future 137–8; hinterland 38; house prices 40; pencil factory 110; parking 138; remoteness 38; theatre 139; tourism **32**, 40; walking to work 66

key actors 40, 54–5, 100, 118, 137, 143–4, 152–3

'key settlements' 43–8, 81–2, 85, 97

King's Lynn 38, 97, 99–101, 112

Labour Party 2–3, 71–2, 82, 85, 89–91

lack of data on market towns 11, 45, 59

Land Registry 5

land use 43–4, 47, 49, 55, 63, 67

Land Use Consultants 47

Leominster 34

libraries 130

lifestyle choices 1–2, 28, **33**, 36, 48, 80, 95, 108, 117, 145, 149; under-employment as 107

lifestyle surveys 1, 112

Littleport **23**

livestock markets 3, **40**, 158

Local Area Agreements 53, 115

Local Development Frameworks 86–8, 93, 98, 116, 160–2

Local Strategic Partnerships 53–4, 115, 144, 161

London 21, 38–40, 59, **64**, **98**, 100–1, 106, 113; *see also* commuting

loyalty 31

Malton 123–4

Manchester 91

Manningtree **23**

manufacturing 14–15, **16**, 18, 28, 40; high proportion of in market towns 106; job losses in 105; moves from urban to rural 106; public sector support for 33

March **23**

Market and Coastal Towns Association 52

Market and Coastal Towns Initiative 142

market crosses 3, 7n1, **36**

'market town', as historical term 3

Market Towns Initiatives 4, 5, 13, 14, 48–9; Action Plans 115; assessment of 54; average size of 54; criticised 55; current direction 44; dedicated officer 143; 'health checks' 120; history of 46–7, 51–4, 90; key actors 54, **55**; role 143–4; and urban areas 35; Yorkshire Forward 41

Market Towns Research Group 51

marketing towns 12, **34**, 70, 108, 112, 114–15, 119, 123–4, 132, 139–40, 153

markets 3, 21, **31**; *see also* trade

Marks & Spencer 141

Martin and Voorhees Associates 44–5, 48

micro-businesses *see* small businesses

migration *see* in-migration; out-migration

Mildenhall **24**

Minehead 7, **33**; characteristics **39**, 110; EYE project 142; remoteness 38; shopping 120; tourism 40, 110

Ministry of Defence 14, 18, 25, 28, **34**, 40, 105, 110; *see also* Royal Air Force

mobile telephones 119

mobility, growth in 1–2, 25, 28–9, 48, 62–3, 66, 106, 145, 148–51, 157–8; *see also* cars; disabled access

mopeds 63

Morpeth 6, 7, **22**, 129, 132, 139; characteristics **39**; department store **126**; expansion 98; housing allocation 99, 104; proximity to Newcastle upon Tyne 38, 97, 111; specialised employment 40; supermarkets **126**; tourism **98**; town centre improvements 141

Mosaic database 70–1

motoring *see* cars

motorways 35, 67, 110

MTI *see* Market Towns Initiative

museums 32

National Parks 15, **16–17**, 28, 37, 87; Lake District 32; Northumberland 75, 99, 131

Neighbourhood Renewal Strategy 90

Newcastle upon Tyne 7, 31, 91

newspapers, local 130

Newmarket **24**

NHS 71, 75, 155; *see also* doctors; hospitals
nightlife 30, 128–9, **129**, 133
North East 4, 7, 12, 20–1, **22**, 93, 96, 103;
     deprivation 97
North/South divide 93
North Walsham 121
North West 92, 106, 113–14
Northern Way 90–1, 96
Northumberland Heritage Coast 131
Norwich **36**, 40, 97–100, 102, **112**, 126–7,
     138
number of market towns 12, 26n2

opening hours **128**, 130
Oswestry 7, 38, **40**; characteristics **39**; youth
     café 142–4
out-shopping 30, **36**, 37, 46, 95, 101, 124–5,
     144, 150
outmigration 2, 34, 37, 104; and ageing
     population 14, 70–1

parish councils **55**, 72, 79, 153, 158
Parish Transport Fund 63, 72
parking, cost of 125, 128, 138, 130, 138;
     disabled 128; free in out-of-town shopping
     centres 66, 76, 118, 126, 138; key issue in
     town centres 125; provision of promotes
     growth 124; shortage of 61–2, 66, 95, 150
parks 131
pay *see* wages, low
pedestrianisation 50, 76–7
perceptions of market towns 7
personal mobility 48, 62, 149–51, 159;
     see also cars; transport
petrol stations 46
planning, contestability 45, 83; defined 49, 160;
     demand 1–2, 40, 42, 82, 85, 91, 93, 95–6,
     104, 151–2; distinguishes between town and
     hinterland 81, 84–6; history 49, 118–19; and
     house prices 87–9, 96; in National Parks 32;
     Planning and Compulsory Purchase Act 46,
     49, 160; Planning Policy Statements 44, 46,
     52, 87–8, 161; policies 27, 44, 56–8, 96, 151;
     regulations 1
policy in market towns 43, 107–8, 148–9, 154;
     see also Market Towns Initiative
population 3, 5, 11–12; and cost of service
     provision 45; density 87, 91; forecasting 94;
     growth 82, 94; and out-migration 71; of
     rural areas 82; *see also* ageing population;
     retirement
Population Census 5
post offices **31**, 46, 63, 72, 77

poverty 89, 108; *see also* deprivation
Primary Care Trusts 155
produce 12
produce markets *see* markets
Prudhoe **22**, 129
public administration 14, 33
public transport 2, 35, 61–2, 64–5, 74, 79, 86,
     150, 156; in case studies 75; *see also* cars;
     cycling; motorways; roads; transport; walking
pubs **31**, 128

Quality Councils 154
quality of life 29, 35, 44; *see also* surroundings
QUANGOs 155
questionnaires **6**

R^2 15–17
racecourses 32
railways 28, **36**, 62, 66, 100–1, 158; closure of
     62; disabled access 77; 'Gateway Stations' 35,
     46, 63; and integrated transport 64
RDAs *see* Regional Development Agencies
real estate 14
reasons for moving to market towns 1, 29
redevelopment *see* regeneration
regeneration 9, 45, 132, 137–44, 148; history
     50–1; key issues 48–50; managing 54;
     policies 51–4, 89–91
Regional Development Agencies 3, **41**, 50–5, 72,
     90, 110, 116–17, 144, 154, 161; Advantage
     West Midlands 110; and deprivation 116; East
     of England Development Agency 96; main
     source of funding for rural development 116;
     South East Regional Research Laboratory 2,
     18, 29–30, 47–8, 95, 105–8, 124, 144; South
     West Regional Development Agency 52, 141;
     Yorkshire Forward 41, 52, **53**, 116, 143, 161
Regional Economic Strategy 97, 116, 154
Regional Housing Strategy 155
Regional Planning Guidance 92
Regional Spatial Strategies 86, 92–4, 97, 99,
     116, 154, 160–2
Regional Sustainable Development Framework
     155
regionalism 81
regression analysis 3, 7, 11, 35–7
relocation 1
remoteness 2, 11, 15, 18, 34
Renaissance Market Towns **53**
renting 41, 84, 102
restaurants **31**, 34, 71
retail provision 49, 66, 98, 101, 104, 124,
     141, 156

retailing, trends in 2

retirement 25, 28, 69–71; and affluence 71; and engagement with community 37; and freedom to choose 36, 69, 71; housing and 36–7, **38**; long-distance commuting precedes 70; and proximity to family 70; to seaside towns 37, 69–70; and services 71; and voluntary work 37; *see also* population

Richmond 7, **34;** Catterick Garrison 34, 110; characteristics **39**; future 137–9, 143–4; house prices 40; quality of life 114; specialised employment 40; theatre 139; website 115

'right to buy' 45, 84

roads historic emphasis on 67; widening 66; *see also* cars; motorways; transport

Rochdale Canal 142

Rothbury **22**, 129

Royal Air Force 20, 98, 101, 112; Brize Norton 67; *see also* Ministry of Defence

Rural Development Commission 2, 45, 50, 90, 115

rural hinterlands 4; decline in services 151; depend on market towns 38, 97, 124; deprivation 89, 151–2; homogeny 81; links with weakened 48; market towns depend on 30, 32, 50; shortage of funding 151; size of 38; *see also* transport

rural idyll 29, 89, 109

rural location 12

rural service centres 21, 27, 43, 80, 130, 146, 148–50; *see also* service hubs

Rural Services Review 72

Rural Services Standard 72

rural settlement policy 9, 46–7

Rural Transport Partnership Scheme 63–4, 72

Rural White Papers 2–3, 43–4, 46, 49–50, 62–4, 72, 80, 82, 87, 115, 153, 155

Saffron Walden **23**

schools 46, 65, 70, 95, 102, 138, 142, 154

Scotland 35–6, 109, 115

Scott Report 44

seaside towns 12, 14–15, **16–17**, 32, **38**; and age of population 18, 21, 37; changing fortunes of **33**; unemployment in 105

seasonal work 32, 107, 151

second best, market towns perceived as 29, 109

second homes 32, **38**, 97; tax on 100

self-contained communities 15, 46, 107, 130, 148, 151–3

self-employment 15, **16,** 36, **41**, 106, 109; and hotels and catering 18

service centres *see* service hubs

service hubs 3, 12, 14, 28, 29–31, 43, 62, 72, 75, 120, 140

services 9, 14–15, **16**, **22–4**, **31**, 157; and age of population 18; cost of 45; decline in 151; difficulty of delivering 72; economies of scale 45–6, 133; employment in 106; greater number than expected 12, 157; key services 46, 118, 154; professional 30, 48; resources 46

Sheerness 66

shopping 12, 97, 150; 'anchor' stores 120–1, **141**, 158; attracting trade 118; central feature of market towns 140; chain shops 122, 128, 130, 132; charity shops 119, 130; choice 118; clothes 14, **17**, 21, 76–7, 119, 123, 127, **128**, **131**, 133; food 30, **31**, 37, 71, 101, 127; comparison goods 18, 30–1, 42, 48, 98, 119, 125, 131–2, 149; environment 120, 124–5; mobile telephones 119; non-food 30, **31**, 37, 101, 127; out-of-town 46, 49, 76–7, 118–122, 125, 138, 146, 149, 150, 156; specialist 12, 74–5, 127, 130–2, 150; and working in town 109; *see also* out-shopping; retail provision; supermarkets

Shorten, James 46, 48, 62, 67, 124

Single Regeneration Budget 89–90, 143

skilled labour, shortage of 108, 114

small businesses **41**, 107, 109, 122

social exclusion 2, 11, 49, 73, 89–90, 99, 110, 145, 153

social inclusion 61, 89–91

social life 1

social services 37, 73, 78, 145, 154

solicitors 12

South East 83, 92, 106, 151

South East Regional Research Laboratory 2, 18, 29–30, 47–8, 95, 105–8, 124, 144

South West 13, 36, 52, 83, 106

South West Regional Development Agency 52, 141

specialised employment 15, 20, 25, 28, 33–4, 40

Stanhope **22**, 129

State of the Countryside 12, 88

stereotypes 11, 20, 148

Stroud 158

Sub-Regional Partnerships 90

suburbs, market towns compared to 13

supermarkets 12, **16**, **31**, **33**, 98, 127–8, 158; 'anchor' stores 120; as employers 78; location 140; out-of-town 46, 119; pros and cons 120–1, 150; range of goods 140; reduce travel to urban centres 34, 140; size of 14–15; *see also* shopping

surroundings 29, 123; stimulate economy 114
sustainable communities 46–8, 59, 85–6,
    88–91, 97, 117, 148, 152
Sustainable Communities Programme 82,
    89–91, 97
sustainable development 2, 30, 56–8, 50,
    53, 60, 117, 152, 154–5, 161–2

teenagers 1, 74; *see also* young people
theatres **31**, 34, 128, 139
Todmorden 7, **41**; characteristics **39**, 110; loses
    cotton industry 110; market **141**; proposed
    health centre 142; proximity to Manchester 7;
    size of hinterland 38; supermarkets 120, 140
tourism 6, 13–15, **16–17**, 18, **21–4**, 40, 97, 105,
    119, 122, 125, 131–2; dependence on **32–3**;
    future 137–8; incentives to visit market towns
    130–1; low-wage industry **32**, 37, 42, 151;
    manufacturing 40; seasonal **32**, 107, 151;
    'tourist towns' 20
tourist information centres 14, 32, 130
Town and Country Planning Act 44, 85, 160
town councils 153–4, 158; Wymondham 100
trade, 'clawing back' 5, 120, **121**, 140, 150;
    'leakage' 2, 34, 48, 65, 95, 107, 127, 132,
    150; maintaining 5, 120
training, scarcity of 106–8, 110
transport 1, 35, 155–6, 158; costs 28, 107–8;
    demand-responsive 59, 65; future 67–8,
    155–6; from hinterlands 59, 61, 151;
    integrated 67–8; policy 61–5; private 30,
    49, 65, 75, 77, 80; technology 60, 62;
    trends 59–62; *see also* buses; cars;
    congestion; environment; motorways;
    Parish Transport Fund; parking; public
    transport; railways; walking
Tring **23**

under-employment 107
unemployment; and immigration 29, 38–40;
    lower than average in market towns
    14–15, **16–17**, 66, 105–6, 108

universities 70, 74
urban deprivation 89–90, 152
urban fringe 12, **17**
urban–rural shift 82, 106
urban services, pull of 1–2, 12, 113
USA 28–9, 35–6, 50, 70, 146

villages, services 31
visitor attractions *see* attractions
visitors 32
voluntary work 37, 78, 90, 95, 102

wages, low 32, 42, 78, 108, 110, 125,
    144, 151
Wales 19, **40**, 46, 50, 115
walking **17**, 30, 59, 62, 66–7; in case studies
    74; networks 61, 64, 67; popularity of 30,
    62; *see also* pedestrianisation
Walton-on-the-Naze **23**
Watton **24**
websites 114, 130, 142
wheelchairs 75–7, 79, 128
'Wheels to Work' 63
Whittlesey **23**
Wickham Market **24**
Wirksworth 50
Wisbech **23**
Woodbridge **24**
Wooler **22**, 129
Wymondham 6, 7, **23**, **36**, 139, 158;
    characteristics **39**, **98**; commuter town 111;
    dormitory town 102; future 137; heritage
    100; housing allocation.100; parking 138;
    proximity to Norwich 38, **126**; Norfolk
    Constabulary Operations Centre 40;
    shopping **126**; town council 100

Yellow Pages 5
Yorkshire and Humber Assembly 143–4
Yorkshire Forward 41, 52, **53**, 116, 143
young people 1, 14, 74; prefer cities 89, 104,
    107; and transport 61

eBooks

eBooks – at www.eBookstore.tandf.co.uk

A library at your fingertips!

eBooks are electronic versions of printed books. You can store them on your PC/laptop or browse them online.

They have advantages for anyone needing rapid access to a wide variety of published, copyright information.

eBooks can help your research by enabling you to bookmark chapters, annotate text and use instant searches to find specific words or phrases. Several eBook files would fit on even a small laptop or PDA.

NEW: Save money by eSubscribing: cheap, online access to any eBook for as long as you need it.

Annual subscription packages

We now offer special low-cost bulk subscriptions to packages of eBooks in certain subject areas. These are available to libraries or to individuals.

For more information please contact webmaster.ebooks@tandf.co.uk

We're continually developing the eBook concept, so keep up to date by visiting the website.

www.eBookstore.tandf.co.uk